from my heart to yours

Part 1

Personal experiences to highlight the supremacy of Christ.

John Constantine

This book or parts thereof may not be reproduced in any form, stored in a retrieval system, or transmitted in any form by any means–electronic, mechanical photocopy, recording, or otherwise–without prior written permission of the publisher, except as provided by United States of America copyright law.

Unless otherwise noted, all Scripture quotations are from the Holy Bible, New King James Version. Copyright © 1982 by Thomas Nelson, Inc. All rights reserved.

Copyright © 2015 John Constantine

All rights reserved.

Cover design by SCHOOLinSITES, LLC

Visit the author's website at www.frommyheart2yours.net.

Constantine, John R.

From My Heart to Yours / John Constantine

(e-book)

While the author has made every effort to provide accurate quoted information at the time of publication, neither the publisher nor the author assumes any responsibility for errors or for changes that occur after publication.

Table of Content

INTRODUCTION	20
Looking at Adult Children	32
With The Whole Heart	32
When The Heart Kneels	33
Why Live?	33
Plus and Minus	33
Loving Non-stop	34
Masterpieces	34
To men, On loving a wife	35
God, The Garden	37
Preparation Required	37
Doing Things Right From my heart to yours –	38
Faithfulness, A Diamond in the sun	38
Heartburns, the Good Kind	39
Suffering Snapshot	40
Love, the Kind That Never Lets Go	40
Hurts Cured	41
Free to NOT Condemn	41
Divine Inspiration	41
The Extent of Suffering	42

To Love By Choice 42

Glory Snapshot 43

Why Do I Love? 43

A New Perspective On Love 44

Love From Above 44

Your Will, Not Mine 45

Mapquest Unacceptable 46

Accepted At The Cross 46

Hurts Abound 46

In Christ Alone 47

Being Crucified with Christ 47

Burdens Lifted at Calvary 48

How Upset 48

Heavy Burdens 49

Worship and Sacrifice 49

Worship Beyond the Cross 50

Glory Crucified 51

Comprehension 52

His Name Shall Be Called 52

Out Of Control 53

Disrupted Fatherhood 53

Complete Commitment 54

Dedication To One 55

Daily Devotion	55
Not of Works	56
True Religion	56
Abundant God	57
The Journey	57
Leadership Snapshot	58
Spiritual Warfare	58
Spiritual Crisis	59
Glory and Power	60
After Easter	60
Easter Takeaways	61
Kingdom Snapshot	61
Hid In His Love	61
His Appearing	62
Love Missing	62
Missing Ingredient	63
Love Never Fails (1Cor 13)	63
Intercession Benefits	64
Resurrection Stone	65
God's Dictionary	65
Salvation in a nutshell	66
True Reflection	68
Arrogance snapshot	69

Precious In His Eyes..69

At What Price 70

Bringing Shame on His Name...70

Maturity Snapshot..70

Pure Heart 71

Comprehensive Yielding..72

Spirit's Only Fruit 72

Self-Control (2)...73

Fruit of Spirit Expressed 73

No Luck..74

Making Changes 74

Changing Places...75

The Potter's Hands 75

Mold Me Make Me...76

In-Formation 77

Deep Gratitude..77

Tweaking Lenses 78

Seizing the moment; and Saving the marriage.....................78

God can use "the least of these" 81

Change and Changeless..84

Ointment Snapshot 86

Scripture Better..86

Gravitational Pull 87

Jesus The Gift	87
Gifts Not Ready	88
Utter Dependence	90
The Father and the Son	92
Lord, Lord	93
Radical Disciples	96
Cross Survey	97
Slowing Down	97
"Whatsoever things are...Think on these things"	98
"He Touched Me"	100
Dying To Live, Living to Die	101
What Really Happened: (part 1 of 2)	101
What Really Happened: (part 2 of 2)	102
Obedience Snapshot	103
I Am No Angel	103
Encountering Jesus	105
Spirit Snapshot	106
Prayer Full Circle	106
True Obedience	108
His Name	111
Dark Night of the Soul	112
Easter - (#2)	115
On Counterfeits	118

Suffering Types 120

Being Awake 123

The Blessings of Bad Days 123

Abort ! Abort ! Abort ! (part-1 of 2) 125

Abort ! Abort ! Abort ! (part-2 of 2) 127

Living Sacrifice 128

Conscience: A Lifelong Eyewitness Companion (part-1 of 4) 129

Not By Shame 135

Discovering Jesus and Knowing Him more each day 136

Right Or Wrong 136

When Prayer Is Not 138

Being Not Of 140

A Heart Filled with Gratitude 141

I Love You, Son 141

Teacher at 87 142

Sovereign Grace 145

Delightful Times 148

Being on the Same Page 149

Good Theology, Bad Living 151

One Thing Lacking 151

Special Moments 155

Sharp Wit 155

Untried Christ 156

Praying Right 159

Sleeping with the Enemy...160

Being Rejected...161

One Mind 162

Dying To Live...162

"Thy Kingdom Come" 163

God Not Impressed..164

God's Priorities 165

Calling Upon His Name 165

"Sufficiency" on my mind..168

Confronting God 169

Let's Not Be Fooled..170

Fingerprints of God 171

DOES IT NOT SURPRISE US ?..172

Pain Is Universal 173

ABOUT THE ONE WE LOVE 174

Fingerprints of God (Pt. 1) 175

Walking Alone in the Crowd...176

On Pleasing God...177

Walking Alone in the Crowd (part 2) 178

Losing To Win...179

On Reconciliation 179

WHY IS IT LIKE THIS ? (3 parts, here's part 1)...................................180

WHY IS IT LIKE THIS ? (3 parts, here's part 2)	181
WHY IS IT LIKE THIS ? (3 parts, here's part 3)	183
The Holy Spirit of God: His Person and Work -- A bird's eye view	185
"NO" Is Clear Enough	188
Two sides of A Coin	188
Thinking of Hell (in the shadow of the Cross)	188
My Amazing Lord	190
Heaven in South Sudan	190
Fellowship of Suffering	191
Shakespeare asked: What's in a name?	191
To Be All His	192
That Resurrection Morning, Never like it, Before or Since	193
Power of Prayer	194
How does the Family of God work?	195
See you next year	196
Until I got home	196
Thinking Clearly about the Gospel of Jesus Christ	197
It's Only Reasonable	200
It is Only Reasonable - (Summary)	201
Facebook Not Appealing	202
Do you know what DTR stands for?	204
Looking from the pew	204
Calvary Snapshot	205

Problem Solved	205
Why do I love Him So?	207
"Are you going to jump?"	207
On "Customizing" God	212
Listening and hearing overlap in meaning	214
What is a "quiet spirit?"	215
My Precious Friend	216
True Identity needs an anchor	217
Water Walk	219
Singleness of heart	219
True Love	220
The Master's Ears	220
Singing Unto the Lord	221
His thoughts and Ours	223
A Question of Faith And Authority	224
Father-Son Specials	226
Mom, Like All Moms	227
Keeping in Mind "Older" Parents (1 of 2) - A New Reality to the Younger generations	228
Keeping in Mind "Older" Parents (2 of 2) - A New Reality to the Younger generations	229
Never Too Late	232
Failure Is Not An Option	232
I Either Wonder or I Wander	234

Beckoning The Broken	235
Doctrines Dead Until	236
Comments on Luke 8:45, 47, 48	237
My Funny Mom	241
Revival takes place	242
Doctrine and Life	244
Preeminence Snapshot	244
My Neighbor	244
True Disciple	245
Time For Sparrows	245
No Specials	246
Building Relationships	246
LOOKING at a Woman the Jesus Way	247
A Character Trait of A Jesus Follower	250
PURE Calling Out to God	251
Sunday, May 18, 2014 at 1:32P.M. CDT	252
Unction: An Old Word	252
The Power of the Gospel (1)	253
The Power of the Gospel (2)	253
My life in Christ	254
To Build Or To Destroy	254
Loving the Jesus Way	255
Better Use of Time	256

Reality of Christ	257
The Funny Thing	258
Skeleton and Muscles Don't	258
Immaterial Distances	259
Keeping Things Simple	259
Masters Demand	260
Wondering Why Worthless Works	260
Touching The Invisible	261
As Sheep Among Wolves	261
Why Persecution?	262
Praying for the Persecuted	263
Persecution	264
Jesus Alone	264
A Member or a Follower?	265
Walking	266
The house of God	267
Helping, Not Enough	268
Brokenness Snapshot	268
On Being Accepted	268
The Meaning of the Cross	269
Building The Church	269
On Being Called By His Name	270
"Hallowed Be Thy Name"	271

Thinking About the Woman Who Was "Caught" 271

Obedience, Not Slavery 273

Obedience (Un)like Rebellion 273

Commission Snapshot 275

Love Held Back 275

We Don't Really Believe 276

My funny Mom, My Praying Mom 278

Bearable Burdens 278

My Mom When She Hurts 280

Seven things that Impress and move God 282

On Knowing God 282

Taking A Siesta 283

Confused About Visions 283

The Good Denomination 285

GPS Not Necessary 285

Forgiveness Snapshot 286

All-Sufficient 286

Smart Praying 286

THERE IS NO SUCH THING (1 of 4) 288

"I'm Blessed". Really? 288

THERE IS NO SUCH THING (2 of 4) 289

Straddling A Fence Of Our Own Making 290

THERE IS NO SUCH THING (3 of 4) 291

THERE IS NO SUCH THING (4 of 4)	294
Global Desire	296
Amazing Savior	296
Faithful Unknown	297
Relevance Relative to Relationship	298
Long Overdue Debt	299
True Passion	300
Pain and suffering	301
Feeling Shame Is Not Good Enough	301
Community in Misery	302
Spiritual "Terms of Endearment"	302
Revival and Worship Missing Jewels	304
Passionate Living	305
One Pure Passion Needed	305
Very Special	306
Love Suffers	306
Light Transmission	306
Not Nets	307
Word and Words	307
True Power	309
Fire or Ice	310
Bearing Witness	310
Adjusting the Lens	311

What Relationship	311
Silo vs. Conduit Thinking	311
Two Are Too Many	312
At What Price?	312
Prayer Snapshot	313
Death Snapshot	313
Starting Right	314
What Does It Mean	314
Visitors and Members	315
Why No Membership Rush?	316
Kingdom Snapshot	317
Saying and Being	317
Some Hard Facts	317
No Such Thing	318
Not For Sale	318
Owner's Manual	319
Proper Loving	319
Who are These?	319
Obedience: A Serious Business	320
Obedient Church	321
Obedient Leadership	322
Serious with God	322
Character Least Discussed	322

Anemic And Discontented 323

Indispensable Spirit 324

Visions Snapshot 324

Holy, Holy, Holy 324

Servant-Leader Snapshot 325

Fingerprints of God (2) 325

Resistance: Good and Bad 326

Wisdom and Knowledge 327

Transparent and Pure 327

Beauty of Holiness 327

Living Contradictions 327

Not Funny 328

Reasonable Reciprocity 329

Life of Hatred, No Life At All 329

Forgiveness Is No Forgiveness IF 330

The Seven Principles of Forgiveness 331

Jesus Down To Earth 332

Saying and Seeing 333

Falling Is Better 334

MYOB 335

Performance Snapshot 335

Attraction Snapshot 335

Always Busy 336

Are you In or Out ?	336
Prayer and Sin	337
A Good Friend	337
Side Benefit of Prayer	337
The Gospel of Jesus Christ	338
Him Alone	338
Center and Circumference	338
On Knowing	339
Failing To See	339
Bird's Eye View	340
The Cross, The Crossroads	341
CHOICES Sum It Up	342
Two Types of Stripes	344
Praying In Persecution	344
Great Errors Leaving The Church Anemic (1 of 2)	345
Great Errors Leaving The Church Anemic (part 2A)	346
Great Errors Leaving The Church Anemic (part 2B)	347
Great Errors Leaving The Church Anemic (part 2C)	347
Great Errors Leaving The Church Anemic (part 2D)	348
Five Great Errors Leaving The Church Anemic (part 2E)	348
Great Errors Leaving The Church Anemic (part 2 - Summary)	349
Can You Count ?	349
Prayer Snapshot	350

PART 1

Introduction

What is it about?

In one sentence, this book consists of daily snapshots, glimpses, and the Holy Spirit's breath on this writer, to experience Christ, *practically, simply,* and to KNOW HIM in His majesty, Humility, Preeminence, Passion, and Love. It's learning daily the meaning of "Longing for Him Ever Day". And, *that's* my heart's desire for you as well.

At the end of the day, it's really "All about HIM".

Why this book? Honestly, it was never intended to be anything for public consumption, for its idea has been decades in the making and couldn't find even a window to take flight; either it hadn't developed mature wings of the soul or its wings unbeknownst to me were clipped prematurely. It's no volcano that erupted but was a heart that has been longing to express the basic idea found in this writing. That idea can be summed up in a word: Christ. Here is why.

I knew, in my humble view, and for no less than four decades, that something was missing, seriously missing, in evangelical churches as a whole, and I couldn't pinpoint what it was yet. I despaired trying to find the words or assemble enough thoughts to capture its substance, but like an elusive dream, a blurred image; it kept fading repeatedly staying out of focus often.

This book is a modest attempt to express regarding the unseen, to know what is readily unknowable by human means. I pleaded with the Spirit of God to know, even glimpses to quench my thirst, until I almost lost everything in life that can be quantified in dollars and cents or otherwise. Then some things began to make sense, slowly but surely. This book has seen the light at the midnight hour on most occasions, and the thoughts tucked in were a delight at first, but like the writer of old, when I swallowed them they were bitter in my gut, and gripped me more as the days went by and would not let go.

Here is what happened when I almost lost everything. On a typical summer day, the family and I got in the vehicle as we've done many times on Sunday to "go to church". But that day was soon to become as atypical as a day can be. Out of nowhere, an unknown car stopped behind us blocking our exit. I thought perhaps they were lost. So I stepped out to ask "how may I help ...", but discovered to my chagrin a hand gun was only few inches away from my face. Its bearer was anger-personified, screaming, cursing, jumping as though struck with an electric current, held the gun like a professional, demanding money and everything we had, and threats were hurled like volleys from his mouth mixed with his spit that found its landing spot on my face often. Shocked could not describe enough our state of mind, changed in seconds, unsure of the direction of life any longer. I chased him with my eyes as he made his way to my wife and son, screaming, threatening more, and looking for easy money to leave with, moving his gun from one to the other wishing it was a triple-barreled gun to point it at us all at once, thinking he was free to do so, not knowing that he was simultaneously gripped in the vice of lostness and hunger for a new day that never came.

In less than four or five minutes, he retreated to the getaway car with the gun pointed at us, threats, warnings, feeling his mission was accomplished, and we looked at him not believing we were still alive. The car disappeared as quickly as it appeared. We looked at each other, breathed a sigh of relief, and thanked God for life with a new perspective on the ease of death and taking for-granted of our day to day life and its blessing. I looked at my wife and son like never before, held them in my arms tighter than ever, cried with relief, thought of the church who were waiting for us at 5:00 P.M. to join them as we did normally for almost twenty years. I realized in a fresh way that I was gazing at a new reality like never before in my life. It was the reality of the earthly family God gave me "until death do us part", and the reality of my heavenly family that even death will not us part. Nothing else had such inherent value.

I realized that Jesus Christ came specifically to affirm these two realities, to establish and build one, and to grant that the home be the incubator of life that gives Him glory, and in which He may dwell sovereignly as well. I also realized that what He gave mankind is priceless, and everything else has a price tag attached to it. I also realized that He loves both so much that He commanded that honor is exercised in both. One is a miniature form of the other, a laboratory in which we grow and learn great life lessons that can be exercised in the bigger family of the church. I was stunned by the fact that the world with all its smarts is very determined to redefine both, the family and the church, and impose its errant ways with the assumption that there is a better way. So far, the world failed miserably and the record of decades bear witness. I don't blame the world at all, but I do fault the church, and more specifically the so-called evangelical church. Here is why.

I expect the world with its systems and mindset to behave like the world, to think different from and adverse to the church, to make every attempt at shredding the last vestige of the church and home, forging a license to what cannot be licensed, and changing, in summary, the good to bad and the bad to good, mouthing platitudes in dogged pursuit of pleasure and loose acquisition of cheap money. Not only that, but they celebrate their accomplishments every chance they have. I don't fault them nor blame them, because they are behaving according to the very nature in which they are conceived and born.

But I do blame the evangelical establishment for many reasons. First, they claim to know the truth and flaunt the accuracy of "and the truth shall set you free", meaning summarily that the world has to become like them for the world to be "right". Second, they claim guardianship over accurate doctrine, and walk about making sure everyone within reach measured properly on their measuring stick of righteousness, and applauding anyone who changes his mind and joins their camp. Third, I have been repeatedly disturbed by the statistics that almost "three-quarters of evangelical adults have questions about their faith". Fourth, the disappointing statistics of drug use, divorces, and other anomalies have become competitively the same between the church and the world, and the differences between the two have become less and less. Fifth, the vast majority of evangelical members have more knowledge of correct doctrine and less acquisition of the character traits that made Jesus Christ so uniquely identifiable by the enemies in His day. It was the enemies who described Him as "lover of publicans and sinners", and it was the Jews at Lazarus' tomb who saw Jesus weep and commented, "Look how much He (Jesus) loved him (Lazarus)". It was the enemies who walked away from the fallen woman whose only refuge was the Son of Man (God Incarnate) who stood taller than all in righteousness and truth and love. They knew He was correct not because of His doctrine but because of his love which they had no inkling of. Sixth, I was puzzled with the simple fact that Jesus did not teach anyone the alleged "doctrines of the faith", ever! But somehow people were attracted to him, young and old, from various classes of society, the religious and the pagan, the upright and the fallen, the rejected found grace abounding in Him, and so much more about Him that brought people to sit at His feet to listen to the words of grace falling from His lips. The evangelical church has anything but grace, and is able to shower the world with all erudite verbiage except the "better way of love", and has lost the art of "him increasing" and them "decreasing", so much so that the world sees denominational names but has not heard of the distinctive "name that is above every other name". Seventh, the evangelical church has become excellent at delineating the doctrinal distinctive and has no clue of the Christ distinctive. Why do I say that? I say it because we are gleeful when someone "joins the church" as though they joined the ranks and can be counted as a statistic of Christendom but we leave them to the intellectual attackers to ravage their weak souls and tear their minds to the shreds of confusion and befuddlement. And the rest of us do worse, we fault them for not "going to church" enough to learn about their version of "Christianity" claiming it is the authorized version, when in fact they are yet to begin slurping the rudiments of what Christ is all about, and discover the power of the Gospel and the filling of the Spirit that enables them to have a changed life and a renewed spirit every day.

I asked myself, why are the evangelical churches having such difficulty flowing with the love of Jesus Christ to the world around? Why are they holding on to the skeleton of doctrines but lacking the muscles and tendons of true Christ-like love that connects the body together? Why do we have difficulty flowing with the love of Christ so much that people are attracted to Him alone, and not to our program? Why have we equated our versions of Christianity to the powerful and holy name of Christ, being duped into thinking that people who come to "us" are the true Christians, not being able to define who "us" really is and what it means?

I asked myself why Jesus didn't teach doctrine in His days. Why did he not prove to the so-called enemies why His teachings were better, more "together", more profound, more lasting? Why did He not start a new school with headquarters and branches and satellite simulcasts? Why did He not publish anything? Why did He not have an army with weapons to fight? Why, Why?? And the only answers I could come up with were the fact that Jesus did not have any doctrines. In fact He *was* the embodiment of all doctrine. The doctrines were hid in Him. And to know the doctrines in the heart, people needed to come to Him and know Him and become one with Him, and know His love, and experience the power of His Spirit that flowed from Him to them. And only then, as it happened often, people were willing to leave everything and follow Him. In fact, His unequivocal assertion was that in order to qualify as a follower of His, one had to leave everything behind. Only then, He becomes their "everything", their sufficiency; and then life happens!

In our evangelical circles, we have become everything except Christ incarnate, yet again, in the flesh, in our flesh, and we experience Him so much that when we breathe we let the world know after His glorious resurrection that He is alive.

I begged to know how to express this nagging reality and stop faulting everyone else why they are not like us. We tried education, we tried dogma, we tried traditions, we tried renunciations of various types, we tried enforcement by various means, and every time we failed miserably, and doubly so for knowing the truth but claiming ownership of it, when in fact we were idolaters of a religion we created in our own images. We tried financial power, moral power, economic power, political power, strategic acumen, programmatic finesse, multiplied arrogance clothed in purple and red, or ties and white collars, or refined words and affinities, or providing humane services of health and shelter almost seducing humanity to be "Christians" and add to our numbers, not knowing, like blind leading the blind, that unless the Lord builds the house, unless the Lord guards the city, all work is done in vain. We blamed everything wrong on the savagery of the Muslims or Hindus or some other group of humanity for not allowing us to have our own utopia of religion. And like the Pharisees of old, we stood repeatedly in the doorway not going in ourselves and not allowing anyone to go in either.

To prove the wrong of our ways, God for the past two or three decades specifically has moved so powerfully across the tapestry of human affliction and suffering, has hovered through His Spirit over the obvious chaos called "humanity", and has breathed often of His Spirit, touched lives, opened eyes, found the untouchable rejects of the world and revealed Himself directly to them. As if discounting us, dismissing us, leaving us outside, and converted them to become His followers, yet again, like the early years. And now, these remnants in every nation, culture, language, and points of a compass, have come to sit at His feet at all cost and declare Him Lord.

The reason, the paramount logic of His cross is simply that all that we do is insufficient to declare His glory. Therefore, He came to give life and make it more abundant, much more abundant. He came so that the principle of multiplication will take place again, meaning, that one grain must go into the ground and die in order to bear much fruit. In many places, the most ill-equipped in every respect are bearing the markings of His sufferings and through His stripes that they carry now many are finding healing in His wings, and are telling the world that there is forgiveness, life, acceptance, and unconditional love in Him who has been from eternity past the "joy of heaven".

I discovered that the truth is all about Him. In fact the totality of truth is simply: Him. And unless we are able to reflect Him alone, we have failed abysmally. Perhaps we evangelicals would do well to resign our state of things, and go back to declaring Him alone as risen Lord, and the Gospel of His Kingdom has over it the banner of love, and His language is not human but divine, and His character does not know nationality or heritage but is supremely preeminent and grand that He still to this day refuses to be counted one among many, but as none beside Him.

To Him I bowed anew, and He is who my heart desired to describe with many variegated colors that only heaven can absorb. The labor pains of recent years have struggled to bring these humble thoughts, as close to reality as is expressed in the title: "From My Heart to Yours".

This document was started with no thought of publishing or making it public. It was a joy to sit during the morning quiet time and write some thoughts which seem at times fairly unrelated to one another.

However, the thoughts reflected a personal journey, a discovery of the kaleidoscopic relation with a discovery of the risen Lord and Savior. This exercise turned into a soul-searching exercise and, through various life experiences, became an examination of heart and soul in light of the Word of the Living God.

Major themes obviously became anchors for the writer's flow of thoughts. The Person of Jesus Christ and His centrality; The person, work, presence, and power of the Holy Spirit; and other themes that are at the core of the Christian life, such as forgiveness, faith, obedience, church life, application of God's love, and what makes the believer's walk challenging and sometimes blurred.

This document has scattered in it personal experiences; many were posted to this author's Facebook page laying bare a soul that's in pursuit of Christ and none other. Over the past four years, many regular readers have encouraged me to convert the postings into a book because it has been a blessing to them. The reason behind this thematic combination is to see the relevance of God's principles expressed in daily life. Much is written about sound doctrine. However, to me, one of the nagging issues in Christendom today is the soundness of doctrine but dead reflection of the life of Christ in everyday life. Surely, there is a bridge that is solidly founded in God's Word. Discovering aspects of that bridge is one of the objectives of this writing.

This author's premise is that doctrines are wonderful and easy to identify, and ascertain their veracity through the objective study of God's Word, but without the indwelling Holy Spirit and daily obedience, discipline, and application, such life is purely pharisaic and counter-productive in personal, family, church, and social life. It grieves the Spirit and produces no fruit. The fact remains that unless the grain goes into the ground and dies; it will remain alone and will bear no fruit. Rightness of doctrine is no guarantee of righteousness that's Christ born and Spirit-implemented. Beginning in faith requires faith for the rest of the journey. Only the Holy Spirit can sustain such a lifestyle, filled with the variegated beauty of Christ's character. Then I can worship in His Spirit (and my spirit) and truth. And then I can enjoy Him forever. The rest of the journey is simply diverse details making each one unique and rich.

May the Spirit who led with the flow of thoughts also grant discernment as each of us walks through the narrow gate and discovers the unique and supreme character of Jesus Christ, to whom be glory forever.

A word of thanks and dedication is in order. First, I lost two friends, Sami and Rodolphe, around the same time I almost lost my family, to the grips of death from a cancer that perniciously nagged them for two and a half years then completely devastated their bodies, and left their families behind to collect the pieces. What made them unique and alike so much was that both died young, both had two children and wives who loved them passionately, both were lovers of Christ, both bore witness to the awesome Savior they loved, both shared a living faith. Both were loved, not only by their local Christian group, but more importantly by those we label as "in the world" who kept close contact to the very end. They surrounded Sami and Rodolphe, not because of the illness but because of the love that Christ instilled in their hearts, and the friends smelled its fragrance and found it powerful and true.

To them this book is dedicated, and to the living proof they presented in a short span of time that Christ can be real in people who are real and are willing to give up all for Him. He bore the curse once for our sins, but will not be replying on human abilities.

A debt of gratitude also goes to those readers who took the time to read and considered what they read a blessing to their daily life and walk with God. The debt extends also to the church of Jesus Christ in many locations with whom this author crossed paths. I dedicate this piece to the suffering church throughout the world, my brothers and sisters, in North Africa and the Middle East. More specifically I stand close to those who tasted death for the sake of Christ and died persecuted and this world was not worthy of them. To all who love His appearing, I affirm to you my love and commitment to know Him more, and to make Him known.

Meditations

Looking at Adult Children
From my heart to yours –

He always called me "Son"; perhaps that's as close and part of his family as I could be. Every time we visited them for few days, and before leaving, he asked me to check the car oil and other fluids. I said: "Daddy, why do you ask me to do that every time?!" He answered every time, "Because you have precious cargo! You have my little girl there!" I still love his "little girl", for his sake too. *(Monday, January 17, 2011 at 4:08A.M. CST)*

With The Whole Heart
From my heart to yours –

An old song says: *Let us love our God supremely; Let us love each other too; Let us love and pray for sinners; Till our God makes all things new. Then He'll call home to heaven; At His table we'll sit down; Brethren pray and holy manna; Will be showered all around."* He said: The conclusion of the whole matter is to love God with all your heart. I trust He will teach us that today! *(Thursday, January 20, 2011 at 10:08A.M. CST)*

WHEN THE HEART KNEELS

From my heart to yours –

Once I asked a man, "Why, when you were praying, you were flat on your face?" He said, "All my life I prayed on my knees to a god I did not know. The true God I now know deserves more; don't you think?" I found silence to be a better answer; and knew firsthand then that God is no respecter of persons. "All who call upon the Name of the Lord . . ." *(Monday, February 28, 2011 at 12:55A.M. CST)*

WHY LIVE?

From my heart to yours –

I challenge the reader to make this year's motto for your life: *IT'S ALL ABOUT HIM*. It's easy to accomplish not by trying harder (and failing), but by complete surrender to His lordship in every aspect of life (no excuses, no comparison, no looking back, no ands ifs or buts), and living daily in His Presence. That's not the supernatural but the Normal Christian life. *(Monday, January 2, 2012 at 3:53P.M. CST)*

PLUS AND MINUS

From my heart to yours –

John Baptist said: "I am not He; he must increase and I must decrease". Paul said: "I count everything but loss for the sake of His knowledge". "To Him all prophets bear witness." To the Emmaus disciples, "He began with Moses and all prophets and told of things pertinent to Him". Isaiah said: "His name shall be called Wonderful ...." Believe me, it's ALL about Him. It Has Been, Is, and Will Be ALL about Him. I can't love Him when I don't live Him. *(Monday, January 2, 2012 at 4:28P.M. CST)*

LOVING NON-STOP

From my heart to yours –

While having breakfast today with Mama and Baba (Arabic for Mom and Dad), I was joking with them about my siblings how they put up with them (as if I were any better). Mama said, "If I carried them here (pointing to her belly), is it difficult to carry them here (pointing to her shoulders)?" Then I remembered that He (Christ) carried us until we were born into His family and he became our elder brother, and through His Spirit, He carries us still to confirm His love from morning till night. Likewise, we ought to do with one another. To Him who loved us be glory forever. *(Friday, January 6, 2012 at 11:51A.M. CST)*

MASTERPIECES

From my heart to yours –

What makes a masterpiece a "Masterpiece" is not the piece, but the Master. What makes a true follower of Christ true is not the following, but Christ. Otherwise, we have noise and human efforts that don't amount to much. And if they persist, can become an annoyance, and are not profitable to participate in an orchestra. I would have loved being with the shepherds in front seats listening to the heavenly choir of angels sing at Jesus' birth. *(Saturday, January 21, 2012 at 4:17P.M. CST)*

TO MEN, ON LOVING A WIFE

From my heart to yours –

What I learned in 35 years so far: (1) Learn and study your wife like your life depended on it, because it does; (2) Love your wife not like you want but like her heart tells you; (3) Loving her requires a *change in the culture* of your heart; (4) Loving her is far more than sex; God said to "delight" in her, not to "demean" her; (5) For your wife alone, God always has reserve energy for you to love her more; (6) Your wife is NOT like any other woman - don't compare. You're not grocery shopping; (7) If you need a servant, hire a maid- it's cheaper; (8) Your goal is not that she be created in your image-again, because God took care of that already; (9) You will be amazed what better job God does if you want her to change, pray for her like never before; (10) One of God's compounded blessings is that if u want her to change, don't do it yourself, she's not a car. Let God change how you look at her; (11) Never treat her based on conditions you put on her, ask yourself if you're changing too; (12) Capture her heart every morning like the earth receives the sunshine every day; (13) Kids don't add what you may think you're missing, because they are mere extensions of what you have already; (14) if you don't honor your wife with class in the living room, don't expect your treatment will be different anywhere else in the house; (15) Ultimatums mean you are ready to burn the bridge. Sometimes a good night's rest helps. Otherwise, try God; he's available 24/7/365; (16) Love is not a chemical term, it never gets toxic; (17) In front of people, always cherish her- and if necessary, use words; (18) When alone, let her know she's all you need and ever hope for; (19) Do you see yourself in her eyes?; (20) if you don't lift her up, don't expect better for your daughter, and you have failed your son; (21) Always, make special time for her, and please dress up; (22) While she is not the stock market, your investments in her always bring dividends; (23) If she smiles at you after 35 years like she did the first year, it means she doesn't need glasses yet; (24) It would be a shame if she still feels cold in your embrace, try taking your heart out of deep freeze; (25) although in heaven there are no marriages, and some men grin sheepishly, remember God gave her to you so heaven can very well begin on earth; (26) your wife is not a business to make profit from, nor a car to rev up the engine, nor a tree to pick the fruit then cut her down, nor a once-in-a-lifetime fireworks then go into dark oblivion, nor a wine glass that has a bitter end, nor a store special on discount, but she is a gift, and a one-carat diamond, don't steal it, she's all yours as much as you're hers; (27) Any alternative is sea water, abysmal, dark, and meaningless, like drinking from an empty glass and catching a handful of wind; (28) If you think the sunrise is gorgeous, just wait until the sunset. Both are yours. Love your wife as Christ loved the church, and gave Himself for her. Love ALWAYS wins. Loving a wife is serious business. *(Wednesday, January 25, 2012 at 9:05A.M. CST)*

GOD, THE GARDEN

From my heart to yours –

A conversation between the great scientist Einstein and his nurse very late in his life: He: You believe in God? She: Yes, yes I do. Do you...believe? He: Do I believe if there is someone who plans the daily life of Albert Einstein? No. Although sometimes I think He may have been leading me up the garden path. She: But didn't he make the garden? He: I think he IS the garden. She: And isn't He the gardener too? He: Yes. And all my life, I've been trying to catch him at his work. *(Monday, January 30, 2012 at 10:12A.M. CST)*

PREPARATION REQUIRED

From my heart to yours –

For everything in life, people have no problem being required and actually pay heavily, for example, to go to school and be trained for years to be prepared for whatever they plan to spend the rest of their life doing, except being prepared for marriage and church. We go in the latter assuming full knowledge and qualification. Could the reason be that marriage and church originated in heaven, and Satan is doing his best to destroy both? Someone said, "If doctors practiced medicine the way some so-called church leaders practice church, or the way husbands practice home leadership, more than half of the doctors will be in jail the first month of practice." God help us! *(Tuesday, February 14, 2012 at 10:40P.M. CST)*

DOING THINGS RIGHT

From my heart to yours –

Since there is a marked distinction between "doing things right" and "doing the right thing", why do people consistently choose to do the first and ignore the second? And, like a nightmare, they major on what doesn't matter, and compare people based on the insignificant. The real sad part though is that we Christians are notorious for watching and approving how people do things, and totally ignore that what really matters most is doing the right thing, and that's not even on our radar screen. I wonder if the reason lies in the fact that, to do the right thing, we need to look to God. And, we choose to ignore THAT. God help us to see what's right in the face of Christ, and do that, and fall in love with Him, and rest. He said: "Come unto me all that are heavy-laden, and I will give you rest." *(Saturday, February 18, 2012 at 10:09P.M. CST)*

FAITHFULNESS, A DIAMOND IN THE SUN

From my heart to yours –

If FAITHFULNESS to HIM is the only criterion for evaluation when we stand before God, does it make any difference whether we are full-time or part-time in ministry? Or did we replace faithfulness with visible effectiveness (likely, and in all honesty, a purely human standard) that won't be taken into consideration in eternity?

FAITHFULNESS is like the word from God in the days of Samuel . . . very rare, for it requires walking alone with God without being lonely. But, we are so busy these days, and always seem to be like the mummies of old pressed for time.

FAITHFULNESS has a twin sister called AFFECTION. Many times we think Faithfulness is synonymous with staying where we are for life (which is not true, because repeating the same actions has nothing to do with Faithfulness); and we think affection is synonymous with infatuation (which is not). Faithfulness is the warmth of a fire caused by the glow of its twin sister, Affection. Simply put, are we so much in love with Jesus Christ that we melt in His Presence, and hold on tight in His seeming absence? Affection teaches us steadily to close our eyes in complete surrender when it's totally dark and we cannot see. The natural result of that life is: Faithfulness. True faithfulness is seeing a smile when we see His blessed face. Then we bow in adoration. And before we know it, it is eternity. *(Monday, February 20, 2012 at 4:33P.M. CST)*

Heartburns, the Good Kind
From my heart to yours –

Heartburns are Necessary to love Jesus right - Remember Jesus on the road to Emmaus? After he told the two disciples about Himself, and disappeared, they said: "Were not our hearts burning within us while He talked to us and opened the Scriptures?" It's amazing what happens when we read the Scriptures... because: It's all about Him. *(Tuesday, February 21, 2012 at 10:02A.M. CST)*

SUFFERING SNAPSHOT
From my heart to yours

> Suffering can only be understood, though in part, in the presence of Him who suffered for no cause of his own making. Maybe that's why He said: "Come unto me all you who are heavy-laden, and I will ..." It's an unconditional invitation, irrevocable promise, and impeccable integrity by someone who said: "I am the truth." *(Tuesday, February 21, 2012 at 10:49P.M. CST)*

LOVE, THE KIND THAT NEVER LETS GO
From my heart to yours

> George Mattheson, upon the loss of his baby daughter to illness while crossing the Atlantic in 1882, penned the words of a song that captured the heartbeat of a follower of Christ through the fiery furnace, and said: "O Love that will not let me go, I rest my weary soul in thee; I give thee back the life I owe, That in thine ocean depths its flow May richer, fuller be. O light that foll'west all my way, I yield my flick'ring torch to thee; My heart restores its borrowed ray, That in thy sunshine's blaze its day May brighter, fairer be. O Joy that seekest me through pain, I cannot close my heart to thee; I trace the rainbow through the rain, And feel the promise is not vain, That morn shall tearless be. O Cross that liftest up my head, I dare not ask to fly from thee; I lay in dust life's glory dead, And from the ground there blossoms red Life that shall endless be." *(Tuesday, February 21, 2012 at 10:59P.M. CST)*

Hurts Cured
From my heart to yours

Hurt people hurt people. They keep trying and cannot stop the cycle of hurts until they come to the cross, and stay there for the rest of their life. Therefore, a changed life, following the Master, is a miracle in and of itself. *(Thursday, February 23, 2012 at 2:35A.M. CST)*

Free to NOT Condemn
From my heart to yours

Having tasted being set free from any condemnation gives us the choice NOT to condemn. As His ambassadors, May we choose, as He did, to deliver and restore others to Him, for THAT is His will for us. Living and Loving His liberty ...means choosing to always be like Him and accomplishing it. I love you Lord, and am eternally grateful for what you have done in my stead. To condemn is a choice, and I choose to filter it through the cross of Christ. *(Thursday, February 23, 2012 at 10:05A.M. CST)*

Divine Inspiration
From my heart to yours

I am learning, yet again, that what I write is not inspired as the Scriptures are. In the last note, I wrote that Jesus cried from the cross "My Father why have u forsaken me", when in fact he cried "My God, My God, why have you forsaken me". And I thought how glad I am that He cried out not using his divine affiliation

with the Father, but using his affiliation and reflecting his complete union with us. For humanity was crying out for centuries in total "lostness" and doom. He took our doom, damnation, and despair and gave us his liberty and freedom to live forever. Now, he taught us instead to cry out: Abba, Father". Completed in Him. He, in us, United. We, in Him, forever, one.
(Thursday, February 23, 2012 at 10:35A.M. CST)

THE EXTENT OF SUFFERING
From my heart to yours

For one insane moment, I want to wish there was no sedation in hospitals so I can hear the real sound of suffering. And, mind you, this is only physical suffering. How much more did He suffer on our behalf. How much more was our burden that bore down and crushed that blessed head that we might be made whole in Him.
(Thursday, February 23, 2012 at 11:07A.M. CST)

TO LOVE BY CHOICE
From my heart to yours

So, it's not that we love others so we serve them, but because He loved us, we have no choice **but** to love others, especially the unlovely...like.... uh...just look around...for that covers all of us.
(Thursday, February 23, 2012 at 11:18A.M. CST)

GLORY SNAPSHOT
From my heart to yours

> All the glorious brightness of angels in the sky could not hold a candle to the incomparable glory that resided in the lowly manger. The shepherds knew that. *(Friday, February 24, 2012 at 12:56A.M. CST)*

WHY DO I LOVE?
From my heart to yours

> On their 50th wedding anniversary, this couple sat in a cozy corner where he first told her he loved her. And she asked with a sparkle in her eyes: "Sweetheart, why did you love me so much in the first place?" He said: "Honey, of all the girls that I knew in the past and looked at, you were the best to serve my purposes." This is of course a fictitious story. Likewise, is any thought that God's motivation resided outside His Own Person as to His choice of people in the OT. In fact, it was purely a love covenant for HIS love's sake, to show His infinite Grace and mercy. Like Hosea taking His harlot wife back an act of sheer mercy and grace (100%), likewise God purchased back unto Himself those who became like sheep gone astray, each going in his own way. His promise was built totally fully completely on faith and obedience. To us also, it still is. For without faith it is impossible to please Him. Without obedience it is impossible to follow Him. The song writer said: "Oh the love that will not let me go". Paul said: "For the love of Christ constrains us". *(Friday, February 24, 2012 at 12:26P.M. CST)*

A NEW PERSPECTIVE ON LOVE
From my heart to yours

It would be incomplete to think that God's love story was between Him and mankind. It's not even the half. For the whole story began and ends in heaven. The union, communion and everlasting love are the essence of the divine nature. It existed before the world began, and will remain forever. So we ask: where do we fit in this eternal masterpiece? Here it is: we obtained the Union with Christ through the cross; we obtained the communion of the eternal Spirit who brought us to the cross; and we obtained the unconditional love of the Father that manifested itself fully and forever at the cross. Peter said that He made us partakers of the divine nature, and held nothing back. Do we need anything else? I think not. For indeed it's ALL about HIM. *(Friday, February 24, 2012 at 5:07P.M. CST)*

LOVE FROM ABOVE
From my heart to yours

The supreme motivation that Jesus had, which consumed his whole being, was not the salvation of man, but doing the will of the Father. The prophets in the OT stated it; Jesus affirmed it. For that reason at His baptism, as on the Mount of Transfiguration, the voice came from heaven saying: "This is my Beloved Son in whom I am well pleased; hear ye Him". And Jesus prayed and said: "Father, glorify your name". The voice came saying: "I have glorified and will glorify". The greatest joy the Father had was that the Son surrendered his will willingly to that of the Father fully empowered by the Holy Spirit. In the Garden he cried: "...pass this cup from me, but let it not be my will, but thine". He was found trustworthy to fulfill what the Blessed Trinity decided in the council chambers of eternity. His word to His followers: "Be faithful unto death and I shall give you the crown of life". He knew exactly the full meaning of those words. Are we true followers? *(Friday, February 24, 2012 at 10:03P.M. CST)*

Your Will, Not Mine
From my heart to yours

Following the example of Jesus, we, His followers, can never accomplish His will if our will is not molded like his, being surrendered constantly, and if our hearts are not being purified completely by His Spirit. Just like Him, so are we. Did Jesus know how His earthly daily life was going to play out? No. How did He do it? How did He manage to accomplish the Father's will? This is how: The Son trusted the Father implicitly, yielded His will intentionally, and loved the Father completely. And that's precisely how He set an example for us. Thank you, Lord, for being the perfect example to follow. By your Spirit I yield, I follow, I listen, I trust, I know that you love me. I love you Lord! *(Friday, February 24, 2012 at 10:29P.M. CST)*

Mapquest Unacceptable
From my heart to yours

The prerequisite to experiencing His faith, hope, and love is that we relinquish our chronic desire to persistently ask Him for the map to our day, our circumstances, our future, our life. God does not believe in mapquest.com. *(Friday, February 24, 2012 at 10:32P.M. CST)*

Accepted At The Cross
From my heart to yours

Following Jesus Christ is categorically a personal matter. Ask Zacchaeus, the woman at the well, the fallen woman, and the blind. We have more in common with them than we are willing to admit...especially after we shed our pride, our fears, our arrogance, and our hypocrisy. The good news: He promised that He accepts ALL who meet Him at the cross. *(Friday, February 24, 2012 at 10:45P.M. CST)*

Hurts Abound
From my heart to yours

When in pain, we tend to hurt those closest to us whom we wouldn't think of hurting under normal condition. When our minds are confused and stifled to the point of despair, we take a destructive path in our behavior. When the soul is suffering in anguish as in a nightmare, the core of one's being has been corrupted. When a culture is steeped in all three types of pain, the night is long and dark. The solution without equivalent is in the cross of Christ. For He saw all the above in that bitter cup of judgment. When a person meets Christ, he knows the meaning of the words: "therefore, there is no condemnation now to those who are in Christ Jesus." thank you Lord for a new day. *(Monday, February 27, 2012 at 9:11A.M. CST)*

IN CHRIST ALONE
From my heart to yours

Why is the solution in Christ and in Christ alone? For starters, because He promised so much that ONLY HE can fulfill those "great and precious promises". He's not a super power for historically these come and go. He simply **IS**, which immediately places Him completely outside our comprehension. That's why when He (the Word) became flesh (incarnate), it was his prerogative of and exercise in absolute condescension. *(Monday, February 27, 2012 at 10:22A.M. CST)*

BEING CRUCIFIED WITH CHRIST
From my heart to yours

Hurt people hurt people. And, what's worse is that they are unable to break that vicious cycle in their own power. Yet it is possible. But, how? To the follower of Christ, we discover sooner or later when our spirits were brought back to life and fellowship with God, His Spirit enables us to live intentionally on a daily basis for the first time in His power and His Spirit. Deliberate living for Him enables us to acknowledge and shed the past, and become daily, and increasingly empowered to thankfully move forward and establish a trail of "small successes" to His glory; not with human fan fair, but with the blessed assurance that inspired Paul to write: "I am crucified with Christ; So I live, yet not I, but Christ lives in me". *(Tuesday, February 28, 2012 at 12:54A.M. CST)*

Burdens Lifted at Calvary
From my heart to yours

> Someone said: "If I overpower, dominate, and abuse you today, it temporarily numbs the pain I still have because I was overpowered, dominated, and abused yesterday." *(Tuesday, February 28, 2012 at 1:17A.M. CST)*

How Upset
From my heart to yours

> To be upset even mad at God when He doesn't do what we want to please us seems to be reasonable ... Only if it works both ways, to be fair to both parties. Or maybe we need to reexamine that picture, for God is good, especially when we don't see His point. *(Friday, March 2, 2012 at 12:21P.M. CST)*

Heavy Burdens
From my heart to yours

It is much easier and lighter to carry the burden of any handicap of the body than to carry the burden of any handicap of the soul. The diagnosis of the body ailment will likely lead to several cure options. And it's repeatable with the same person and over a span of a lifetime. So, when there is a headache, we take our favorite pain-reliever. And with time, we become experts with what works and what doesn't. But what can we suggest to someone who says, "My soul is downcast (depressed and crushed) unto death"? What analgesic is available? Is there a balm in Gilead? The mystery of the cross is that the very experience of suffering became the very path to a new life. The glory of the cross is that there is no other path than the path of the cross. That's why Jesus said: "if any man wants to follow me, let him deny himself and carry his cross and follow me" (as if Jesus was saying…"for I am carrying mine as well"). *(Monday, March 5, 2012 at 4:54A.M. CST)*

Worship and Sacrifice
From my heart to yours

Throughout the Bible, worship is associated with a sacrifice, with an animal tied to the altar (in the OT), or with total personal abandonment of the soul crushed beyond recognition in the presence of Almighty God. Paul said: "I beseech you therefore, brethren, by the mercies of God, to present your bodies a living sacrifice, wholly and holy acceptable, which is your reasonable worship". The visible piety is no reflection of the invisible crushing of the soul in worship in the presence of the Almighty, for then it is not who I am but truly who He is. Oh the sheer mercies of God, capable to sustain for a lifetime. "Surely goodness and mercy shall follow me all the days of my life. And I shall dwell in the house of the Lord forever." I had to ask myself: "how did I get into the house of the Lord in the first place, were it not for a life of worship?" For it's really all about Him. "That He might increase, and I might decrease." May His holy Name be blessed forever. *(Monday, March 5, 2012 at 5:19A.M. CST)*

Worship Beyond the Cross
From my heart to yours

The most crushing act of worship took place when the greatest sacrifice was offered to God on the cross. It was crushing to Jesus, to Mary, to John the beloved, to his disciples, to all who expected a man-made salvation. The problem is that the sacrifice had to be acceptable to God, not man. It had to be a God-size sacrifice, not a watered-down human remedy. And since when we transient humans of 70 or 80 years were able to come up with solutions to last into eternity?! The day God died on the cross was the day we came to life through His great sacrifice. It was on that day that God identified with man, becoming one with us, that we might identify with Christ, becoming one with Him. Oh, the unspeakable gift that hung on that cross for an eternal moment so that we, in worship, may be suspended in all our earthly life and for eternity between His grace and mercy in total worship of Him, in total abandonment to Him, in total adoration of Him. *(Monday, March 5, 2012 at 5:36A.M. CST)*

GLORY CRUCIFIED

From my heart to yours

The glory of the cross, which Paul insisted on as the crux and hinge of our faith, rests not in that Jesus Christ was lifted up for all to see, but in that Christ in the full power and presence of the eternal Spirit descended to the lowest parts of hell, faced the most pernicious of sins, found the most abhorrent of sinners, endured the most horrid of agonies, and drank the full cup of God's wrath to the point that Satan was intoxicated with the mirage of victory; but then Christ emerged from the grave in true, complete, vindicated, irreversible victory over sin and death, offering himself as our permanent representative in the innermost sanctum of heaven itself making intercession on our behalf until we go home. And this is only the beginning. "He that glories, let him glory in the cross of Christ", to whom be glory forever. *(Monday, March 5, 2012 at 7:05P.M. CST)*

Most times, we Christians treat the Bible, God, and church the same way. *(Wednesday, March 7, 2012 at 10:16A.M. CST)*

COMPREHENSION

From my heart to yours

I read a fascinating article about how the brain processes our reading that made my heart worship Jesus Christ in a fresh way. One paragraph from it says: (Note: Nothing Misspelled) "Reading is mental.You might not realize it, but your brain is a code-cracking machine. "For emaxlpe, it deson't mttaer in waht oredr the ltteers in a wrod aepapr, the olny iprmoatnt tihng is taht the frist and lsat ltteer are in the rghit pcale. The rset can be a toatl mses and you can sitll raed it wouthit pobelrm. S1M1L4RLY, Y0UR M1ND 15 R34D1NG 7H15 4U70M471C4LLY W17H0U7 3V3N 7H1NK1NG 4B0U7 17." And I thought: WOW! Jesus said: "I am the first and the last, the beginning and the end, the ALPHA and OMEGA". In addition to other thoughts about the verse, HE is what gives us meaning, the glue that keeps us together, what enables us to keep pressing on in life. Paul said: "And the peace of God that passes understanding shall keep your hearts and minds (together and protected) through Jesus Christ our Lord". To Him I bow my knee in worship, adoration, and gratitude forever. Have an awesome day! *(Friday, March 9, 2012 at 5:56A.M. CST)*

HIS NAME SHALL BE CALLED

From my heart to yours

Why His name shall be called "Wonderful"? Because He is the Servant-King; He is the Savior-Judge; He is the Lion-Lamb; He is the Royal-High Priest; and He is the God-Man. No wonder He is the Wonder. And I wonder why some people still wander and wander. How sad! *(Friday, March 9, 2012 at 4:23P.M. CST)*

OUT OF CONTROL
From my heart to yours

Someone said: "there is a direct correlation between people who are out of control in their own life and their hatred of the word 'No' ". Proverbs 19:19 says: Don't rescue an angry person, because you may have to do it again tomorrow." but there is a cure, and it's in Christ. Why? Because at the cross of Christ God taught us visibly how to hate the sin and how to love the sinner at the same time. He did that well. He did that perfectly. He did the right thing. Now, He said, "we are ambassadors for Christ, as though God is speaking through us". Let's do the right thing today. Then, thank Him for the right thing that He did. *(Saturday, March 10, 2012 at 4:38A.M. CST)*

DISRUPTED FATHERHOOD
From my heart to yours

I thought, by now I should have forgotten, or the episode should have been folded back with other pages past, or at least the pain, anguish, even the horror of the moment that lasted 2-3 minutes would be bearable by now, two years later. But, not so, and here it comes again, rushing like a tidal wave as I tossed and turned in bed at 3:00A.M. Looking down the barrel of a gun, watching as the guy pointed the gun inches from my only son's face, then moved toward the front seat where my wife was and brought the gun within an inch of her face. Then, before I could go any further, while still in that light sleep state, another image slipped into my thoughts non-invasively at the moment. It was the image of another Father who did in fact experience the disruption and total disconnect of an eternal love and union and fellowship with One he loved. Then I realized that walking through the valley of the shadow, was now more bearable. Then, I realized how insignificant my life was, for it could have ended in less than a second. I realized how horrible, how UN-acceptable was the thought of my only son slipping through my fingers to the sound of a bullet. And I realized how alone I would have been to lose the fellowship, union, and love of my wife of 35 years. I thanked God deeply for sparing us. But, as if for the very first time in my life, I thanked God more for not sparing His only Son. I will thank Him forever. Oh, the love that will not let me go! *(Saturday, March 10, 2012 at 5:05A.M. CST)*

Complete Commitment
From my heart to yours

I'm learning that Christ asks for nothing less than total devotion. Devotion to Christ happens continually in the atmosphere of love with a pure heart and in obedience without reservation. Its object, Christ, has the brilliance as on the Mount and the demonstration as in the Garden. Its cost is simply everything. Once we grasp that, only then can we comprehend his devotion to doing the will of the Father. *(Monday, March 12, 2012 at 8:07P.M. CDT)*

Dedication To One
From my heart to yours

> Devotion is loyalty tuned, as a musical instrument with love; so much so that it creates a bond that binds two in a covenant relationship. May I remind us that our devotion to our beloved Savior, Jesus Christ, derives its richness and freshness and meaning from the depth of His bond to us in His incarnation. And on the cross He sealed it complete and forever. *(Monday, March 12, 2012 at 10:24P.M. CDT)*

Daily Devotion
From my heart to yours

> Devotion (a daily necessary growing heart condition), when mixed with humility (a condition which if I discover I have, I lose) and love (gazing into the audience of One), and uncompromisingly focused on its object ("unto Him"), will make the subject (the leader-in-training, the follower-at-all-cost) usable, teachable, moldable in the hands of the Holy Spirit whose commitment is also primarily not to us but to the same object of our devotion, Christ. The rest (the hearers, the content, and the results) will fall in their proper place every time. The result (singular) is the sheer glory of Christ. Oh, that He might be preeminent in all things. Any additives will contribute to spiritual adultery of the heart, whose shameful outcome is also known, though in part. *(Tuesday, March 13, 2012 at 6:40A.M. CDT)*

NOT OF WORKS
From my heart to yours

As I grasp that true devotion to Him in my daily life, I realize that all my day is spent in worship of Him regardless of where the Spirit uses me. Though He may not say a word, yet to break the heart of the one I love (see Songs 5:2-5ff) is costly. But, still, my heart devotion is willing to pay the price, because: it's ALL about Him, and I learn that my comforts coming first have no part in worship. The motive: Love. The audience: Him. The Spirit: His. And whatever I do, even the most menial of tasks, is an act of worship toward Him (5:5). *(Tuesday, March 13, 2012 at 6:57A.M. CDT)*

TRUE RELIGION
From my heart to yours

There is nothing formal, official, or global about true religion if we go by the biblical definition. For it is defined as: "Religion that God our Father accepts as pure and faultless is this: to look after orphans and widows in their distress and to keep oneself from being polluted by the world." (James 1:37). Writing the same definition in keeping with today's organized church, it becomes: Religion that God our Father does not accept as pure and faultless is this: to look after the outside and be acceptable when it's convenient, self-serving and keeps me in my comfort zone; and, as far as "keep oneself from being polluted by the world"...well, each is entitled to his own opinions and feelings. *(Wednesday, March 14, 2012 at 2:07P.M. CDT)*

ABUNDANT GOD
From my heart to yours

God is the God of the "more", the "better", and of the "second chance". He said: "I came that they might have life and have it MORE..." (Mt 6:31); He said: "I will show you a BETTER way" (1Cor 12:27). Third, although he *knew* what Peter was about to do to Him at the end of His earthly ministry, he said: "and I prayed for you that your faith is not eradicated, and when you return, be sure to strengthen your brothers". Oh, the sustaining power of His love! *(Friday, March 16, 2012 at 4:24P.M. CDT)*

THE JOURNEY
From my heart to yours

Forty years ago, when I was in a youth choir, the pastor's wife closed her eyes, tears flowed at times, with radiant face as though transported to a different realm and sang this song: "Since I started for the Kingdom, Since my life He controls, Since I gave my heart to Jesus, The longer I serve Him, The sweeter He grows." Chorus: "The longer I serve Him, the sweeter He grows, The more that I love Him, more love He bestows; Each day is like heaven, my heart overflows, The longer I serve Him, the sweeter He grows." "Ev'ry need He is supplying, Plenteous grace He bestows; Ev'ry day my way gets brighter; The longer I serve Him, The sweeter He grows."

Today, the words came rushing into my memory, and I'm starting to understand, and the reason why she closed her eyes could be because she saw His face. The pastor's wife, in her 80s, stricken with Alzheimer's, when I asked her recently if she remembers that song, she only smiled and closed her eyes. Oh, the glory of His face! *(Friday, March 16, 2012 at 6:59P.M. CDT)*

LEADERSHIP SNAPSHOT
From my heart to yours

Here is a true mark of a Christian leader. While he is grateful that he receives the devotion of his people, he knows that they are following the Lord. For the devotion to serve truly comes from the Lord. And in worship, the Christian leader cultivates and nurtures their devotion. The pressing need is for a unified heart toward the Lord. *(Saturday, March 17, 2012 at 8:08A.M. CDT)*

SPIRITUAL WARFARE
From my heart to yours

There has been a concerted effort recently by satanic powers to annoy, attack, and destroy those who have made a genuine, transparent, and all-out commitment to be sold-out to the Person of Christ, yielding fully to the dominant power and presence of the Holy Spirit, rejecting totally any desire to say 'No' to what the Spirit desires to change in their lives. The conclusion they expressed in the sampling of expressions (verbal, written or otherwise) is that they willingly acknowledge their inadequacy, incompetence, and total wretchedness apart from Christ the Lord and the prompting of His Spirit. Perhaps, they discovered the first steps of what it means to be "led by the Spirit". For as Jesus said many time that the Son of Man MUST suffer and die, in like manner, they rightly concluded that they likewise MUST be emptied in order to be filled again. May that be the desire and reality of more and more among the portion of the 'Church' who speak Arabic. *(Sunday, April 1, 2012 at 11:37A.M. CDT)*

SPIRITUAL CRISIS
From my heart to yours

When a Christian experiences a true spiritual crisis of faith, his train of life stops and his pure devotion passes by faith through repeated moments of silence, and he utters only what is understood by Him who drank the bitter cup and was baptized with fire. Only then, he enters into His 'rest' and, through scorching tears, he smiles for he has seen His face. The true spiritual crisis for a follower of Christ is not when the Christian practices his Christianity but when the Gospel of Christ becomes the new reality in which he survives and thrives and finds his rest. *(Tuesday, April 3, 2012 at 12:53A.M. CDT)*

GLORY AND POWER

From my heart to yours

His power was shown when He established the earth with the power of His word. But His glory was shown when He established our salvation with the power of His cross. Today, after He died and before He rose again, we worship Him for He is not in the holy of holies on earth made by hands, but He is in the Holy of Holies of heaven itself, with His own blood, making the case on our behalf, settling our massive debt forever. If we don't grasp the size of our debt, we can never grasp the depth of His love or the richness of His grace. Oh, what a wonderful Savior! *(Saturday, April 7, 2012 at 12:50P.M. CDT)*

AFTER EASTER

From my heart to yours

Today, that Easter weekend is over, have you ever wondered: What now? Will it be another year before we celebrate it again? Maybe we need to change the way we look at Easter. For it never was intended to be an annual tradition of the Risen Lord but a daily celebration of a new life in Him, a radical beginning of the Kingdom of God in our hearts made possible exclusively by means of the curse accepted on the cross and the grace completely delivered from the empty tomb. More soon on: What comes after Easter. *(Monday, April 9, 2012 at 10:16A.M. CDT)*

EASTER TAKEAWAYS
From my heart to yours

What are the "takeaways" after the Easter event, things for us to chew on? Here they are: 1. Jesus, the Incarnate Son of God, on the cross lost the infinite love of the Father because of His infinite love for you and me. Try to live with that unique Reality, and you will discover, if you accept His alternative, that your hardness he can change to tenderness, your darkness he can change to light, and your death he can change to life. He said: if the Son of Man is lifted up (on the cross), he will draw all people to himself. He becomes the galvanizing "Center" around which all revolves. More to come. *(Tuesday, April 10, 2012 at 1:20A.M. CDT)*

KINGDOM SNAPSHOT
From my heart to yours

Fact-based resurrection event makes faith-based Kingdom living possible. *(Wednesday, April 11, 2012 at 12:41P.M. CDT)*

HID IN HIS LOVE
From my heart to yours

I may not understand my own, or my loved ones', sufferings AT ALL. But one thing I can be sure of; and that is that God for the sake of Christ will never keep his love from me. Why? It is because Christ lost the privilege of experiencing the Father's love from eternity past, so that we will always dwell in His love forever. Not because I understand it but because He promised, and so far He kept every promise He made. That's what Easter/Passover made possible through Christ. If you are a true follower of Christ, Won't you thank Him today? *(Thursday, April 12, 2012 at 10:06A.M. CDT)*

HIS APPEARING
From my heart to yours

After His resurrection, the Lord didn't come or go anymore. He simply appeared or disappeared. To Mary He said "Touch me not", but to Thomas He said "Bring your finger and touch me so you can believe". Now, it became a question of Faith. With Faith we can touch the resurrected Lord. That's another of what Easter/Passover accomplished for us, forever. Won't you pray today: "Lord, help my unbelief", so you may touch the face of God, and live... *(Friday, April 13, 2012 at 6:33A.M. CDT)*

LOVE MISSING
From my heart to yours

As our congregation has been reading aloud every Sunday 1Cor 13, our focus has been turning, slowly but surely, to the awesomeness of the love of God. Our fascination in its words gradually became a grinding examination of our hearts. I arrived so far face to face with the truth that Love is a cover (not a cover-up) for a multitude of sins. Otherwise, there isn't enough alternate covering of any kind to suffice as a cover for one sin. His love abounding! *(Sunday, April 15, 2012 at 11:01P.M. CDT)*

MISSING INGREDIENT
From my heart to yours

The greatest challenge to the follower of Christ is not that we won't have love, but that His love is truly ALL that we have. For His love cannot be partial, temporary, conditional, tangible, self-serving, or dependent on or in partnership with any human trait. It must be ALL of Him, because it's ALL about Him. The beauty of His love is that anyone can have it if he/she puts on Christ. *(Monday, April 16, 2012 at 9:57A.M. CDT)*

LOVE NEVER FAILS (1 COR 13)
From my heart to yours

Why? Because it's the infinite love of the father; it's the sacrificial love of the Son; it's the sustaining power of the Spirit; because it's unconditional; it's the source and driving force behind many precious promises from Him to us; it's the only practical way to live; because it overpowers enemies, it deepens the relationship with God, it elevates the human soul, it fills the emptiness in mankind, it disarms every enemy and empowers every follower of Christ to reach for more; it shuts the mouth of hell and it opens the gates of heaven; it puts a smile on any face and it gives a new song in the night; it reaches to the depths of the broken human heart, and it enables us to touch the face of God; it gives every satisfaction and fulfills every longing; it brings people together and it sets His followers apart; it reaches to the highest mountain and it flows to the lowest valley; it meets the yearning of every human being and brings the lost person home. THAT'S the start of why His Love Never Fails. The amazing thing about His matchless love is that it has no substitute, no alternative, no match, no end, no beginning, no height too much, no depth too low, no void too big, no stony heart to callous, and no ugly sin too sinful. It ALL flows from Calvary and covers the un-coverable, and recovers the irretrievable. It conquers, it changes, it quenches, it empowers, it delivers from sin, and it gives life everlasting. That's why NOTHING shall separate us from the love of God in Jesus Christ our Lord. Can we thank you anew? Can we stop thanking Him ever? Maybe that's why there is eternity! *(Tuesday, April 17, 2012 at 10:07A.M. CDT)*

INTERCESSION BENEFITS
From my heart to yours

To understand intercessory prayer, we need to consider that Human difficulties are Divine necessities that train us to discipline the flesh to the point of crucifixion and have true audience with God, and indeed have our prayer answered. It constantly shapes out spiritual character to be more like Christ. *(Thursday, April 19, 2012 at 5:42A.M. CDT)*

Resurrection Stone
From my heart to yours

The rolled-away stone is sure grounds for the solid Rock. The "living sacrifice" lifestyle is Christ in us at His best. The cross of Christ is unquestionably the crossroad of mankind. Celsus, a second century Greek philosopher and staunch opponent of early Christianity was first to mount a full written attack on the Christian sect. He said that the fact that women were the first bearers of the resurrection news is proof that the story is certainly unreliable claiming that women are hysterical by nature. And we think in the 21st century that the world altogether is less hysterical? That's crazy! *(Tuesday, April 24, 2012 at 4:09A.M. CDT)*

God's Dictionary
From my heart to yours

Isn't it interesting that we will never catch God saying things like: "I never thought of that", because everything is present before Him; or, "Let me think about it" because He said My thoughts are not your thoughts; or, "Good luck" because He holds everything in the power of His hand; or, "I'm running out of time" because He dwells in eternity; or, "I'm behind and need to work overtime" because he never sleeps and He never slumbers; or, "Why nobody told me about that?" because He's far above the heavens; or, "You're beyond help" because his love reaches to the lowest valley; or, "God doesn't love me" because He died for you and me; or "Where is my iPad, iPhone, my contact list" because He's the great I AM. Won't you praise Him today? He deserves all our

gratitude, adoration, worship, love, and praise forever and ever.
(Thursday, April 26, 2012 at 7:27A.M. CDT)

Salvation in a Nutshell

From my heart to yours

If someone is wondering: what exactly is "Salvation"? You may want to think of it like this:

- It's created and delivered in heaven at manufacturer's expense;
- 100% guaranteed to work without any fine print;
- It's 100% personal, non-refundable, non-customizable, non-transferable;
- Cannot be loaned or borrowed, never gets old or ruins;
- Will never have recalls;
- Doesn't discriminate by age, color, race, religion, national origin, gender, or sexual orientation;
- Minorities and women encouraged to receive it;
- One size fits all because His love reaches to the highest mountain and flows to the lowest valley;
- It's not seasonal and is not for sale;
- No advertising or special coupon needed;
- You don't need to "Google" it because it's at Calvary;
- The URL is "www.U-R-Loved.byHim";
- You don't need a super star or a movie star to tell you about it because they may likely become fallen star;
- It is backward and forward compatible automatically;
- It wasn't the result of some research and development department, or clinical trials on monkeys;
- No need for co-signor or co-sponsor;
- Has no spiffs ever;
- Has no side effects except one which is a life changed into His likeness;

- It is PAID IN FULL IN ADVANCE because mankind was in total foreclosure;
- The forecast was definitely NOT good;
- Wall Street was up the wall hedging their bets, and economists did not find it in their charts and psychologists were going nuts trying to replace it with behavior modification;
- The sociologists suggested better self-esteem but that theory quickly ran out of steam;
- No killing is needed to attain it, or a sacred place to stain it;
- It is not affiliated with any prayer cloth or cheese cloth;
- It's not to be taken (or stolen or bought or bartered or negotiated) because it's a gift;
- It is not financed because the debt is too big and the applicant (you or me) is already bankrupt;
- Chapter 7 and 13 bankruptcy do not apply because we were beyond protection from God's wrath and not fit for re-structuring;
- It's never been in draft mode or beta testing;
- It's not a la carte;
- It's all or none because it cost the blood of the Father's Son;
- It has no denominational pull or push;
- It's not in a piece of wood or at a place to visit if you could. Well, you may ask, "So, What is it then?"

Answer: Salvation is:

- A cry of faith from the bottom of the human heart,
- A cry that says by faith 'God, I need your kind of faith to believe what you did on Calvary's cross for me; and bear with what I'm about to say, but would you, dear God, for the life of me, have my heart and life in exchange for the life you gave to me on the cross? Would you, God? And I have no guarantees of my own because I have failed so much, but I have your promise to hold on to that you, God, have covered my debt completely and will forgive me for the asking with all my heart, will accept me, will make me whole again, will breathe in me your Spirit of life, will make me your child, will give me your name, will grant me to live again, to love you again, to

serve you gladly and to worship you forever. Will you have me, Lord, as I am?"
- Then, listen, for He was heard saying all along: "Come unto me all you who are heavy-laden and I will give you rest".

This is where you and I say, if we accept Him, "Thank you, Lord. I accept by faith what you've done. Lead me every day as you promised. My desire is to live for you, and to do your will in my life even if it cost me what it cost your Son Jesus." *(Friday, April 27, 2012 at 2:14A.M. CDT)*

TRUE REFLECTION
From my heart to yours

This past week I have been completely overwhelmed by a simple truth that kept visiting me like a nagging toothache. It has three parts. Part One: that the love of the Father was manifested in Christ. Part Two: That every person we meet needs to see it in its simplest form. Part Three: that Christ gave his followers His Spirit dwelling in us to convey that same love untarnished or absolutely captivating. Then I faced the question: What's keeping me from showing His love? Is it a hurt, a hang-up, a loss, a complaint, a negative emotion, a fear, failure, or any other excuse? For I should know that in Him I have everything I need that I may overflow with His amazing love. *(Tuesday, May 1, 2012 at 10:58A.M. CDT)*

ARROGANCE SNAPSHOT
From my heart to yours

Since the Holy Spirit is the only person who succeeds in glorifying Christ 100%, it is sheer arrogance and pride on our part if we think that the Holy Spirit does his work on a part-time basis. Furthermore, what we think is glorifying to Christ is not necessarily what the Holy Spirit thinks. *(Wednesday, June 20, 2012 at 1:02A.M. CDT)*

PRECIOUS IN HIS EYES
From my heart to yours

Last night, I received a message to let me know that the wife of a dear pastor I knew when I was 19 (and he has been with the Lord for over a year) has gone on to meet the Lord she always loved. She played the piano when the youth choir travelled about twice a month. She sang a very precious song that said: "Since I started for the Kingdom; Since my life He controls; Since I gave my heart to Jesus; The longer I serve Him; The sweeter He grows." Chorus: "The longer I serve Him, The sweeter He grows; The more that I love Him; More love He bestows; Each day is like heaven my heart overflows; the longer I serve Him; The sweeter He grows." Now at 60, I'm discovering how true her words have always been. Lord, make me a blessing like she was, and let me see your lovely face when it pleases you, like she is gazing now and has arrived home. *(Wednesday, June 20, 2012 at 11:02A.M. CDT)*

AT WHAT PRICE
From my heart to yours

> The least costly and the most productive lifestyle in any local church is when the focus is on learning, loving and living the Word; loving the believers unconditionally; loving the company of the Lord at His Table; and Praying like the church depended on it for it does and like heaven can't wait to answer. What about everything else? It'll all fall in place once the priorities are set. *(Wednesday, June 20, 2012 at 11:31A.M. CDT)*

BRINGING SHAME ON HIS NAME
From my heart to yours

> It is shocking at times beyond measure, for a true follower of Christ, to realize that when he/she is not reflecting Christ, automatically we are disgracing His name on a personal or corporate level. Put differently, and without alternative, we are always part of the construction or part of the destruction within the body of Christ. May our eyes remain open and our hearts diligent in loving Him from a pure heart. *(Friday, June 22, 2012 at 11:20P.M. CDT)*

MATURITY SNAPSHOT
From my heart to yours

> The success (maturity) of a local church or a single believer alike depends, neither on what we do for Him nor what He does for us, but rather on how much the Holy Spirit did IN us to reflect

Christ's image to the world. Satan is diligently working 24/7 to keep the local church and believer busy with religious duties driven by feeling of guilt when we fail rather than the believer is being guided by the Spirit of Christ. The fact of the matter is that He (the Holy Spirit) is not impressed by our creativity for Christ but by our maturity in Christ. *(Friday, June 22, 2012 at 11:30P.M. CDT)*

PURE HEART
From my heart to yours

To love Christ from a pure heart requires a heart purified by the Spirit of Christ. From Romans 12:1-2, and since a sacrifice can never place itself on the altar but is in need of someone to place it there, we must yield to the Spirit daily (complete surrender) for Him to bind us like a sacrifice then place us on top of the altar. Result: a holy fire descends, the sacrifice burns, what's worldly dies daily, and a new life from the Spirit of life is infused in us, the life that's filled with Christ, totally, and then He lives in us, is glorified through us, is pleased with us, and reveals Himself to us. What did we do? We just burned, and we died daily for Him. And he lives daily in us. "I have been crucified with Christ; and, I live, yet not I, but Christ lives in me." He gives me His DNA by the work of His Spirit in me. *(Friday, June 22, 2012 at 11:46P.M. CDT)*

COMPREHENSIVE YIELDING
From my heart to yours

Coming from many cultural backgrounds enables us to understand the meaning of "tribes", "languages", "dialects - those unique variations among the sub-groups", "traditions", "personal values and preferences", "personal opinions, rights, and privileges", and "family name". ALL the above must be yielded to Christ and His supremacy is granted full rights and governance over us for one simple reason, namely, because now we who claim to be His followers have His Name on us, His Spirit in us, and have become members in his "tribe". To-date, any person cannot be a member in two tribes but in only one. So, this simplifies things, doesn't it? It boils down to this: who is yielding to whom? Do I really belong to Him? May we bring Him glory in all things! (Friday, June 22, 2012 at 11:57P.M. CDT)

SPIRIT'S ONLY FRUIT
From my heart to yours

True Love, which is the only fruit of the Spirit, shows its beauty, taste, and grace in several areas of life. One area is SELF-CONTROL or self-discipline. Lack of self-control has definite "side effects" and "ugly friends", such as, Indulgence in all areas of life, Defensiveness about sinful lifestyle, Unmanaged daily living, Self at center-stage, Slothful habits of life, Waste of time, Cover-up by faulting others, Poor testimony to Christ. How can we even begin to glorify the Lord with these characteristics in our lives? Are we lying and don't even know it? For it's not OK to have

SELF out-of-control. There is no excuse. The world thrives on it. Satan loves these types of people. The Holy Spirit is grieved. God help us! *(Sunday, June 24, 2012 at 10:14A.M. CDT)*

SELF-CONTROL (2)
From my heart to yours

The beauty of self-control is not that we can make it happen, but that by submitting to the governance of the Holy Spirit in our lives enables Him to make it happen, and brings glory to Christ. Let's stop looking at others because all that leads to nothing more than a life of self-made righteousness. *(Sunday, June 24, 2012 at 10:18A.M. CDT)*

FRUIT OF SPIRIT EXPRESSED
From my heart to yours

Self-control means: saying NO in the power of the Spirit; it's saying YES to loving and knowing Christ and anything that leads me to serve and live for Him; it's being CONSISTENT in small steps that bring me closer to Him; it's having a DISCONNECT from anything that distracts me from Him. And if you ask me why all this, the simple answer is: Because it's ALL about HIM. Then in the Spirit I can worship Him, love Him, serve Him, know Him, adore Him, Run to Him, Listen to Him, and fade into Him because of His immense love for me, and all people see will be...Him. What about others and how they live? When Peter asked the Lord about John living forever, Jesus said: "What is it to you?" So, about everybody else, Leave them alone! That's a distraction from our supreme objective, which is HIM. *(Sunday, June 24, 2012 at 10:28A.M. CDT)*

NO LUCK
From my heart to yours

In an article by Maggie Hendricks, on Yahoo Sports News, she said: "Allyson Felix and Jeneba Tarmoh finished in a dead heat for third place in the 100m dash at the Olympic Trials in Eugene, Ore., on Saturday. The tie has to be broken. Shockingly, U.S. Track and Field does not have tie-breaker procedures in place." The option of a coin toss was rejected, she continues, because "Too much depends on the decision for it to be settled by chance.". But yet, it's Ok to determine the origin of the human species by chance. The problem is not with the coin tossed; but that the coin doesn't have anything on either side. And the hand of the one tossing it hasn't evolved completely yet. Yikes! *(Sunday, June 24, 2012 at 10:56A.M. CDT)*

MAKING CHANGES
From my heart to yours

If I have a serious desire and determination to change my wife, coming up on 36 years, I discovered that it is easier, more enjoyable, and of greater worth and sure success if I yielded to the Spirit to change me totally into the image of Christ for love's sake than to waste all my energies in total vain. Then instead of being impressed by the changes accomplished in my wife's life, I am captivated by His love for me, and that's when I get a good glimpse of how much my Lord loved the Church, His bride. And I also discover that even with time, my wife still has the glimmer of a bride throughout my days. All the rest is mere details. *(Saturday, July 7, 2012 at 1:05P.M. CDT)*

CHANGING PLACES
From my heart to yours

There was a time when she put her arm around my shoulder to walk me through rough days. Surely goodness and mercy shall follow me. As she hastened to make Turkish coffee, she skipped taking her medication, but seemed content that an arm was around her shoulder... as there will be yet another day for the meds, just didn't want to miss the quiet cup of coffee. Her rationale goes like this: "one more, one less, doesn't matter. It will all even out at the end." I'll take that anytime :-) *(Sunday, August 19, 2012 at 1:49A.M. CDT)*

THE POTTER'S HANDS
From my heart to yours

I was gently awakened a little while ago with a line from a favorite Arabic song on my mind. (Translated: Remake me into a new vessel, According to your good pleasure) and kept repeating the words again and again.... . Then uninvited thoughts came rushing, screaming, flooding my heart and mind, words that stopped me in my slumbering tracks, words like: Crushing, Fire, Kneading, Yielding, Submission, Vessel, Ownership, Nothingness, Suffering, ... and I thought "I need to push the NEXT button and play another song on the platter of my mind ...something milder, more happy, less intrusive, more enjoyable, less painful," but I couldn't, and I didn't want to because I remembered ... I remembered Him – Crushed alone in Gethsemane for me, passed through The Fire of Holy Anger, Kneaded in the grips of Holy Love, Yielded His Sacred head for me, Suffered beyond compare on my behalf, and at the end Surrendered even his very spirit. And tears rolled down my face as I asked: Why? Why?! and sensed my whole being was wanting to know...why. And like never before, the answer came as in a holy hush, and I remembered how He presented Himself a sacrifice in that sacred and eternal Council of the Godhead for my sake, for me, because He loved me, because he never stopped loving me. Then I was constrained, as it were, in the vise of His love, and didn't want to let go, not because I wanted to, but because He wouldn't let me go. Then I sang it again. !!! "Amazing Love, How Can It be." *(Sunday, October 28, 2012 at 3:44A.M. CDT)*

MOLD ME MAKE ME
From my heart to yours

God NEVER destroys us in our pain and suffering (of any kind). Satan ALWAYS tries to destroy us through every pain and suffering (of any kind). I'm grateful that God ALWAYS has the final word. This morning I was thinking on: "I am the Alpha and Omega", and was humming a song that says: "How can I say Thanks for the things you have done for me; Things so undeserved; Yet you came to prove your love for me; The voices of a million angels; Could not express my gratitude; All that I am or ever hope to be; I owe it All to thee." May we always be...thankful. *(Monday, October 29, 2012 at 11:18A.M. CDT)*

IN-FORMATION
From my heart to yours

Do I come before God because I believe right or because He is? Do I stay in His presence because of who He is or because of who I am? Do I love Him because I desire Him or because I desire something from Him? Is my longing for Him driven by who He is or by what I am? Is He my Lord because I insist loudly or because I know in my heart that He is? Am I a follower of Jesus because of information about Him or because of formation by Him? Lord, "search me, O Lord, and know my heart; test me and know my anxious thoughts. See if there is any offensive way in me; and lead me in the way everlasting." *(Thursday, November 1, 2012 at 6:53A.M. CDT)*

DEEP GRATITUDE
From my heart to yours

On Thanksgiving Day, or any other day, how can one be thankful when there is suffering, pain, hurt, death, abuse, shame, or you-name-it ? The answer is not on earth or in heaven. It is in Christ Alone, for if He's not enough alone, he's not good at all. Please look at Him on the cross, for He identified with us, carried us, lifted us with Him and loved us with all our suffering, pain, hurt, death, abuse, shame, or you-name-it, and gave us Himself to be in Him safe and secure, clothed and our shame covered. He became one with us so that we become one with Him. For that, I am eternally thankful. Any alternatives?! Now, look at Him as King of Kings who loved us with an everlasting love. Isn't He Awesome?!! *(Thursday, November 22, 2012 at 11:56A.M. CST)*

TWEAKING LENSES
From my heart to yours

Why do I love Him? It's, as the song says, "Not because of who I am but because of what He's done; not because of what I've done, but because of who You are." For His love endures not when things are going well, but especially when things are not well at all. *(Thursday, November 22, 2012 at 1:01P.M. CST)*

SEIZING THE MOMENT; AND SAVING THE MARRIAGE
From my heart to yours

I have a confession to make. Since it is 1:47A.M. now, I can refer to the 23rd as yesterday. Yesterday, I made a big blunder. In 42 years this month, I always knew that my wife's birthdate was Nov 24th. I don't know if the sun stood still yesterday or what, but I said that wife's birthday was yesterday, when in fact it is today. To the average bystander on the streets of life, this is such a silly matter. To me, however, this was a crisis situation! And for the past 24 hours, I was waiting for the moment when I can make it up to her. Throughout yesterday, she would walk by me and simply give me that look that says: "I can't believe you'd do this to me!" I thought maybe going to a restaurant for dinner would help remedy the situation. Not so! It became a critical matter when I looked at the clock and it was 11:00P.M.. I resigned myself to a miserable sequence of future years when I just knew she was going to remind me of this episode every chance she gets, and usually it will be in front of people discussing the joyful bliss of married life. Then, at 11:40P.M., the break came in the ever-darkening clouds of misery and utter shame over my head. I had my pjs on, throbbing headache from thinking too much, gloomy outlook loomed on the horizon of my remaining years. I kissed her goodnight and laid my head down, looked at the ceiling, knowing that not even a prayer for a miracle will help now. Then she says: "I wish I have some ice cream!" The sweetest words to my ears, indeed! I tried to control my emotions, and said: "Honey, you're not pregnant, are you?" Ha-ha She said: "No, because if I was, I would ask for pickles with the ice cream." Ha-ha! I'm a man who believes in looking at options when possible! So I said: "Honey, would you like me to get two small pints, or a gallon of three flavors?" She said, "how about if we get both, the pints and the gallon?" Of course! I should have thought of that one! I laid back; it was approaching midnight! Suspenseful music was playing in my head, and the biggest grin was about to break on my face! But I played Mr. Cool, and said, "You ARE going to stay up while I'm gone to get the ice cream, right?" Very matter-of-factly, she says, "Yes". Those who know me, know how much I LOVE ice cream, but in this experience I was sacrificing even ice cream for the sake of building relationships, of course! I would have you know, the car engine revved up, the headlights flew wide open down the highway, and between 11:40P.M. and 12:23, I was singing my joyful hymns going and coming, thankful for how a crisis can be avoided. . . with a little bit of ice cream and finesse. You just have to seize the moment and save the marriage, you know. Once at the store, I parked the car and looked around making sure I didn't know any creature around, human or otherwise. I sneaked in to the supermarket store, and navigated my way to the ice cream aisle (no GPS needed). Then it hit me, which flavors should I get?? I forgot to ask, but oh, well, again, I believe in options! So I picked up butter pecan, Dutch chocolate and three-flavored pints (vanilla, chocolate, and strawberry). I picked up the gallon as well, a little further down the aisle, and made my way to the cashier like an Olympic skater skims the ice and swings around the corner with a swish of icicles spraying into the crowd. Gladly paid for the frozen treasures! To the cashier it was money. To me, it was saving myself embarrassing future moments for years to come. I walked in the back door at home, placed the items on the kitchen table, went straight to the bedroom. And lo, and behold, my Honey was sitting straight up in bed like a princess waiting for her Prince Charming. "Which flavor would you like, Sweetheart?" I said. Genius words to show I cared! Ha-ha. After I told her the options, we both settled down in bed, sitting up at 1:45A.M., blanket draped over our legs, long-neck spoons in our hands, dipping delightfully into the pints of priceless frozen delights in total silence except for the clicking sound when the spoon hit our teeth. We finished almost together, me a bit sooner. She dipped into her pint of butter pecan and dropped a scoop into my empty bucket. A sign of approval and pleasure from her! To me, now I can look forward to years of utter marriage bliss, enriching the meaning of the phrase: ". . . and they lived happily ever after". Then I lay back, looking at the inside of my eyelids, thankfully repeating in deafening silence, "November 24, November 24, don't ever forget: November 24". And now, it's 2:40A.M.! My November 24 Sweetheart was worth it all. Goodnight...... *(Saturday, November 24, 2012 at 2:52A.M. CST)*

GOD CAN USE "THE LEAST OF THESE"
From my heart to yours

Please Meet Ricky! Yesterday, November 24, we took a trip to Tennessee to visit some dear friends we haven't seen in months. As we sat enjoying dinner together at a cafeteria, toward the end of the meal, someone tapped me on the shoulder. I turned; it was Jonathan. He said, "Dad, I'd like for you to meet Ricky. Ricky is a new friend." I shook hands and said, "Hello Ricky, good to meet you". But I noticed tears in Ricky's eyes. "Are you ok, Ricky?" "Oh, yes I am," he said. "Your son here came up to me while I was working back there, introduced himself, and was telling me about the dental surgery he had a month ago, an' all. And told me about y'all here having dinner. Then out of nowhere he asked me if he can pray for me. And for a moment there, I froze in my place thinking 'now of all the people in this cafeteria, why me Lord?" I smiled and said, "that's my Jonathan; he did that recently at a KFC when we went to eat-in, and he walked up to place an order and suddenly he looked at the assistant manager and said to her 'hello my name is Jonathan, what's your name? How are you?' And she said 'Fine, fine, how are you Jonathan?' And Jonathan said, I'm fine, I'm here with my parents eating." I went on to tell Ricky that Jonathan asked her 'is there anything I can pray with you about?' And she said, 'As a matter of fact Yes, my husband is having cancer surgery tomorrow, and his heart is weak, and I wish you'd pray for him.' So Jonathan, pulling his little notepad out of his back pocket, said 'and what's your husband's name?'. And she told him. He wrote it down. 'And what's his phone number', Jonathan asked her. And she gave him. Then he said, 'I promise I'll pray for him". Ricky interrupted me and chuckled, and said, "Yes Jonathan took out that little notepad from his pocket again and wrote my name on it too". Then Ricky went on to say, "I just want you to know that I thank God for your son and his boldness and discernment to walk up to me and of all these people to tell me he wants to pray for me." Then Ricky went on saying, "ya know, when my 9-month old baby grows up, I want to tell him about your son Jonathan, and I want to tell him how thankful I am that someone cared enough to stop and tell me he wants to pray for me." And as he fought back the tears, he said, looking up, "and ya know, I love the Lord but I've been away from Him, but now all I want to do is come back to Him and want Him to know that I love Him. I just want to love on Him and tell Him so, because He's been so good to me here through your son." And again, he looked at Jonathan and said, "and it's all because of this young man who dared to stop me and pray for me. I just love him, I love him. And, as they hugged, Ricky said 'Now, I have a little brother in your son." I choked, not expecting a holy moment like this to happen. I really didn't know what to say further, because all that needed to be said WAS said. So I said, "I'd like to take a picture of you two so we can pray for you." Click! But I suppose that was not all that Jonathan had on his mind at that moment, for he turned to Ricky and said, (almost in a whisper) "Hey Ricky, you want to walk back here to this empty table and let's pray?" Ricky couldn't hold his tears back anymore, and said, 'Yes, Yes, I wish you would'. And they withdrew from us gently for a greater moment with Him who answers prayer. They locked hands, and I heard them pray. I don't know what they said, but when they finished I saw tears in their eyes. As I snapped a picture during prayer, I felt like an intruder on a sacred hush moment in time when perhaps I needed to take my shoes off instead because the ground where I was standing was holy. They finished, hugged, and said goodbye. I remembered and started humming to myself the words of a song my wife and I learned many years back that said: "There's a sweet, sweet Spirit in this place; And I know that it's the Spirit of the Lord. There are sweet expressions on each face; And I know that it's the presence of the Lord." The chorus said: "Sweet Holy Spirit, Sweet Heavenly Dove, Stay right here with us, Filling us with your love; And for these blessings, We lift our hearts in praise; Without a doubt we'll know that we have been revived, When we shall leave this place". I know God can use the least of these. I know that the world is filled with a Ricky somewhere who is waiting for someone to pray with and for them. I also know that God answers prayer. Now, I need to get me a notepad. Personal note: On the day when Jonathan was born, six or seven newborn specialists stood in the room around my wife's hospital bed trying to give us some input and comfort about what to expect as Jonathan grows up. And one by one, as I asked them "what do you expect his future will look like developmentally?" they would say "we really can't say, because we don't know enough". The cardiologist told us Jonathan needed heart surgery when he gets to be six. The eye doctor told us that we can have the surgery on his eyes shortly after his heart is repaired. The geneticist could not assure us of anything, neither could the other experts. After they left, my wife said "Honey, didn't the Lord give him to us when the church in Ohio prayed? Let's give him back to the Lord." "Yes, I think we should", I said. I remember holding her hand and praying, not knowing what the future will hold. I have a mind that the Lord answered our prayer. I just didn't know how he was going to do that. We just had to wait a few years. I know God is faithful. His love is enduring. That's why I love Him so much. *(Sunday, November 25, 2012 at 6:34A.M. CST)*

CHANGE AND CHANGELESS
From my heart to yours

What I've been thinking lately is that . . .

1. Change is unquestionably expected if I'm truly a follower of Jesus Christ.

2. Change into His likeness is expected if I'm truly obedient to Him.

3. Change is expected in ALL areas of my life. Everything must be on the table. Yes, especially my favorites!

4. Holiness and Obedience are not optional. He does not require actions or reactions; I'm wasting my breath trying to change his mind.

5. Holy Anointing is the only method by which I learn His desire for me.

6. True change happens only when the Holy Spirit does that work.

7. The results of true change are: genuine worship, implicit obedience, and unconditional love. All must be dedicated toward the person of Jesus Christ.

8. His work in me always begins small, and grows commensurate with my love, worship, obedience and faithfulness to Him; and only He knows whether I'm faithful because he always tests it with fire.

9. He is never impressed with what religion I do for Him. But He is always impressed with what the Spirit does, for the Spirit glorifies Him constantly.

10. What He demands of me is nothing less than absolute surrender. No questions asked. None! Until then, all I do amounts, in fact, to absolute worthlessness.

11. Comparing myself to people is futile, for it has no eternal value whatsoever - not on earth, not in heaven.

12. Seeking the kingdom of God and His righteousness is neither a part-time nor a full-time task. In fact, it's not a matter of time, but of being. It's not something I do, but rather it's something that I am.

13. My consuming passion for Him filters all my other passions.

14. Touching the hem of His garment causes me to shy away from touching anything else that does not bring forth His power.

15. Loving my Lord always is simply true worship. Thus, what I do for Him is always measured by my motive which is loving Him, and by the outcome which asks whether my action has led me to worship and adore only Him. *(Sunday, December 16, 2012 at 1:01A.M. CST)*

OINTMENT SNAPSHOT
From my heart to yours

I prayed this morning to be emptied of everything that does not find its fountain in the cross of Christ. Someone said: "All of our relationships are restored and prioritized by the cross." May we always remember that the Christ of the manger is the Christ of the Cross. *(Wednesday, December 19, 2012 at 7:58A.M. CST)*

SCRIPTURE BETTER
From my heart to yours

Christian songs can move me and may point me to Christ, but not necessarily so, because they reflect human emotions and thoughts. Scripture, on the other hand, is the very thoughts of God the Holy Spirit, lifting the writers above error, using their unique personality and style, to convey to mankind and place in our hands the fully inspired Word of God. It's His Word that I "hide in my heart" to guide and fill. Many songs I've found lately are like beer commercials: canned, Less filling and Lite. *(Monday, December 31, 2012 at 1:16P.M. CST)*

GRAVITATIONAL PULL
From my heart to yours

All religions without exception have a physical center from which they derive their identity. However, the Center of Christianity is a Person, not a place. That Person is Christ. And He always moves His habitation to where there is an altar and fire. For all He seeks is people who worship Him in Spirit and Truth. In the heart of a true follower is His temple. That's where He makes His dwelling. That's where He pours His love. That's where we open the alabaster box and pour all its content in complete surrender and worship and adoration, for He is worthy! May 2013 be just that for all who love Him. *(Tuesday, January 1, 2013 at 2:30A.M. CST)*

JESUS THE GIFT
From my heart to yours

The greatest GIFT God gave the world is Himself in Jesus Christ. The greatest HONOR He gave those who follow Him is to be living members of His Body and be vessels of honors to Him. The greatest JOY He gave those who love Him is to love one another. The greatest POWER He gave His followers to live victoriously is the power of His Spirit. The greatest REWARD that awaits those who love Him is to worship Him forever. However, what breaks His heart the most after seeing Him hanging on the cross is that there is no reason any longer to still be running away when He's become our refuge, or to be hiding from Him when He's become our hiding place, or to love Him conditionally when His love was convincingly demonstrated on our behalf. Some people say THIS love is SO out of this world. But He says THIS love is exactly what the world needs most. Some guitarist may sing "Imagine there's no heaven". I say, Imagine there's no Calvary! Imagine there's no cross! Imagine there's no love of God. How dark! How lonely! How doomed we would have been! "But God demonstrated His love toward us". Love so amazing! And to think that He has the capability and wants to empower us to love with THAT kind of love?!!! WOW! *(Sunday, January 6, 2013 at 12:17A.M. CST)*

GIFTS NOT READY
From my heart to yours

IF the gift(s) of the Holy Spirit, according to His Word, belonged to every believer and true follower of Christ, IF indeed the Bible describes all believers as living members, useful and serving one another, and IF The Lord God who paid her debt forever and "purchased her with His own blood" is indeed the One building His Church firmly one stone upon another, I must ask: Why don't leaders of evangelical and traditional churches open their church doors much more and give the Spirit of the living God the opportunity to invade their stony altars and empty pews and shaken hearts and extract the fears deep within each soul, and enable willing members to breathe the fresh air of the Holy Spirit, and bless all churches and memberships if indeed they are alive in Christ? Why doesn't the world see in the "one-day churches" who revolve around a one-hour performance a better and more dynamic life that speaks everyday of Jesus Christ alone, in ALL His beauty, and in His true and superlative Person and unique personality, and reflect His image to the world in numbing simplicity and eternal truth? I must ask: Has God relinquished His plan to work through the organism called the Church, through individuals, and left the matter to organizations and programs requiring rework and perpetual maintenance so as to "maximize exposure" in the marketplace ? Why would the Holy Spirit, I ask, give His gift(s) to every member of the Body of Christ if He had no intention of using those gifts to reflect Christ in the world and give Him glory? Has the visible church shirked its sacred duty of telling its membership about the Person and work of the Holy Spirit in each one? Did we leave the Person and topic of the Holy Spirit to avoid controversy or flaunt a more "religiously correct posture" over a group who by default have monopolized the Holy Spirit's name and presence in the church? Since when has a corrupt world become the referee, arbiter, judge and jury over the life and work of the followers of Jesus Christ who truly desire to follow Him? How long does the pulpit insist on paralyzing the pew, usurp power that belongs only to Christ, and fear the results of a true and holy fellowship where Christ supremely reigns? Has the love and grace of our Lord become a commodity, and a trinket marked cheaply from a popular source, just to peddle abuse in the corrupt human markets of the world? I pray that every group and church upon whom that blessed Name is called would open their doors asking the Spirit of God to enter, to hover over its face as in the first creation, and blow on it as on the dead bones in Ezekiel's vision to bring them together to life, and no one knows from where He came or his destination? I pray that every group or local church would open their windows so that the light and Spirit of Christ may come in, remove the religious dust clogging its lungs to breathe Him fully, and its stubborn worn-out rags covering its shame to be clothed with His beauty and become useful again in His image. So, what can we say, what should we say, when we sense the whiff and breath of the Spirit coming over us and we are, as it were, in that strange but real state between wakefulness and sleep, conscious but not fully ? For we truly believe that He is able to do exceedingly abundantly more than we can ask or think. May I suggest with my whole being that we be found like Hannah, mother of Samuel the prophet, who with "sorrowful spirit" poured out her soul, "spoke in her heart, only her lips moving but her voice was not heard", and in deafening silence say: COME, HOLY SPIRIT, WE NEED YOU COME, HOLY SPIRIT, WE PRAY COME WITH YOUR STRENGTH AND YOUR POWER COME IN YOUR OWN SPECIAL WAY. COME LIKE A SPRING IN THE DESERT COME TO THE WEARY OF SOUL, LORD LET YOUR SWEET HEALING POWER TOUCH US AND MAKE US WHOLE. *(Sunday, January 6, 2013 at 12:30P.M. CST)*

UTTER DEPENDENCE
From my heart to yours

It became clearer to me in recent days, when Jesus said: "As the Father has sent me, I am sending you", that the Father did not depend on the Son, but the Son depended fully on the Father. For the Son of Man said: "I do not speak of myself, but what I hear, I speak unto you". Also, from His younger days, He was fully aware of His relationship with the Heavenly Father, for he said to Mary and Joseph "Don't you know that I must be about my Father's business." The mission for the Son of Man was not his own independent project, but it was to know and then to convey the heart and love of the Father. The method was by means of and in the full enablement of the Holy Spirit who filled and led the Son. The fully self-sufficient and reciprocated love and union and fellowship in the Triune God was demonstrated, was His desire for His followers to partake in; and now it makes perfect sense. When Jesus sends His disciples and followers to be His ambassadors, He has shown them in a practical way how it can be done successfully. Complete emptying from self, complete fullness of faith and trust, and continual experience of the Spirit's power are the three essential recipe ingredients to know and to show the love of God. A Hindu professor said to a Christian student once: "If you Christians lived like Jesus Christ, India would be at your feet today." Iskandar Jadeed, a former Arab Muslim, once said: "If all Christians were Christians there would be no more Islam today". Christlikeness is God's purpose. His Holy Spirit accomplishes that purpose in His full power. The value of my effectiveness and worth in the world today is commensurate with being Christ-like. It's not what I do, but what He does. At the end of the day, It's not about ME, but it's about HIM. Anything else, regardless of the value we humans place on it, is man-made and nothing less than sheer idolatry in religious form. *(Tuesday, January 8, 2013 at 12:43P.M. CST)*

THE FATHER AND THE SON
From my heart to yours

I cannot presume to know much on how the Father and Son in the Godhead relate to one another, and still what I do know is frail at best. Yet it's clear enough to give me awe and drive me to worship deeply. What I know is in Scripture, and of no direct or special revelation. It's important to cultivate a growing knowledge about this relationship, even somewhat, so that when we pray and say: "Our Father who art in heaven", we will stay at any cost away from senseless expressions of selfish motives glazed with a "form of godliness", yet knowing fully that what we say when we pray is simply self-serving and goes unanswered (see James 4:1-4). The Father-Son relationship is absolutely unique in its essence and eternally holy in all its beauty. Why is it relevant to the followers of Christ? It's because that kind of relationship is what Christ always desired for His followers once they unite with Him at the cross. For through that unbreakable union with the eternal, and now Incarnate, Son we can have the same union with the Father through Him. For that reason, and for a thousand others, if the candle brags about its light in the presence of the sun at the noon hour, Christ's followers can claim a value for any earthly accomplishment in the presence of Him who loved us and gave His own life for us at Calvary. The eternal Father and Son, the two most sacred dwellers of the most holy place, we know, loved one another completely, unconditionally, unreservedly, and from everlasting to everlasting. Why is that relevant to us? It's because that was Christ's desire for His true followers when he said: "And I have declared unto them your name, ... that the love with which you have loved me may be in them, and I in them. (John 17:26).

Therefore, the union between Christ and His followers becomes an integral part and an extension of that sacred and timeless union and love between Father and Son. (more to come) *(Tuesday, January 8, 2013 at 2:14P.M. CST)*

LORD, LORD
From my heart to yours

Why would Jesus say in Matthew 7:21: "Not everyone who says to Me, 'Lord, Lord,' will enter the kingdom of heaven, but he who does the will of My Father who is in heaven will enter". Jesus is saying:

(1) It's not what we say, but it's who were are;
(2) Who we truly are is known 100% accurately only to him;
(3) Who we truly are is never known 100% to us, which is why we always yield to His searching in and verdict on our human heart.
(4) What others think about our hearts is totally immaterial because the others, legally, are not "material witnesses" of any human heart.
(5) Furthermore, what we think of the hearts of others is equally immaterial and irrelevant for the same reason, because, unless we are the Holy Spirit of God, we don't really and fully know.
(6) That's why he said judge not lest you be judged; meaning, if you wish to judge, then, to be fair, you must allow judgment to be reciprocated.

(7) When you judge others, you're not giving a full assessment, nor you are capable of doing that, but you are certainly exposing the very thoughts of your own heart.

Doing the will of the heavenly Father is:

(1) A personal responsibility;
(2) An individual, and never a group duty;
(3) conditional, in that it demands allegiance and commitment;
(4) It's never subject to personal interpretation, collective bargaining, or high-powered negotiations.
(5) doing the will of the Father is definitely possible;
(6) It's rewarding in the short-term, and in its eternal dividends;
(7) It affirms a maturing personal relationship with the Father, through the Son;
(8) It's non-transferable and does not require maintenance because its new and fresh every day.

Price? It's been paid for. And THIS is where faith comes in and moves the true follower of Jesus Christ day by day, empowered by the Holy Spirit. For abiding in Christ alone, ALONE, makes it possible. Bearing fruit is a fait accompli ("an accomplished fact"). The signs of personal maturity in the follower of Jesus Christ are that he/she receives training from the Holy Spirit in four areas. They are: Worship, Faith, Love, and, Obedience. They have nothing to do with behavior, but everything to do with being. All personal; All from the heart. That's why the whole story, God's Story, is about Him, about Jesus Christ; not about me, the fallen struggling failing searching desperate vacillating temperamental imperfect and you-name-it more and more creature. To the contrary, Jesus alone rose from the dead and is alive forever, was full of faith, always knew the Father's will, was obedient with His whole being, was filled and controlled fully by the Spirit of God, never hesitated, always knew how dependent he, the Son of Man (like us), was on the Father, confident and without sin, and on and on, and on. He emptied himself to fill us with a never-ending love, became hungry so we never will, became poor so we be made rich in Him, traded His righteousness for our filthy rags, suffered unto death so we can find our rest in Him for eternity, was alone so that we never ever have to be, and when he looked fixedly into that cup of wrath, he was shaken to the core of His being, so much so, that His sweat was like drops of blood. He faced the horror of our Sin nature, and sinful acts, and guilty conscience, and separation from the Heavenly Father that He cried from the cross: "Abba, Father, Why have you forsaken me!!" Let's not think for one fleeting moment that he has any difficulty showing us the will of our heavenly father and giving us success in doing it. He went through hell so we can be assured of everything He brings our way (with no fine print nor conditions since He signed our eternal deed with His blood). And, Why? There is no reason more powerful to guarantee His effective work in us than His everlasting love toward us. The beauty of it all is not that He did it only, but that He brought us into Him to the point of becoming one with us, and that He empowers us daily, as we yield to Him, to experience that same love in action. What do I call that? My accomplishments? Forget it. It's far better. It's called: Worship. And, according to Romans 12:1-2, He calls that worship "reasonable". It's really, truly, and eternally ALL about Him. When we become impressed and captivated by what He did, we cease to be impressed by anything we do, because He becomes the focus and the center and the lover of our heart. *(Saturday, January 12, 2013 at 12:06A.M. CST)*

Radical Disciples
From my heart to yours

John Stott said in his book, The Radical Disciple, what spoke to my heart that a true radical disciple of Jesus Christ reflects three of many characteristics:

(1) He/she is thankful, often and always, because thankfulness is the soil in which pride does not easily grow.
(2) He/she is sure to confess one's own sins. For criticizing self before God lets a person experience proper self-examination, and being criticized by God in His presence lets one experience proper confession.
(3) He/she is ready to accept humiliation, for small and bigger humiliations bring one closer to the humble and crucified Lord. Some are more difficult than others, but they are not the most difficult. *(Monday, January 14, 2013 at 9:42A.M. CST)*

CROSS SURVEY

From my heart to yours

> The meaning of the cross of Christ: Approaching the cross gives us an historical perspective of where it began. The sum total of the cross is the very heart of the Gospel message. The accomplishment of the cross is a final verdict on man's abilities. And life at the cross is the changed life of Christ in us. A true follower of Jesus Christ remains at the foot of the cross, captivated not by the wooden cross but by the Blessed One hanging on it. *(Thursday, January 17, 2013 at 12:18A.M. CST)*

SLOWING DOWN

From my heart to yours

> A young man who lived about 135 years ago attended church in the town where he lived, but decided to leave that church because he was sorely disappointed with the quality of the sermons he heard. He spent the next several months going from church to church, very disappointed again and again because of lack of preparation and depth of sermons. He concluded that none of them was satisfying to him, and decided not to attend church much, if at all. He attended law school, and travelled the world. But he spent much of his life during that period at home and seldom left the house for 20 years! We may conclude with a gasp: how sad! This young man must be so depressed and introvert, and of no use to society whatsoever. Aren't his actions terrible? Isn't this young man a bad example and bad influence on his peers? You and I might think also, if we were members in any of

those churches where he attended, that such behavior is unacceptable, and we may need to address this dilemma in our next church council meeting, and find ways to correct such attitude. And we may not succeed even, because we may conclude that this generation of young people is so disappointing anyway and hopeless and pathetic, and potentially genetically messed up. .....until we realize that this young man's name was James Strong, who compiled the first comprehensive and "exhaustive" concordance to the English Bible because he realized how deprived was the library of the pastors and Sunday school teachers of such tools. And the reason he seldom left his house during those years was because his fragile and sickly body and weak health that limited his movement outside. Do you still think the same thing now of this young man? Or, shall we call off that church council meeting? The Bible says: "Therefore judge nothing before the appointed time; wait until the Lord comes. He will bring to light what is hidden in darkness and will expose the motives of the heart. At that time each will receive their praise from God." (1 Corinthians 4:5 NIV) *(Thursday, January 17, 2013 at 6:18A.M. CST)*

"WHATSOEVER THINGS ARE...THINK ON THESE THINGS"
From my heart to yours

This morning, I was reading "100 Prison Meditations", by the Romanian pastor, Richard Wurmbrand. He joins a "cloud of witnesses" that spent between 12 and 45 years in jail, tortured, beaten, starved, isolated, abused, cold, sleepless nights, and underground for weeks at a time, and other types of persecution only known to the depraved mind of the human species. In it he reflected, many years after his release from the Romanian prison, on an incident that took place in a meeting with like-minded pastors in Australia. Their melancholic conversation was about the mission and ministry problems behind the iron curtain. His granddaughter, as she played with her toys nearby, overheard parts of the conversation, sighed and asked: "Oh, Papa, what is a 'problem'? Where is it in the Bible?" He immediately said, "Nowhere". She replied, "Then why do you pastors worry about something not in the Bible?" Even though we haven't been in jail for Christ yet, one of our favorite phrases in many conversations is: "...but the problem is..." Other times we say more emphatically, "I will tell you what the problem is...". "Be not conformed to this world, but be transformed by the renewing of your mind." May we, today, see his feet on the cross where we are called to lay our "problems" for good. "Casting all your cares upon Him, for He cares for you." By the way, What exactly is a "problem?" (NOTE: As I was about to upload this to FB, I received an email from a dear Brother, from a Muslim background and became a follower of Jesus. I stopped to read the email first. He was jailed for many years, and many were praying for his release. The email was long, sharing much detail, but I will share two pieces: first, he said the official in their local "justice department" received him in his office, and they spoke "like friends", (and he said) "...as if he - the official - was afraid of someone". After the official released him, he asked our brother if they can meet at the official's house soon, this time for coffee. WOW! This is one of those moments where it's OK to talk to yourself, ha-ha. I laughed and said to myself "YES, and I know that someone's Name too" ha-ha. This "someone" is the same yesterday, today, and forever, who also opened the outside door to the prison where Peter was too. His word is every official's command! The second thing I want to share is that this dear brother said there were so many people praying for him; and as a result, his dad now has seen and has opened his heart to the King and Savior, Jesus Christ. May you be encouraged to press on! Let's not forget the persecuted Church! They ARE our brothers who suffer for the sake of That Name! *(Saturday, January 19, 2013 at 1:56P.M. CST)*

"He Touched Me"
From my heart to yours

The reason I post this song is that this is its 50th anniversary. In November of 2011, someone from Saudi Arabia gave testimony that he heard it and was touched by its message, because its message is about Jesus the Healer of everyone who comes to Him. May it be a blessing to you. Here are the words by its composer, Bill Gaither. "Shackled by a heavy burden, 'Neath a load of guilt and shame, Then the hand of Jesus touched me, Now I am no longer the same." CHORUS: "He touched me, oh He touched me, And oh the joy that floods my soul, Something happened and now I know, He touched me and made me whole." "Since I met the blessed Savior, Since He cleansed and made me whole, I will never cease to praise Him, I'll shout it while eternity rolls." "He touched me, oh He touched me, And oh the joy that floods my soul, Something happened and now I know, He touched me, and made me whole." *(Saturday, January 19, 2013 at 8:23P.M. CST)*

DYING TO LIVE, LIVING TO DIE
From my heart to yours

It's one thing to accept His death for my sins; that's required substitution, and I became alive in Him. It's a whole different matter to accept my death with Him; that's required fellowship, and I became dead with Him and He became alive in *me*. I cannot do the first without the second for proper understanding of redemption. For in my redemption, He paid my debt. In fellowship of His suffering, He lives through me. There is no alternative. The reason Christians are ineffective today is that they want the first but not the second. *(Sunday, January 20, 2013 at 1:32A.M. CST)*

WHAT REALLY HAPPENED: (PART 1 OF 2)
From my heart to yours

Unless a believer truly realizes what happened at the cross of Christ, and that he/she is a crucified person with Christ, there can never be a true expression of the resurrected Lord nor of the Church of Jesus Christ of Everyday Saints. The Bible says: "I have been crucified with Christ; and I no longer live, but Christ lives in me." *(Sunday, January 20, 2013 at 10:23A.M. CST)*

What Really Happened: (part 2 of 2)
From my heart to yours

What makes every person totally unique is: his mind, his emotions, his personality, his will, his heart, his strength, his soul. At the cross of Christ, Jesus says to whoever comes to Him: "Here, you have come to the end of yourself, and I shall begin my life in you. Here, you have died with me. Do you accept?" And there, at the cross, a true believer confesses and says: "Yes, Lord, I believe that you have accomplished everything, and there is no need for me to add anything. I accept that I am done there on the cross with you, and that you have begun your life in me here." Then, I hear Him say to me, "I have put my Spirit in you, and He will change you day by day. He will change your mind so you will think my thoughts according to my Word. He will change your emotions so that you will feel about everything and everyone like I do. Your personality and character will be changed so that you will look like me. Your will doesn't belong to you any longer for you have surrendered it to me and you can truly pray 'Thy will be done on earth as it is in heaven'. And your heartbeat will pulsate with what moves me. And there, at the cross of Christ, a person is created again in the image of Him who came to give him a second chance at life. And man begins a life with Him who loved him and died for him. And day by day, man will practically become taken more and more by Christ who loved him, and man will focus on loving Him with all his heart, and mind, and soul. And man forgets all and truly becomes a "follower of Christ". *(Sunday, January 20, 2013 at 10:52A.M. CST)*

OBEDIENCE SNAPSHOT

From my heart to yours

> Success: The success and sign of a true follower of Jesus Christ is determined, not by what he does for Christ, but by his obedience to Him. The rest is the details of living in Him (See Heb. 5:8). *(Sunday, January 20, 2013 at 11:24A.M. CST)*

I AM NO ANGEL

From my heart to yours

> Just Trying to Grasp the Reason, because I'm no angel --- If an angel from heaven flew down to earth one morning, looked into my eyes, and said: "I love you and wish to be with you forever; I'm very strong and will fight and destroy anything and everything to spend eternity together", I would likely decline the offer. The angel is no human, and I am no angel. I may be impressed but he doesn't move me. On all levels there will be lingering question marks, hesitation, reservations, and possible disappointments. But God, on the other hand, became incarnate, human, a baby whose face Mary kissed and held warmly close in his early years. If I were close to him, I would have kissed him too. He travelled light on earth, and no one even heard Him raise His voice (Isa. 53). His ties to me ran deep from day one. He came into the world like every other baby. Obedience was His middle name. His Father in heaven always took precedence and preference. His only motivation was His everlasting love for me. So, I stood amazed, totally consumed by this panorama, especially that I had nothing to offer Him back. Nothing! And I thought ... The Divine became

human to give me His nature. The Pure remained pure while among us so I can be made like Him, Pure. The Guiltless hanged on the cross, condemned for me, so that I, the guilty, may be made guilt-free. The Free was bound with no chance of escape so that I, the captive, can be bought with a ransom and set free, never to be a slave again. The Clean, like drifting snow and fresh mountain spring, came and washed my dirty heart with His shed blood and made me clean. I looked at Him on the cross, very unclean, it can't be, and asked: "...but, Why? Why all this? Why me?" And his eyes pierced my very soul with compassion when he opened his mouth and said: "...because I loved you from day one, even when I thought of you, I loved you, and want to be with you. Will you come to me? I asked, "Heaven?" He said, "Yes, but by way of the cross". I thought of the angel and I thought of Immanuel. And, fighting my tears back, I said: "but I don't deserve you". And He said: "But I made you worthy". He swept me off my feet, for He loved me completely. I cried and said: "Take these filthy rags of mine, Lord, and wash me, wash me clean from your fountain that never runs dry, for I want to be with you too". I had nothing to offer Him back. Nothing! And now, I can't imagine having anything except for what He gave me. In lifelong gratitude, I say "I'm deeply thankful!" In lifelong servitude, I say "You're completely Worthy!" In lifelong worshipful attitude, I say "Holy, holy, holy, forever holy"!
(Wednesday, January 23, 2013 at 10:22A.M. CST)

Encountering Jesus

From my heart to yours

Unless an encounter with Jesus Christ challenges and shakes everything we stand on and consider foundational in our life, we can never stand on anything that lasts forever and worship Him properly. In the story of the Samaritan woman (John 4), He equally did just that to the woman and to the disciples. She spoke selectively with words. They spoke selectively with their eyes. They thought they belonged to the "haves", and that she belonged to the "have-nots". But when he shook both foundations in his conversation, both were found lacking. For it never was a question of who was fallen and who was standing, but a question of Worship and Presence. She, the woman, who was far, was consistently wrong in guessing who He was until He revealed Himself to her as the expected Messiah. The disciples, who were close, were consistently wrong until He revealed Himself to them as the Messiah. Both needed His Spirit to bring them to a place of true Worship. She then proclaimed to her countrymen, "Come see a man who told me everything" after He declared how His Spirit is needed for true worship. They also proclaimed at Pentecost, "This is That" referring to the outpouring of His Spirit." After both foundations were challenged and shaken, true worship happened. Then both were equally at home, in His Presence, and worshipped Him. They both discovered that nothing was really about THEM, but that everything was really about HIM. Then, they were ready to go and tell because they all were in the Presence. They never really left His Presence. For all they said, all their life, was summarily that they know Him, Christ. The details are just that - details. The song is correct: Jesus, Jesus, Jesus, there's just something about that Name / Master, Savior, Jesus, like the fragrance after the rain / Kings and kingdoms will all pass away / But there's something about that Name. *(Thursday, January 24, 2013 at 6:00A.M. CST)*

SPIRIT SNAPSHOT
From my heart to yours

At the cross of Christ everything was made possible. For being born of the Spirit unites us with Christ. Being taught by the Spirit delights us in Christ. Being filled with the Spirit equips us for Christ. Being consumed by the Spirit brings all the glory to Christ. *(Friday, January 25, 2013 at 7:46A.M. CST)*

PRAYER FULL CIRCLE
From my heart to yours

Praying for everyone is good. Praying for the ones we love is a joy. Praying for our spouses is a must. If you are reading this, urge your spouse to read it too. John Piper urged men to pray these specifics for their wives, but (with adaptation) I ask wives to do the same for their husbands, perhaps because they need it most. The poet said: "How do I love you, let me count the ways". Here are a few ways, but then, there are a thousand others. Pray specifically that:

1. God, be her/his God —her all-satisfying treasure and all. Make her jealous for your exclusive supremacy over all her affections (Psalm 73:24–25).

2. Increase her/his faith —give her/him a rock-solid confidence that your incomparable power is only always wielded for her/his absolute good in Christ (Romans 8:28–30).

3. Intensify her/his joy —a joy in you that abandons all to the riches of your grace in Jesus and that says firmly, clearly, gladly: "I'll go anywhere and do anything if you are there" (Exodus 33:14–15).

4. Soften her/his heart —rescue her/him from cynicism and make her /him tender to your presence in the most complicated details and a multitude of other needs you've called her/him to meet (Hebrews 1:3).

5. Make her/him cherish your church —build relationships into her/his life that challenge and encourage her/him to walk in step with the truth of the gospel, and cause her/him to love corporate gatherings, the Lord's Table, and the everyday life of the body (Mark 3:35).

6. Give her/him wisdom —make her/him see dimensions of reality that I would overlook and accompany her/his vision with a gentle, quiet spirit that feels safe and celebrated (1 Peter 3:4).

7. Sustain her/his health —continue to speak your gift of health and keep us from presumption; it is by blood-bought grace (Psalm 139:14).

8. Multiply her/his influence —encourage and deepen the impact she/he has on our children. Give her/him sweet glimpses of it. Pour her/him out in love for our neighbors and spark creative ways to engage them for Jesus's sake (John 12:24).

9. Make her/him hear your voice — to read the Bible and accept it as it really is, your word... your very word to her/him where she/he lives, full of grace and power and everything she/he needs pertaining to life and godliness (2 Peter 1:3).

10. Overcome her/him with Jesus —that she/he is united to him, that she/he is a new creature in him, that she/he is your beloved in him. . . No longer in Adam and dead to sin; now in Christ and alive to you, forever (Romans 6:11). In Jesus' Precious and Holy Name, Amen! This is where we need to start. *(Thursday, February 7, 2013 at 4:22A.M. CST)*

TRUE OBEDIENCE
From my heart to yours

I ramble in words as I try to understand in thought ... On Obedience - Obedience, by definition, is not true obedience unless it's from the heart and unless it's 100%. Meaning, if I obey 99% of a given command, or if I obey 99% of the time is never enough, and is never true obedience. It's impossible for obedience to be relevant. Its definition requires it to be absolute. It applies 100%, not in a hypothetical realm of thought, but in reality. A judge is never satisfied that I obey the law 99%, and make allowance for the 1% without consequences, unless he redefines truth. How much allowance he makes is absolutely irrelevant. The only way Jesus could say, in the spirit of prophecy, "I have come to do Thy will, oh God" is because He was governed by the Spirit of God, and not His own. Obedience can only be TRUE to retain its definition. Does it not strike us as odd that in the Garden of Eden

God did not ask Adam to love Him, to trust Him, to rejoice with Him, to be humble before Him, and He, God, will be pleased? Why obedience? And, furthermore, why ONLY obedience is what he requires? And it appears that God hasn't changed His mind (compare Gen 2:16 with Rev 22:14). The truth is that Obedience is the "head of the class" and it brings all the rest of the attributes with it. That's why even though He was Son, the Eternal Son, he learned obedience, not love, not faith, not joy, not peace, but obedience. But that was not enough, for it says (Heb. 5:8), "and when He was 'perfected', [and only then], He became to all that obey Him the cause of eternal salvation." He had to obey to death, even the death of the cross (as if to say, to be specific, THAT death). And in His love, from that cross, there is no more the loneliness of the Garden of Gethsemane, but joy and peace, long-suffering and kindness, rightness and gentleness, and self-control. For the fruit of the Spirit is love. And with that love comes, as fringe benefits, all the rest. Now, I can be alone, but never lonely, for I know He loves me. Karl Barth, shortly before his death was asked what was the highlight of his learning and scholarship. He said, I learned the meaning of that line that says: "Jesus loves me this I know, for the Bible tells me so." Doing things right is not true obedience (Pharisee style), but doing the right thing is. Our chronic human dilemma is an fractured inability to do the right thing. The extent that true obedience only knows is to the uttermost, to the end. In the absence of obedience there is genuine fear, intentional hiding, irreverent self-righteousness, and irreversible path to "the way things were". A cracked or a shattered crystal vase never asks how much the shattering or cracking was, and does not distinguish between a small fracture and utter destruction. For its value has already been reduced to worthless. Only in antique auctions it finds a buyer, only to spend all he has, and only to place it on a mantle as a reminder that he gave all for it. The strange thing is that no one in his right mind gives to his beloved a cracked crystal vase as a token of his love, I dare say, not even that same antique auction crystal vase. For perfect love never settles for less. Freedom of choice can be in practice, but does not mean as to its essence, choosing the opposite of God's desire. To choose the opposite of His heart's desire, He classifies that as sin. Intentional choice contrary to the desire of God's heart is the nature of depravity, that irreversible condition of man's heart. To worship Him in spirit requires us to worship Him in truth also. Otherwise, any other redefinition of worship is sheer idolatry. Likewise, love. And to truly love Him is to worship Him in truth. To truly serve Him, when we serve others, is to simply love Him visibly. The tendency to choose consistently what is contrary to God's desire shows how far we have drifted from Him. Nature has become the undercurrent; hence, a natural selection. The freedom to choose contrary to God's desire, even once, is sin; and more than once is "the nature of things". Man's utter inability to choose the perfect desire of God's heart except by the Spirit of God demonstrates how desperately we need Him in our lives. In the beginning, Obedience was the one virtue that the first Adam needed to stay in the Garden of Eden (Genesis 2:16) in fellowship, in communion, in worship. At the end, Obedience was the one condition, in Revelation 22:14, for man to eat from the tree of life. Between the beginning and the end stood the Garden of Gethsemane where Obedience was the singular heart's desire of the second Adam, Jesus, where He uttered "let it not be my will but thine". Between Paradise lost and Paradise regained stands the cross of Christ. The symbol of death becomes the path of life for the follower of Christ in the valley. Does it not strikes us as odd that God gave the Ten Commandments only for all of us, without exception, to break at least one? I must ask why! To break "the one" is to fail in all. And the "one" is the first of the Ten, for from the first the nine are derived. Does it not strike us as odd that God gave the Golden Rule only for all of us, without exception, to break it? Does it not strike us as odd that God invites man to come near Him only for all of us to stay at a distance? Why would He do that to us? To coerce us somehow? I think not. To mock our inability? I doubt it for that would be out of character. And as if that's not enough, even Jesus came saying, "Love your enemies", as if we really can. And he, Jesus, doesn't settle for adultery to be merely a physical act, but says, "if anyone even looks at a woman lusting, he has committed adultery in his heart". And he knows we cannot accomplish what He asks. So, WHY does he even bring up the subject? The only reason I can find to satisfy my pursuit is this: He wants us to realize that without Him we can really do nothing. But, with Christ, "I can do all things." And both are true. I'm still rambling ... *(Thursday, March 21, 2013 at 6:06A.M. CDT)*

HIS NAME
From my heart to yours

Christ the Son of God could not have saved us from a distance, from heaven, without coming closer, and becoming Jesus the Son of Man. And AT ONCE, God the eternal Son became flesh, one with us, the bridge between the two, to bring us close, and make us one with Him. He reconciled us to Himself through His cross. IMM = with ANU = us EL = God Immanuel = God with us. May He who bore our sorrows on the cross of shame bring everlasting joy to many who seek Him this Easter season. "For God is near to them, near to those who seek Him in truth." *(Friday, March 29, 2013 at 11:39P.M. CDT)*

DARK NIGHT OF THE SOUL
From my heart to yours

I was awakened early today and looked outside. My first thought was: "this is a very dark night still". And instantly, another dark night came to mind, actually a much darker night, and to be more accurate, the darkest night in all of history. It was the night when Jesus held in his hands the full cup of the wrath of a thrice-holy God and began to drink. It was the night when he gasped in shock as a human, he who knew no sin, at the sight of the horror of sin. It was the night when he agonized alone for me, for us. It was the most cursed night of all history, the night when the filth of that curse that infested and corrupted man's heart was beginning to gush out in his blessed face, and be poured on his blessed head. It was the night when his closest friends were sound asleep; the night when he was a "stone's throw" from humanity, when knowingly he discovered his feet leading Him further and further into the depths of the hellish and most demonic fight of all eternity; the night when "he who knew no sin" began sensing, bearing down on him, the loads of sin from the Garden days until that hour in Gethsemane; the night when all the fallen angels gathered in conference and Satan at their head like mighty Goliath hurling mockery and derision at the sight of beautiful David. The full force of Satan's anger that consumed him from the day of his creation (Ezk. 28 and Isa. 14) was gathered like a perfect storm to totally decimate his arch enemy, the Christ, the Eternal Son, the Beloved of the Father, the Rose of Sharon. It was the night when the only consolation he found was a moment with the Father, when he had one more lesson in obedience to learn, the lesson of utter obedience, obedience unto death, yielding his very existence into the hands of the Father. And nothing new, for he always knew the path to the Father's bosom, where his soul always found comfort and strength, where his mind found refreshment. He sweated, he cried, he moaned, he groaned, he reached in the dark and found none to hold his hand on earth, not even the bosom of his mother, not the cheers of crowds, not the serene company of the teachers of the Law, for the judgments of that Law like mountains of indictments against us were being transferred from us to Him...in that night. The rose was being crushed, and no recourse. "All we like sheep have gone astray; we have turned everyone to his own way; and The Lord God has laid on him the iniquity of us all." It was the night of the shadows, when he faced the biggest temptation of all - the temptation of 'quitting', of changing his mind, of 'taking his destiny into his own hands', of exercising his eternal right as the Son of God to rush back to his 'comfort zone' in heaven, the temptation of exercising his will and stepping back from the chasm that separated man from God since Adam upon seeing more clearly the depths of the horror of sin and evil. He's never been there before. It wasn't just a 'difficulty' he was facing, or a few days' trauma, or the sour taste of bitterness in a thimble. The curtain was being slowly removed uncovering the shame of many cultures, the grief of many colors, the tears that could fill an ocean, the despair of generations. He began to see more clearly the shattered dreams and broken hearts throughout humanity caused by sin, and he found himself beginning to step into the valley of Ezekiel's bones. He was the object of the Father's love from eternity past, the sole delight of the Father's heart, and the supreme joy of unnumbered multitudes of heavenly hosts. He always and fully knew the Father and his love in close and holiest communion. But now, now he finds himself calling on the Father from the distant land of the ones he pursued for love's sake, the ones whom he desired to bring into that same love he shared with the Father. What he did not know, and the price he had to pay, was that to love us to the uttermost enough to cleave to us, he had to leave his Father in order to bring us back into the joys of the Father's house. Staring into the gaping mouth of that old Serpent, seeing the glistening venom of jealousy and hatred from eternity past, smelling the stench of death itself, he was stretched to the uttermost. From his younger days, his heart was set on delighting in the Father's will, but now his heart was being shred to pieces ... for me, for us. And he's not hanging on the cross yet ... *(Saturday, March 30, 2013 at 7:11A.M. CDT)*

EASTER - (#2)

From my heart to yours

Imagine Jesus close to committing the sin of idolatry in the Garden of Gethsemane. The horror of such idea! Really? Yes! How? This is how. Furthermore, we're guilty of that sin many times. Think of the heathens who stand before an image or pray to an idol. The material out of which the idol is made is really immaterial, although we use good stuff...gold, silver, etc. Think of Elijah on Mount Carmel, and the prophets of Baal. They prayed loud wanting the Baal to answer what they were asking, which is, to send fire from heaven (or somewhere) and consume the sacrifice. Elijah laughed at them saying: Shout louder, he may be asleep or on a journey. They were trying to get the Baal god to answer them right there and then, and do their bidding. And the sad part is that they really believed what they were practicing. Think of James (4:1-3) speaking to Christians, he says: "What causes fights and quarrels among you? Don't they come from your desires that battle within you? You desire but do not have, so you kill. You covet but you cannot get what you want, so you quarrel and fight. You do not have because you do not ask God. When you ask, you do not receive, because you ask with wrong motives, that you may spend what you get on your pleasures." Notice the words: "fights...quarrels...your desires...battle... kill... covet... when you ask, you do not receive, wrong motives, spend on your pleasures". Back to Gethsemane! What Jesus was committed to throughout his life, was never to ask for the sake of His own comfort, His own pleasure, His own desire. He always kept his motives in check. He learned that from the beginning of his life, by always yielding consistently to the desire and will of the

Heavenly Father. Never His will, NEVER, Always the Father's will. And he pursued that passionately with his whole being. So much so, that it became his "food", meaning, that which sustained his life. So, to his parents he said: "don't you know that I must be about my Father's business?" To the disciples at Jacob's well he said: "my food is to do the will of him that sent me". To the crowd and Pharisees he said: "I don't speak of myself, of my own will, but what I hear, that I speak". In the spirit of prophecy he quoted the OT saying: "I have come to do thy will, O God". And many other occasions show how completely he submitted his motives and will to that of the Father. And he was always successful. And that's what the Pharisees hated. They knew the Law. They monitored how people behaved, absolute control using the very instrument given by God. (Lesson: the Bible is not a chain of many links that we can use to control people with, and tie them down into bondage, but it's the truth and revelation of Christ which sets them free.) So far, Jesus won. He obeyed when all was going well, when the crowed loved his miracles and ate the food he gave. Then in John's gospel (Ch. 6) Jesus left them, and they followed him wanting him to do what they wanted, to feed them more. It's amazing how many are the ones who go after Jesus so they can eat and fill their belly. Then suddenly, the passage said that Jesus turned to the crowd and said: "I am the bread that came down from heaven". "From this time many of his disciples turned back and no longer followed him." The tables turned now. Jesus is the one in dire need for the Father to hear him, promptly, completely, not asking much, but just one thing..... to pass "that cup [of wrath]" from him. That's it. It definitely was no formula he repeated. It was his whole being going into the wine press. And he had the option to retreat, to quit, to leave, and go back to being just "Christ the Son of the living God". The song paraphrases what he said to Pilate: "He could have called ten thousand angels". The only way He was able to win the case on our behalf was to obey unto death, the death of the cross. "Not my will but thine", he cried in anguish. And He knew at that point that he won, because his compass never wavered. His commitment stayed rock solid. Never to ask for what made his life easier, what comforted him. There was no "plan-B". There was no contingency alternative. What is idolatry? Simply put: it's the ultimate commitment to self to get even God (or some version of a god) to do what we ask, knowing deep within our conscience and heart that the reason we keep coming before this god and what we're asking for is ultimately "in our best interest". Think about what we pray for sometimes. Let's not rush to rationalize or justify, for I'm not condemning here, but just stepping through a potential minefield of cosmic proportions. Insisting on "what I want", and practicing that regularly like an addiction, is the idea behind idolatry. The idol can be gold or silver. It can be God the Father, Son, and Holy Spirit. If what we ask is not in keeping with his will, that is leading us in the wrong direction. If we insist on that idea of trying to get him to do our bidding, we soon approach an addiction of using, even God, for our self-comfort and self-centered desire. Jesus, as he prayed in the Garden, realized what was potentially about to happen, and also realized that suffering, and yielding to the Father's will, even the death of the cross was his only option to secure eternal redemption for us. Then he could truly validate the truth of what he taught the disciples to pray saying: "...Thy will be done, on earth as it is in heaven". Our Master...obeyed. So must we. Haven't you wondered why, after an entire letter to believers on the subject of love, John ends his first letter (1 Jn 5:21) by saying: "little children, keep yourselves from idols"? Can God become an idol? Yes, when we use him, coerce him, for our purposes. How to avoid that sin? Taking Jesus' role model, Jesus would tell us: (1) Be filled with and led and dominated by the Holy Spirit continually; (2) Be immersed in the living Word of God day and night (Ps. 1); (3) Let the Spirit change your deepest desires and character into the likeness of Jesus; (4) Let your life always be, not about yourself at all but, about Him. Jesus was consumed with the Father's desire for his life on earth. He gave us a successful model, promising us to be in us as we are in Him. May we be consumed with doing His will in our life...without "plan-B". May our prayer, with the psalmist, be: "Let the words of my mouth and the meditations of my heart be acceptable unto thee, Oh Lord and my redeemer". *(Sunday, March 31, 2013 at 1:10A.M. CDT)*

ON COUNTERFEITS
From my heart to yours

The idea of "counterfeiting" must assume and accept as true the fact that there is something (source/original) for which a "duplicate with a twist" is created. This applies across the board, in all areas of life, whether it's a document or money or a certain lifestyle or belief. Otherwise, if there is no TRUTH, no original, then "counterfeit" loses its very meaning and essence. Counterfeiting can never replicate 100% of an original so as to have "two originals". Counterfeiting is always intended to deceive or mislead. That's why counterfeiting prefers to operate in the shadows, and never comes into the light. Counterfeiting never lasts. Counterfeiting always causes separation among peers. A person who encounters a Counterfeit may genuinely think/believe that it's the truth/original. Hence, he's described as "misguided" or "deceived". A deceived person who is not aware he is being deceived can mislead/deceive others without really knowing or acknowledging he is in fact doing that. Paul is an example. Counterfeit (or deception) - on its own - can never become the original, can never become "truth", not even by force. A deceived person can never find truth on his own, in his own power, especially when the deception, which began at a very shallow level, is now at the level of the heart and at the level of the conscience. To know the truth, as true, truth requires a revelation from its (truth) source. The harder a counterfeiter/deceiver tries to be convincing, the more entrenched he becomes in the deception and lie, and the deceived are there with him. The darker the prison cell becomes, and the chances of successful self-help tactics become nil - impossible. Counterfeiting and counterfeiters are FALSE, pure and simple. Think of that in the context of: Counterfeit gospel (1Cor 11: 2-4) Counterfeit teachers 2 Cor. 11:13-15 Counterfeit doctrine 2 Tim. 4:1 Counterfeit communion table 1 Cor. 10:19-21 Counterfeit righteousness Matt. 19:16-18 Counterfeit manner of life ("living the beautiful life") Matt. 23 Counterfeit power 2 Thess. 2:8-10 Counterfeit gods 2 Thess. 2:3,4 How can I, as a believer, know or detect a counterfeit? The counterfeit has a false facade. Matt. 7:15; Rom. 16:18. The counterfeit tries to get close to believers. Gal. 4:17,18; 2 Tim. 3:5,7. The counterfeit appeals to human pride (2 Cor. 10:12).

The counterfeit promotes idolatry because it is a quick way to demon influence. Hab. 2:18,1 The counterfeit promotes legalism. 1 Tim. 1:7,8 The counterfeit/false teachers continue to operate throughout Satan's rule on earth. 1 John 4:1 To know that the counterfeit is just that, counterfeit/false, a person must be very acquainted in his heart and mind, not with the counterfeits but, with Truth. Nothing but the Gospel of Jesus Christ can set a person free (from counterfeits) and alive unto God. Jesus himself said: "if you abide in me, and my words abide in you; and you will know the truth, and the truth shall set you free". That's how much He loved us, and paid the full price of our debt on the cross of shame. So that we no longer live in shame for counterfeits, but in what pleases God by faith. *(Monday, April 1, 2013 at 10:40A.M. CDT)*

SUFFERING TYPES
From my heart to yours

Three kinds of Suffering we Christians may endure, but need not be confused about their differences. Usually we don't like to talk about the first because it's embarrassing and brings shame. We also don't like to experience the second because there is still that "I-want-to-be-in-charge" feeling. Further, we make every effort to avoid the third kind because it requires being totally sold out to Christ, and even though we like to share our faith and the Gospel of Christ, we would rather stay within our comfort zones. The summary is below, and the details will come later.

1. There is Suffering for Sin. This is called Punishment. (1 Cor. 3:11-15). If we as Christians live for ourselves

(selfish motives, attitudes, thoughts, actions), we tend to be of little use to the Church, God's kingdom that He is building on earth, and will likely fall into many temptations and sins. Suffering follows.

2. There is Suffering for Christ. This is called Persecution. (Phil 1:29). The Scriptures say: "it was granted unto you not only to believe in Him, but also to suffer for Him". Also, Jesus Himself said: "Blessed are you when they persecute you and revile you for my Name's sake, for this is what they did to the prophets before you." It's not the "persecution" so as to draw attention to the person suffering that is front and center, but the "for my Name's sake" part. That's what matters.

3. There is Suffering with Christ. This is called Fellowship. (Phil 3:10). The Scriptures say: "To know Him and the power of His resurrection, and the Fellowship of His Suffering". This kind of suffering goes beyond the physical pain inflicted on a follower of Christ. The fellowship of His suffering calls for refinement of our Character through fires not of our own making. They maybe deep anguish, indescribable and unexplainable. It maybe burdens too heavy to bear alone without His sustaining Spirit always rushing to aid us. It maybe grieving near the point of death as we meditate upon the cross of Christ and the burden He carried and the never-before separation He endured from the Father in heaven. This fellowship comes in different colors, yet they all carry a lasting stain on our

hearts and spirit. A beautiful girl of 18 or 19 years was sentenced to death for her faith. (Note: Execution in this particular prison always took place at midnight). The Christians called the firing squad "the midnight bride". This is how she described her final moments as her friends reported. She said: "Jesus said, 'Whoever lives and believes in Me shall never die.' And I believe these words of Jesus more than the rifles that will be pointed at me tonight. I believe them more than the open grave that is already waiting for me. Tonight I shall not die. Jesus is a gentleman; He will keep his word. Tonight, by His grace, I will enter through the gates of pearl into the golden city. I will see and hear angels singing. I will be with the saints of all the centuries. I will rest my head on Jesus' bosom waiting for others to come." As she walked through the vaulted corridors of the underground prison, she was reciting the Nicene Creed which from her mouth gave it an entirely different significance. "I believe in One God ... I believe in One Lord Jesus Christ". Her last words that her friends heard were "I look for the resurrection of the dead and the life of the world to come". The one who reported this whole event concluded about this beautiful young girl saying: "After this, a few shots were heard. The poor executioners believed they killed her. They did not know they had sent her into the embraces of the most beautiful Bridegroom of all". Fellowship of His Suffering. Are we still concerned and is our first priority what matters here on earth? The truth is that on our list of priorities there should be only one item. It's Him, Jesus Christ, and only Him. For he's not in competition. He bought us with a price, his blood. Where is the distant second? Nowhere. So, the question simply is: is He not worthy of being our consuming passion? Keep in mind, there thousands, like seeds, are falling to the ground and dying for His Name's sake and in fellowship with Him every day. *(Tuesday, April 2, 2013 at 9:55A.M. CDT)*

BEING AWAKE
From my heart to yours

Does it not strike us as odd, when the disciples were at sea in the middle of a raging storm, that Jesus was asleep; and, when Jesus was in the raging storm of the ages, in Gethsemane, the disciples were sound asleep? There is indeed time for everything, a time to be awake, and a time to sleep. May both be in keeping with the Father's will. *(Tuesday, April 2, 2013 at 12:24P.M. CDT)*

THE BLESSINGS OF BAD DAYS
From my heart to yours

One thing for sure, whether we like it or not, whether we admit it or not, is that we WILL have bad days. It is not true to think that we will experience perpetual victorious living. There are nights that come into the life of a believer, a true follower of Jesus Christ when, for one reason or another, there are no stars and no possibility of morning. The question is: Why? What for? Here are some thoughts, even though I'm still learning:

(1) Bad days are good, because we can understand others better who have them, and be able to hear them out. We too have feet of clay after all.

(2) Bad days are good, because they are times when we can be (and perhaps need to be) quiet. They are times when the Holy Spirit of God speaks to us in whispers. He does exist outside our bad days but does not hesitate to come close.

(3) Bad days are good, because they teach us to worship when we don't have words to say. That's when God receives our heart cries best.

(4) Bad days are good, because they teach us the value of being alone with God. In fact, they teach us - to walk - alone and not be lonely. For maturity in Christian fellowship is learning to walk alone ... together.

(5) Bad days are good, because in our loneliness we draw near-er to God and have nothing to rely on except Him. We may hate that lonely feeling, but learn to love God altogether differently.

(6) Bad days are good because they are the times when God strips us of everything earthly, and clothes us with what brings Him all the glory.

(7) Bad days are good because, as with Gethsemane, He brings us totally to the end of "ME", and the beginning of something new, of His own making. The question revolves around whether I'm willing to yield to His will in complete surrender.

(8) Bad days are good, because after their chaos, confusion, despair, and misery are done, we live humbly before Him, treasuring every moment we spend with kindred spirits in God's family.

(9) Bad days are good, because they teach us to worship Him carrying nothing in our hands to offer Him except that which He places in our hands. There, He teaches us a new song.

(10) Bad days are good because, while they draw us nearer to death, sickness of the soul, crises and cries of the heart, and questions with no earthly answers ...

We discover that we can take off our sandals and step into His presence like a baby curled up in his mother's embrace claiming nothing but her love. Better yet, nothing shall separate us from the love of God in Christ Jesus our Lord. *(Wednesday, April 3, 2013 at 2:32A.M. CDT)*

ABORT ! ABORT ! ABORT ! (PART-1 OF 2)
From my heart to yours

This is the signal troops find themselves giving when the fight gets too risky, too dangerous, and the mission, if it continues, will very likely lead to serious loss of life. Timely assessment of the situation takes place by "the powers that be", and then a decision "to abort" is reached. Bear with me, for I know talking about Easter stuff yet again has become in the minds of many an out-of-season item, and we have changed the furnishings of our stores already. Now imagine this aborting scenario in the Garden of Gethsemane. Although the matter of man's salvation was "predetermined" (technical term) in eternity past, it was clearly a whole different matter now for it was missing the "on the ground" element until this very moment. Did he know about it? Absolutely, 100% Yes. To be sure, this was the "mother of all battles", the struggle of all ages, and the likely sure possibility of the death of the incarnate Son of God (in human form and flesh and likeness). The temptation to abort was staring Him, Jesus, in the face squarely, and He had that option to take it. His decision on the ground determined His accomplishment, perfecting, and completeness of mission on the cross. Every other man failed the test of living. And He wasn't about to do the same. He could have followed suit. But He did not. The decision was reached - Not as the Eternal Son of God - but as the Son of Man totally. To die specifically on the cross was a necessary detail. To obey unto death was the real decision. He came to the settled conclusion that: to leave the Father because He loves us so much was better than to hold on to what was rightfully His; to give us life, it was necessary that the Son of Man must die. And in doing that, He did the Father's will in every last detail. To be crushed under the full weight of God's judgment and curse of sin at the cross was chosen so that all who are created again and abide in Him by faith will be crushed no more, but will be loved by Him for evermore. That's why we love Him alone, we worship Him alone, we adore Him alone, and we serve Him alone. We learn to make decisions in daily obedience like He made, and put aside everything that distracts us from Him, so we can live always in Him. Oh, the HORROR of the thought that He could have aborted. Oh, the blessedness that He loved us so! (Please go to part-2). *(Thursday, April 4, 2013 at 6:29A.M. CDT)*

ABORT! ABORT! ABORT! (PART-2 OF 2)
From my heart to yours

Although the entire Easter event has been filed away in the dusty cabinets of our minds (tradition), I caught myself this week repeatedly going back to "Good Friday". I'm sure few of us care to ponder why it was called Good Friday. Maybe we should call it Labor Day. It is the day after all when in Gethsemane our Lord Jesus started, like a mother, having those recurring contractions, as it were, in the depths of his soul, and His heart was in death-stained agony alone in the Garden. For He was "being perfected through suffering" (Heb. 5:8) one final time before he delivered this beautiful organism called the Church, full of life, after having been in eternal gestation in ages past. No one understands the real torment, and the nagging anguish of a birthing drama like a woman about to have her baby. Men may teach it, but only a mother truly knows it. Maybe that explains why she wishes to be left alone at times. For she, for all intents and purposes, dies as the baby is being born; then, she comes back to a new life with her newborn, reunited, and inseparable. A mystic communion of sorts takes place between mother and child that none other may comprehend. We can discuss it. We can describe it. We can debate it. But only the mother looks with eyes that say to us, "you just have no clue what you're talking about until you walk in my shoes". So was the birthing of the Church through the passion of the Christ. And the darkness of the second Garden, Gethsemane, delivered the eternal remedy to the loss of the First. For in the first Garden, Eden, judgment was pronounced, and in the second, judgment was delivered its fullest blow upon His blessed head for us. So he says [in the spirit of prophecy], 'Here am I, and the children God has given me.' (Heb. 2). It's all of Him. It's all about Him. That's why I bow my knees in numbing silence and worship Him. He loves me so. I love Him so. *(Thursday, April 4, 2013 at 6:31A.M. CDT)*

LIVING SACRIFICE
From my heart to yours

Worship has to do with BEING the sacrifice, not with OFFERING a sacrifice. "Present your bodies a living sacrifice, which is your reasonable worship". Therefore, offering sacrifices is not a sign of true worship; obedience that willingly anticipates suffering is. Mary, the blessed one among women, heard a prophecy in the Temple of a sword piercing her heart; and Jesus was only a baby. Not your typical baby shower gift. Throughout Jesus' ministry on earth, many times, we read about Mary 'keeping things in her heart'. But at the cross, as she stood there watching front and center, her heart was totally and slowly shattered, play by play, with anguish and agony at the horrible sight of her Son hanging on the wooden cross. She kept that sight, as it were, in her heart also. Then she was at the empty tomb with no son inside. There was emptiness that she kept in her heart, the emptiness of the tomb, an atypical sight. We can truthfully say that nothing was "life as usual" for her. This one child stretched her in every direction, so much so that she arrived at the upper room with one thing she could still do. She with the disciples prayed, and did not stop, until the Spirit of the living God was poured out on them, anointing them, preparing them fully, not to tell how they felt but to tell the story of the ages, the true Gospel of Jesus Christ. Now, after she was totally transformed, after everything she kept inside started to make sense, she was among those who worshipped as her and their Risen Lord ascended to heaven. He whom she carried in her womb and sang for Him to sleep is now seated at the right hand of the Father. And now, she can worship with a new song in her heart. *(Saturday, April 6, 2013 at 12:28A.M. CDT)*

CONSCIENCE: A LIFELONG EYEWITNESS COMPANION (PART-1 OF 4)

From my heart to yours

During this past year, I caught myself unintentionally making mental notes about one particular and unusual type of news from here and there. It wasn't exactly a fun-filled Easter egg hunt. The matter got really annoying to me to the point where I was waking up at night thinking about what I read just from the 2012 records. I concluded that this type of events was reported just as much on in prior years; and with little research, I began wading at the shore of thick piles of ugly human realities from around the globe. Then I could see that this was getting really filthy all around me even to read as the list was getting longer by the day. Here is a tiny tidbit and snapshot of records; then some observations that, admittedly, haven't fully matured, but getting there. To be sure, according to dictionary references, the word is borrowed from Latin "conscientia" (meaning "knowledge within oneself"); hence, the title referring to an uninvited partnership and a sure reality. News bit #1: A Detroit, Michigan paper reported on February 16,

2006 that a man walked into a police station and confessed to a 1975 house robbery where a grisly triple murder of three adults took place involving a gun and a hatchet". He said that he was "unable to live with his conscience any longer" after all these years. He said, "the only thing I could not remove from my memory was the sight of the mother begging me 'please don't hurt my children' ". She was shot at close range. The children were spared. One daughter, 6 at the time, now 42, confirmed precise details. News bit #2: In March 2013 a murder which took place twenty two years ago was reported on the outlets of a worldwide news agency. An innocent man was selected from a lineup and sentenced to 37 and 1/2 years to life for a gold robbery and murder. Then 22 years later, a man came forward and confessed saying, "It was on my conscience for all these [22] years". He identified two others who committed the crime with him. Investigations confirmed the details. News bit #3: a journal article that appeared in 2012 reported that in 2004 528,480 felony convictions were reported in only one state, and 92,645 criminal cases were prosecuted in federal courts in 2007. In all these cases, 95% or higher entered a guilty plea. In the same article, entitled: "The Lawyer's 'Conscience' and the Limits of Persuasion", one trial lawyer said: "I like to tell these trial stories because it makes me a much more interesting dinner guest or conference speaker." Then he said: "I confess that I tend to tell these stories to my colleagues to show that I'm keeping up, to my students to increase my credibility, and to friends and family because everybody loves a good story." Then he added, ". . . But the truth is that I spend much of my time-much more than I like to admit, counseling clients about guilty pleas". The article goes on to say that in most state and federal courts the single most important decision they make in 99% of the cases is whether to go to trial or enter a guilty plea." This is the so-called "the civilized world" in which we live. News bit #4: In January 4, 2013 an article appeared in the New York Times entitled: "Lance Armstrong Said to Weigh Admission of Doping". The article said even after the prosecution laid out the evidence from a variety of sources including teammates, financial records, emails, laboratory analyses and eyewitness testimony from various sources, that he, Lance Armstrong, the holder of seven world records bicycling at the renowned Tour de France and the recipient of gold trophies "vehemently continued to deny ever doping". Then the article said after many of his major supporters pressured him before they deserted him to confess, and the major donors to "Livestrong", a charity he founded after surviving cancer, have been "trying to persuade him to come forward and clear his conscience and save the organization from further damage". News bit #5: A Nashville, TN newspaper reported in May 2012 of a man, age 72, who came forward and "was welcomed with open arms" as he confessed to the theft when he was 18, of "the most beautiful, perfectly formed potted hydrangeas [plants]". He confessed saying, "I knew that it was wrong. I thought all along that I was borrowing them. But this stayed with me all this time". Interesting facts about this incident: he was 18, newly married, and didn't have a Mother's Day gift for his mother who lived in another state. He pulled out of the ground the entire two plants from their roots. When he confessed 54 years later, he returned the same plants "and the roots. He said, when his stolen goods were accepted by the owners, that "now he goes by the same park without any feelings of guilt". News bit #6: In 2013, a young lady in Seattle, Washington, , age 23, came forward and confessed that she lied in 2001 when she was 11 about a rape crime for which she falsely accused her father who has been in jail for nine years already. The Seattle Times article said that the girl "was prompted by guilt had to come forward and reveal the truth". The truth was that she was very upset about her parents' divorce. News bit #7: Last year, a man walked into the police station in New York, and confessed to a crime which he committed 33 years ago in which he strangled a 6-year old boy who was on his way to the school bus stop. There was no DNA, physical, or forensic evidence because long ago he put the body in a dumpster, and the body was never found. The criminal, 76 now, said that he couldn't take the burden of guilt anymore, and confessed what he did in a prayer meeting where there were at least 50 witnesses. News bit #8: A television affiliate in Stockholm Sweden in 2012, and "The Local", which is a Swedish paper in English reported about a man who walked into a police station to confess to killing a 51-year old man in 2000, saying "he needed to clear his conscience". The TV reporter said that the man confessed because "of the heavy burden of having killed a man". One of the victim's four sons "expressed his disappointment in the Swedish legal system" because for over a facade this case remained unsolved. Some of the remains were found at a construction site in 2006, but not enough to convict anyone. News bit #9: In New Delhi, India, in December 2012, "The Hindu" online news website reported about a gang-rape that took place of a 23-year old woman. One of the perpetrators confessed saying, "I have done a horrible thing. I have done a bad thing." One of his two accomplices who is a gym instructor also said, "I confess to my guilt. Hang me". The paper described the incident like this: "Two suspects of the gang-rape case that shocked the conscience of the nation confessed to their involvement to this gruesome crime". Some observations: I'm sure it is easier to read about a happy social event like the birth of a child, or tell about a trip to the glorious mountains, or describe a vacation in a cozy spot somewhere. But surely these incidents above have some elements in common:

(1) Conscience encounter is a universal experience, not a local tradition.
(2) No one can eradicate Conscience it as long as they are alive (with one exception).
(3) When Conscience files a complaint in the legal courts of our mind, it wins every time.
(4) Conscience comes roaring like a lion when it does. There is no stopping it, and it demands full settlement.
(5) Conscience attaches itself to every person. I'm not sure when it begins its activity, but suffice it to say that it does so very early in life.
(6) Conscience serves as a continuous observer. But it reserves the right to clothe itself with the robe of a judge on a moment's notice, and of its own choosing.
(7) When the conscience begins its justified objection, human efforts may attempt to quiet it down.
(8) It runs the full spectrum of the human experience. Meaning, nothing is considered trivial. It cannot be dismissed or applied at will.

(9) Conscience does not discriminate by race, culture, gender, religion, level of education, or any other variable.

(10) Normally, when truth at its core is violated, the conscience responds.

(11) There seems to be this universal acceptance, a propositional given, that fighting the conscience and winning is an exercise in futility.

(12) Conscience is outside anything related to mankind, but is fully capable of interacting with every conceivable human experience, and without a learning curve either.

(13) Conscience operates totally independent of human emotions or other capacities, as if it has its own triggers, its own movements, its own lingua franca that every person inherently understands.

(14) Conscience is given by God and can only be appeased by provision from God. Reason being, that all scriptural references clearly remove every decision-making related to conscience out of human hands. (See part 3 of 3).

(15) When Conscience makes its voice known that something has been violated, the guilty party is very likely making an attempt to cover-up, or falsely self-vindicate, or refuse the charges. Then, war is declared in the sense that the conscience will entrench itself in recurring memories and, when least expected, surfaces to remind the guilty party of its errant event.

(16) Responses to Conscience objections include: fear, running away, seeking pleasures, and attempts to transfer the feeling of guilt onto someone or something else. The motivations are: pride, anger, injustice, universal good,

false humility, associate with credible persons so as to acquire credibility by association, and a few other such subtleties.

(17) The final battle launched by Conscience is usually kept for another "Day".

(18) Conscience points to the error but does not have the capacity of a solution.

The solution must come from elsewhere. (Please go to part-2) *(Sunday, April 7, 2013 at 6:48A.M. CDT)*

NOT BY SHAME
From my heart to yours

When we don't cooperate with God the Holy Spirit and change like He wants us to, He's not quick to judge. God doesn't shame us to do what pleases Him, and look at us and says, "what a dirty rat this one is because he/she messing up; I need to throw him out". We are labeled as "beloved" in His eyes, for His Beloved Son's sake. He takes His time to build our character properly. He takes His time to learn humility, listening and discerning His voice, responding to His promptings driven by His love, basically skills we lack even on a good day. May we dwell today on the fact that He loves us, and be willing to change for His Beloved's sake, driving us to worship not out of duty but out of single-minded love. *(Wednesday, April 10, 2013 at 3:48P.M. CDT)*

Discovering Jesus and Knowing Him more each day
From my heart to yours

Discovering Jesus daily is not trying to think about something He did and do the same, but it is being what He desires for me to be and worship Him. The rest is details that make us unique. This lifestyle enables me and you to worship Him, not because of what I've done, but because of who He is as I discover Him daily. Here's a new simple spotlight on His amazing and pure passion: Jesus went to the Father all the time. And the Heavenly Father was the ONLY person to whom Jesus went for everything. Doesn't that surprise us? From His early years in the Temple, Jesus seemed comfortable talking to the priests and leaders, for He was very comfortable talking to the Father. He never discussed theological matters with them, for He Was the theological Center that they ignored. His passion was not being after something on earth so He could get to heaven, but His passion was being after Someone in heaven, the ONLY One who really mattered, so He could live on earth. His passion was being with the Father fully clothed with the Spirit, and all else found its proper place in His life. We can be the same, for that was His true desire towards us.
(Thursday, April 11, 2013 at 2:24A.M. CDT)

Right Or Wrong
From my heart to yours

Is it really right or wrong to have my own plans and make my own decisions when I choose to? Or, could it be that I'm asking the wrong question. If I choose deep in my heart to run my life on my own schedule and on my own agenda, it may not be sin, and I justify that by taking for granted that it's not hurting anyone anyway, but I have made two mistakes at least, and one if not both ends up being sin. First, I have removed myself from living my life on God's calendar and actively experiencing His mercy and grace. And the nature of calendar sync'ing, we know, should be and will always be that of my calendar on His, not His calendar on mine, because He is not interested in my calendar in the least. He takes note, not of my calendar, but of my heart's affections. Besides, we read that we are like lost sheep, we have gone each one in his own way (our own calendars and agendas). I have also removed myself from experiencing His daily provisions to me (which are usually outside my limited capacity of comprehending) that bring Him glory, and sought to provide for myself, which is good by human standards but not His standards, the thing that normally leads me to bring glory to me myself and I because it was my efforts and hard work that accomplished, not the energy and power of the Holy Spirit. The nuances of sin are more deceptive than sin itself. We know also that the Holy Spirit's desire is always to glorify the Son, and not me. And this is where I fail and sin for inadvertently I have sought my own glory without possibly knowing that I am intentionally doing that. For if I am intentionally doing that toward God, then I am committing idolatry of the worst kind, the idolatry of the heart, and no one knows and sees the heart but God. That's why the Scriptures say that God left the visible things to us to know, but He knows the deep secrets of the heart (meaning, He knows what we never have the capability of knowing). And that's what really matters, for that is truly the heart of the matter. That was the calendar, and, as if that's not enough, we observe also that we have devised agendas with skilled craving, and have ironically a healthy appetite and propensity to generate our own agendas at numbing speeds. Furthermore, on many occasions, we Christians do that unaware that perhaps, just perhaps, God has something else in mind, and we should find that out first. We gladly recite "thy will be done on earth as it is in heaven", but we either assume that normally the prayer refers to global, big picture, matters and not necessarily what's happening directly in my own life, or that what we are doing is in fact His will when in fact mostly likely it is not. Or, that we bypass seeking His will first altogether because He just might ask us to wait on Him, and we simply hate waiting. We are content with obtaining business in the kingdom of God, when we know the challenge is to seek God's kingdom, His rule, His governance, His Presence, His resources, and nothing from us. Yet we pray and say, "Give us this day our daily bread" as we are sheepishly trying to do what the children of Israel did in the old days, hoarding the Manna for tomorrow too because God just might not have enough for us tomorrow. And we live chasing the abundance of tomorrow but failed to live today, today with and for His glory and grace in my life. It's all about choices, we say. *Or, is it ? (Friday, April 26, 2013 at 6:34P.M. CDT)*

WHEN PRAYER IS NOT
From my heart to yours

This picture was taken at the prayer time, at the June 2013 Conference, totally and authentically at peace, in the Presence. She, like her "look-alike twin sister before her" (many know of whom I speak), taught me to speak to God as a friend speaks with a friend. At 87, that sacred moment was captured as she was stepping into audience with His Majesty on High. In one place, the Scriptures speak of Jesus speaking to the Father "alone while the disciples were around Him". Those who were there can testify that she was more in His Holy Presence than she was in theirs. Many talk "about" God these days, while few talk "to" God. Many deny His very existence, but somehow many still manage to speak to Him every day. May God help us to learn what brother Lawrence of old called: "Practicing the Presence"... not because we are worthy but because He is. She loves to speak to God while looking out of the window toward heaven. I have a feeling she wanted to look right into His beautiful face each time, for I know how much she loves and adores Him. However, recently, while she was recovering from a fall that brought tears to her eyes (never before) from the pain, She told me of times when the pain was so severe and recovery was taking so long that she told God she didn't want to talk to Him. Reason: too much pain. I couldn't help but grin at the thought of it, thinking, how silly we act at times, and yet, He goes on loving us. Then she came back to Him later, she said, in tears missing the moments when she prayed in secret. She leaned over toward me with an innocent but sheepish grin on her beautiful face and, almost in a whisper, she said, "I talk to Him many times more than I talk to your Dad these days." (Ha-ha!) That day, she was totally broken and asked me: "Do you think God minded that I didn't talk to Him for so long?" Then, like someone whose best friend is always there listening regardless, she answered her own question and said, "Of course, He heard me. I know Him. He doesn't mind my fragile brain when I ramble. Who am I to stand before Him anyway?" I asked her, "So, you're back talking to Him?" she smiled and said, "Of course I'm back. How can I not be? I felt so dry when I stopped. But He knows me and I know He loves me." What an awesome God we have, people!!! Mom is very precious to, and loved by, many. Yet to her, being captured by the love of God exceeds all loves. I know, as I rambled here, that this is not exactly considered among today's hot topics of discussion. Even the weather gets more attention. But I also know, her topic is out of this world! My desire for everyone who calls Him "Father" is to never stop talking to Him but seek Him with our whole heart, and, perhaps, we can even get closer than we think we can. For being close to Him teaches us to love one another with a pure heart. *(Tuesday, June 11, 2013 at 7:14A.M. CDT)*

BEING NOT OF
From my heart to yours

To be "in the world but not of the world" has a double responsibility. Being "in the world" means to live, serve and to witness as followers of Christ. Being "not of the world" means to avoid being contaminated by the world. We can do neither without the daily work of the Holy Spirit. Do I not have freedom of choice? Of course I do. For as a slave of Jesus Christ I have chosen to love Him with my whole heart. Therefore, everything else holds the value of the dust in the scales compared to the weight of His love for me on the cross. If I'm unwilling to show that kind of love, I don't deserve to be called a Christian. I'm a mere rebel in religious clothing. Could it be that that's why there's little of the church in the world, and much of the world in the church? *(Sunday, June 16, 2013 at 12:04P.M. CDT)*

A HEART FILLED WITH GRATITUDE
From my heart to yours

From us to you, our dearest family and friends, we thank God for you. We treasure your being part of our life. Most of all, we are grateful for Him who loved us enough to unite Himself with us so that we may be one with Him. Pure Awesomeness!! With the unknowns of the New Year, we are reminded that nothing catches Him by surprise when it comes to His children. So, we love Him, we adore Him, we worship Him - whose name is Emmanuel. Although there are billions of stars and Milky Way, one star was found useful, because it pointed to Him in a Bethlehem manger. *(Wednesday, January 1, 2014 at 2:43A.M. CST)*

I LOVE YOU, SON
From my heart to yours

I will never forget the first words out of my mouth in 2014, because I found myself caught again in one of those "transcendent moments", when God catches me unawares. My words were to Jonathan, my only son, when he walked in the bedroom to wake me up. I looked at him and said: "I love you, son". And immediately God spoke to my heart, this time with a series of questions: -Do you have any doubts about your love for him? (No) -Do you have any malice or even a hesitation toward him? (No) -

Do you have any thoughts toward him that are not all good and tender? (No, Lord) -Is he completely precious in your eyes? (Of course, Lord) -Anything you wouldn't do for him? (No) -Remember how long you waited for him to be in your family? (Yes, Sir) -Remember when he first walked around your home? (Yes, yes) -How you stayed up nights watching over him when he was weak or fragile or sick or in surgery? (Yes, definitely) -How he would walk in at night when he was 2 of 3 and just stand on your side silent and you wake up sensing his presence? (Yes) -How you raised the cover and he slipped in beside you and slept the night through? (Yes, Lord) -For how long would you love him? (Oh Lord, I know I would for the rest of my life) Then the Lord whispered: "That's only the beginning of my love for you. And you have eternity to know how much." I hugged Jonathan tight again, my eyes welled up, and for the first time I wished I could hug God. As if for the first time, I realized the immensity of God's love through Christ for me, that it's real, complete, pure, and eternal; that his thoughts toward me are all for good and blessing. Then I closed my eyes and worshipped, and whispered as I hugged, "I really love you, Lord. Thank you, Thank you, for your great love for it's beyond my comprehension." *(Wednesday, January 1, 2014 at 10:52A.M. CST)*

TEACHER AT 87

From my heart to yours

Mama at 87+ is still teaching me well: (1) My mom is a very special woman, not only to me but to all who know her. However, at her age now she has reached many milestones. One, is that she has obtained a license (with honors, I might add) to say pretty much anything on her mind to anyone and at any time she pleases, and she is always well-received. One of those incidents had to do with me yesterday morning. As I sat down at her kitchen table, she pleaded with me that it's been a "very long time" since she had a decent cup of coffee with me. A "very long time" on her calendar/watch, mind you, can be anything from few hours to a day or two. But this time, it REALLY was a very long time as it exceeded 2 days (2.5 days to be exact). Time at this stage in her life is a very precious commodity. To her, every minute she spends with someone is timeless and every word she heard is priceless (but that's for another time to elaborate on). So, I confirmed to her that I missed her coffee as well, and I hurried to make coffee. Of course, she got up immediately to come and help me, so I thought. But to her, when I asked her to wait at the table and I will bring the coffee when ready, she said: "I've missed you so much and I just want to be around you and look at you and smell you." [I want to assure the reader that I did take my shower that day, and it was not the yonder years of childhood where the moms smelled their kids to ensure good hygiene under the guise of "oh-my-baby-I-love-you-so-much" innocent parental deception-kind of thing.] :-) My mom really wanted to spend every minute she could with me now that I'm at her house. But I assured her that I will be back at the table in no time. She waited on pins and needles, and raised her volume so I can hear her well across the chasm that separated us at that moment (which was actually the width of the stove across the opening). When I sat across from her with the steaming brew in hand, she started this barrage of questions about the time I was gone. How are your brothers? Did you see your sister? Is she doing ok? Are they doing ok? Is anyone sick? How are the babies? (Then she interjects her own words by stating that the only mistake she made in her life was that she stopped at seven kids instead of 12). I told her, "Mom, God really wanted you to give other people a chance too". She chuckled and said, "let them have their own kids; it has nothing to do with me" :-). In the middle of her nonstop questions and comments, my Dad made the mistake to let us know the audience is three not two, and said to her, "Give our son a chance to say something...". And without missing her focus or needing to catch her breath, she glanced at him from the corner of her right eye with the quivering lid, and said "I'm talking to my son, not to you"...:-) and she continued her momentary one-sided conversation without missing a beat. We laughed. But I choked a bit and asked myself a question or two: would I be willing to long to spend time with God like that? Would I reject any interruption, even from the dearest to my heart? Would I be as focused and intent to savor every moment with Him? Does time stand still for me when I'm in His presence? Do I long to be just me and Him? Do I love God at least as much as I know my Mom loves me? When will I be content in the Presence of one, The One? And I whispered a prayer of confession to God with eyes open and still focused on her eyes, knowing how much she loves me. To her, she didn't care even about the coffee. To me, it was good to be in their house. In Matthew, Jesus said, "When you pray, go into your room, close your door, and spend time with your Father who sees in secret." Prayer is time well spent - with God. *(Sunday, January 5, 2014 at 11:27A.M. CST)*

SOVEREIGN GRACE

From my heart to yours

The Difference Between Theory and Practice in the Christian Life: (A true Mom story) -- Recently, a missionary came back from the mission field, and sent me an email that she's in town and would like to meet and share what God has been doing in her life the past couple of years. So, my plan was to stop by my parents, have breakfast with them, give them their meds; then go to N's restaurant to my meeting with the missionary. I asked my Mom if she would like to go, to get out of the house too, and have an opportunity to meet this lady. "I'll go with you anywhere". Fancy that!! :-) It was a delight to see Sarah (not her real name) at the restaurant, and was very eager to hear her story. Sarah brought with her best friend, Beth (real name). After the greetings and general inquiry about her stay overseas, she shared for a while in her animated manner about her experiences and the challenges she encountered. Mom and Beth were listening for a while. Then it happened. Without advance notice, Mom seized a quiet moment and began to share about her (Mom's) experiences while serving in Lebanon. I figured it was sweet of Mom to join in and share a bit, but---not Mom. The "little bit" ended up about 30-35 minutes, sharing about all kinds of events that she had during her and dad's ministry time in Lebanon, starting in 1953 and all the way to 1979. She relived many of the experiences with details, the houses we lived in, the mission locations we went to weekly, the people who hated us or loved us, and those who sent their kids to Sunday school, the sicknesses and trials, the persecutions and rewards of ministry, what Jesus Christ had done, and how important He is for people to believe in Him and trust Him because He is our only hope and we have to trust Him and love Him, and he will give us mercy and forgive us for everything, and... and..., and I had the feeling it was going to be another 27 years of Mom sharing what happened in Lebanon before she stops :-). So I decided to gently interrupt her to let her know that Sarah and Beth probably needed to go, but it was awesome to see Sarah again. We said our goodbyes, and went our separate ways. Although Sarah shared plenty about her trip, I felt that Mom probably took too much time, but still it was good for her to get out of the house. I thought the story was over, until we had a call from Sarah the next morning. Unexpectedly, Sarah said her friend Beth called her early that next morning, and here is part of the exchange: Beth: hey Sarah. Remember the lady yesterday that we met at the restaurant? Sarah: yeah, what about her? Beth: after I got home last night, I couldn't sleep thinking over everything she was saying. I started going over some of the stuff she was saying..... Sarah: yeah...? Beth: the way she was talking, and all about God and what happened in her life, and she just came across so real, so genuine, what she was saying seemed so true, and everything she shared about what God did in her life...was like it happened yesterday, and was as real to her as us sitting together. I realized how much I don't have it either. What I didn't know is that Beth was in fact an atheist, but what she heard in an hour the day before shook her to the core of her being, made her restless for God, and caused her to reconsider her views of what Jesus Christ had done, and can do. Sarah: so, what do you think now? Beth: I really want that faith this lady has, and whatever she had inside her to cause her to live that kind of life, I want in my life. I don't think I can go another day without it. They prayed over the phone, and Beth accepted Jesus Christ as her personal Savior. Simply put: She wanted what was real. This is what Jesus meant when He said: "...so is everyone who is born of the Spirit". To this day, Mom does not know that Beth made a genuine decision to become a follower of Christ. Mom goes on living and loving. But I have a feeling that she will see Beth when she steps into glory one day. Then I went through a checklist in my head: - Is God that real in my life? (day by day). - Is my faith REALLY real? (Yes). Jesus, one day, asked some people: "is this what you have witnessed yourselves, or what you heard others say about me?" Paraphrased: Are you holding on to ME or to what others said about me? - Can God use a genuine person without that person knowing the outcome? (Obviously, yes. He said: "My ways are not your ways, and your thoughts are not my thoughts). Paraphrased: don't try to second-guess God. - Is Mom perfect? (I KNOW she's not). - Am I genuine in my walk with Him, or giving lip-service? (Daily walking). - What exactly did Mom do that morning? (What she did had nothing to do with people. She simply told about God's goodness and mercies IN HER life). - How did God use her? (She walked with Him every day) - On what basis? (She made a heart commitment to follow after Him). - Did she check her doctrine making sure it's correct, lined up, and conveyed her doctrine to the lady point by point? (Definitely not). - How can doctrinal accuracy be part of life without having the attitude that "I want to make sure the other person 'gets it' first"? (That's the simple difference between being taught by people and being taught by the Spirit of God. The Spirit gives life, people's plans don't. No wonder why Jesus never taught doctrine; He conveyed the love of the Father to all. He said: "if the Son of man be lifted up, He will draw all people to Him". So, the real (perhaps, the only) question is: "is my life really about Him, or about me?" The rest is simply -- details. In 2014, may we ask Him to make it happen in us through His Spirit. I KNOW He will answer that request. *(Monday, January 6, 2014 at 3:10P.M. CST)*

DELIGHTFUL TIMES
From my heart to yours

Thirty seven years later, as of yesterday, she still loves me and puts up with me "warts 'n all". I got upset with myself last night, as we had quiet time at dinner, and I asked her: "Sweetheart, after 37 years, what would you change?" (Risky, I know :-), but No nail-biting or head-scratching). Without hesitation in her voice, she said, "I would have gotten married sooner". I thought: YESSS!! :). But I thought I could really kick myself now for not pressing my question upon her more emphatically when I first saw her. Now the way I look at it, I would say, it's a healthy combination of love, mercy and grace, and it's all good. "Surely goodness and mercy shall follow me...", and at times live with me :), all the days of my life. I wonder if there are 100 couples who promise, before all-knowing all-loving God (and Facebook or other seemingly all-knowing-wannabes") that they will love and cherish each other until "death do them part"... Please say "I Do". :-) *(Thursday, January 23, 2014 at 6:28A.M. CST)*

BEING ON THE SAME PAGE

From my heart to yours

From my heart to yours this day: When people cry out to God, they take hold of him. When revival comes, God takes hold of people and doesn't let go. When God's people pray, God listens. But when God speaks, people change. When God's people pray, they step into His presence. But when God moves, His holiness consumes everything in its way. When Isaiah stepped into the Temple, a familiar place which he respected, expecting "the usual", he encountered the unusual and was in shock. Then he had the proper view of God, the proper view of his heart, and the proper view of the immediate religious culture in which he lived. Isaiah encountered the unusual presence of God, the unbelievable sinfulness of his heart, and the abysmal condition of his own society. He recognized the meaning of having the "form of godliness", but denying and being oblivious to its power. He discovered that whatever the condition on earth was, heaven had the answer. And the answer was nothing less than consuming fire. Isaiah learned that he could not go to speak to people about the life-giving God unless God came to him and burned every last vestige of sinfulness in his heart. Isaiah was petrified in the awesome Presence of God, and then purified by the awesome fire from the altar. The altar has always been the place where worship took place. But no worship can be without fire from God. It's more common and even easier for people to gather in front of altars where there is no fire. Isaiah stepped into the Presence and his honest response was: WOW! He looked at his heart and his honest response was: Woe! He stepped into the Presence to see God. He got an added bonus and encountered his own heart too.

That's why when man steps into the real Presence of God, his life won't be "business as usual" any longer. He is stunned and stops asking, because God begins to speak. Uzziah the king (Isa. 6) began his life with greatness as long as he listened to God and beheld God's glory. He had great accomplishments throughout most of his life. But Uzziah took things into his own hands, and that's when he lost everything... everything on earth, and everything in heaven (Isa. 6:1, he died). The high priest threw him out of the Temple. God threw him out of His Presence. The power of the Alpha is when God initiates his work on earth. For nothing is determined on earth without His will in heaven. It's not how our journey begins with God that matters as much as how it ends. God waits to the end to determine the presence or absence of faithfulness. That's the power of "the Omega". Uzziah's reach may have been long with friend and foe, but he fell short where it mattered most. Being successful with men gives no rightful access to tamper with holy things. Uzziah may have been invincible and infallible with men, but when he entered the holy place, he was found deeply in-trouble. When man goes after God, he finds God. When God goes after man, He crushes him, then remakes him in His image and brings him back to life. It's better to be crushed by God than to crash in front of people. His skill set does include: "perfect ability to create". Abraham's life had two items that stood out above all else: the Tent and the Altar. The first helped him to dwell on earth, and the second helped him to dwell in the presence of God. Abraham knew that secret, and lacked nothing. Thus, he excelled on earth, because he excelled with God. Isaiah, the prophet of God, knew his place before men because he knew his place before God. Isaiah's words burned because his lips were purified with fire. Isaiah stood before men because he fell on his face before God. He preferred to fall before God than to fall before men. God mattered to him, men didn't. God's pleasure was his sole desire, and God granted him his desire. A heart pleasing to God does not seek the pleasure of people. A heart longing for God loses interest in earthly things. A heart captured by God is set free to love God and love neighbor properly. *(Monday, January 27, 2014 at 6:35A.M. CST)*

GOOD THEOLOGY, BAD LIVING
From my heart to yours

Good theology without the love of Christ is indeed Bad theology. For the love of Christ is not one of the subjects in theology. It is, in fact, THE subject. That's why only the Spirit of Christ was entrusted fully with the effective teaching of THE subject. He breathes and breeds life; and unless we are filled with the same Spirit of Christ, we are nothing more than a bunch of dignified Pharisees. *(Friday, February 7, 2014 at 8:32P.M. CST)*

ONE THING LACKING
From my heart to yours

I have good news. I finally found a people of God who did things right. Upon further research, I was able to confirm also that they live a perfect life too. They:

(1) Studied the Bible every day;
(2) Assembled to worship God every day;

(3) Gave, not only money, but of everything they had;

(4) Were generous to the poor;

(5) Worshipped the one true God regularly;

(6) Kept every single word in the Bible;

(7) Taught the word of God to their children;

(8) Made sure their kids were just like them;

(9) Sang beautiful songs, lifting hands to God;

(10) Cared for one another and admonished one another;

(11) Made sure they had no sin in their life or in the life of anyone in their group;

(12) Presented publicly an enviable way of life;

(13) Kept everyone else out because others could not be as good as they;

(14) Were precise in their conversation with one another;

(15) Did not let just anyone teach God's word;

(16) Were very disciplined in their daily habits;

(17) Admonished others because others were not as good as they;

(18) Prayed daily, and many times;

(19) Have a very solid tradition which they passed on from generation to generation with perfect precision;

(20) Did in-depth research about the identity of each member;

(21) Kept a very clean and decent life;

(22) Others recognized that it's virtually impossible to be like this group...too perfect.

Wouldn't you like to be part of this group who were so sure they were the people of God? The good news is that their descendants are with us until today. They were the best from day one, and they can document it too. Wouldn't you like to live the perfect life and be an example to others? Wouldn't you like to be the envy of the town, friends and family? Wouldn't you like to be among the few, the brave, the strong, the well-established? Wouldn't you like to be born in such a group? They did not call themselves evangelical, Catholic, Orthodox, Maronite, Baptist, Presbyterian, and a thousand other flavors of Perfection-Wannabes. The reason is that they were far better than these Johnny-Come-Lately-Groups. Don't you and I aspire to improve so much and be like them as we come closer and closer to God, so much so that no one is as good as we?

Now, the bad news -- really bad news. Jesus called this group by what would not be exactly labeled as "politically-correct". We know about whom He is talking. To Him, they were vipers, liars, they stink, cheaters, fake, country club fanatics, coming short on all counts. He actually called them evil, fathered by Satan, and missed the whole point of being followers of God. They were so closed up on the inside and were content with the outside that all people saw was the "face-book" (pun intended). Why? Because they were perfectly convinced that God accepted them and everything they brought before Him, but in fact He rejected them and all they brought. Why? Because God did not want what they did for Him on earth. He did not want their gifts and generosity; not their precise words and separation from others; not how THEY determined what true religion was (and is). Why? Because what God wanted, really desired, is not what they brought or had or gave, but God was interested in them personally, to give themselves completely to Him without reference to anything they had or their lineage or even their theology. He wanted their heart to be yielded to Him, filled with Him, perfected by Him, when obedience is truly possible. To Him, His true followers have broken hearts, broken lives, broken homes, broken relationships, broken dreams, broken minds, broken wills, even smashed on the rocks of religious perfection and our shores are littered with such. He takes them all, and offers to mend them, to build them even from scratch, and to fill them with His Spirit, and is willing to work with this crowd daily so they will be like Him, just like HIM, JUST like Him, in heart, in life, in relationships, in thought, in desires, and all they have to do is ask. After all, He's got time, and He's got the skill to accomplish it. He promised. And He is faithful to fulfill, so far, every promise He made since day one. May we never aspire to "find ourselves" only to find out we have to deny that which we found, for His sake. May we never feel content with our own confidence or strength, for He has a far better way of making things happen. His way is called: Love. And true love begins and ends with Him. It brings us back to Him to say to Him: I love you, Lord, And I lift my voice To worship You Oh, my soul, rejoice! Take joy my King In what You hear Let it be a sweet, sweet sound In Your ear. If you think you can't, He can make it happen in you. Just ask. And when we look in His face and say with all your heart: "I love you Lord", we will hear Him say: "I loved you first, and would never want even eternity to be without you!" May today be worship time! *(Saturday, February 8, 2014 at 5:45A.M. CST)*

SPECIAL MOMENTS
From my heart to yours

On a couple of occasions, some people (with eye sight problems, I might add) thought when they saw me with Mom that we were brother and sister. Of course, Mom looked at me and grinned, and said: "that's not my problem!" For the record, Mom is close to 88, and I'm ... ah... much younger ... (Smile). I don't know what to say, but I'm wishing that somehow when we get to heaven, age marks will fade away, but I'm sure I would still consider it an honor to open the gate for her. :) *(Monday, February 24, 2014 at 11:15P.M. CST)*

SHARP WIT
From my heart to yours

In one of the many friendly encounters at the kitchen table with my dear Mom, I decided to check and see how sharp her wits are. So, we went back and forth about my birth date. To avoid month-day confusion in filling out the 1001 forms, I changed the date from October 8 to Oct 10. And I assured her that that's when I was born, not on the 8th. She looked at me with a quizzing look, thought for a minute, (make that 30 seconds), squinted her left eye, broke a smile on her face, and said: "I'm sorry to tell you that you're wrong, but you were born on the 8th". I leaned toward her and with presumed confidence said: "Mom, I would have you know that I-Was-There!" I thought I was able to corner her now. But, Not Mom. She leaned toward me, pointed her shaky index finger toward me, and said: "Are you looking at me?" Yes Ma'am, I said. She said, "I would have you know that before You Were There, I-Was-There! And I have the scars to prove it. "My Cute Mom! WHAM! BAM! Fell flat on my face. K.O. Fat chance of winning a single round with her. :) So, I licked my wounds, poured her another cup of Turkish coffee, and decided to wait few more years. My Mom, the Margaret Thatcher of our home. *(Tuesday, February 25, 2014 at 8:15A.M. CST)*

UNTRIED CHRIST
From my heart to yours

To Those Who Care About Truly Following Him: (from my heart to yours) G. K. Chesterton said, "Christianity has not so much been tried and found wanting, as it has been found difficult and left untried." Dallas Willard speaks of "The Way of Christ". Gandhi said: "Give me your Christ, and take away your Christianity". Luke (in Acts 9:2) speaks of certain people being "in The Way" - referring to following Christ in a new-found way. In Acts, the only way the disciples were recognized as genuine was because they were "with Jesus" (e.g., Acts 4:13). Dietrich Bonhoeffer wrote in Nazi prison his masterpiece "The Cost of Discipleship", found more these days on the shelves of used bookstores for a penny, and costs $3.99 for online shipping, than in the hearts of followers of Christ. My, my, my! How great value is always given to the cheap in the world, and the priceless fades into oblivion. The abundance of workshops, seminars, books, articles, videos, training, and other such content on the subject of discipleship and leadership gives the impression that all is well in Christendom. Then we hear church leaders at the highest level from China, Africa, and South America, where God is truly saving large numbers of people, say that while the large numbers give the impression that there is tremendous church growth, this growth is merely in numbers, but lacks growth in depth in a very alarming manner. I bypassed America completely because, for the past two years, records show that Bible literacy and church attendance (and much more so true followers in "the Way") has been on the decline despite all efforts made, financial or otherwise. How sad! And to cover our pettiness, we blame the stars of evangelical television who fell from grace, knowing fully that falling stars always attract more attention for a moment than the great wonders that faithfully shine in the heavens night after night, and we don't even acknowledge so much as their existence sometimes. There is something wrong when around us there is so much content outside our hearts to benefit from, but little penetration to show a radically changed life that truly reflects and clearly indicates transformation within. This *Transformation* is based on Re-Formation, and not on IN-Formation. But we must realize that there is absolutely No acceptable change in our hearts and, in practice, in our life, unless brought about 100% by the working of the Holy Spirit in us. For He, the Spirit, seeks to glorify Christ exclusively and always in whatever is of eternal value. The difficulty we have is simply this: We refuse to surrender completely to governorship and ownership of our life. Yes, I'm looking in the mirror. For that acceptable surrender to happen we must experience what Oswald Chambers and Hudson Taylor described as "Total Abandonment" of ourselves to Christ. Total, not partial! And that won't happen in our own strength or power at all, but when that moment "happens" and we hear Jesus Christ call us by name saying: "Follow Me". Then, and only then, the transformation journey of our life - Begins, for to come after Him by faith is not the end, but the beginning. Genuine discipleship is recognized -- When the Holy Spirit brings true glory to Jesus Christ in others, not by visible efforts of the moment, but by the promptings in people's hearts when the Spirit whispers; Genuine discipleship is recognized -- When others are invited to become followers of Him, not of us and our trappings and our denominational biases, for He who dwells in the hearts has no use for mailing list, and we relish dissecting the butterfly even to death; Genuine discipleship is recognized -- When others invite, yet, others to "come and see a man" (as the Samaritan woman said of Jesus to her people; Genuine discipleship is recognized -- When man is frustrated and cannot explain what happened by human means; Genuine discipleship is recognized -- When whatever happens leads to worship, to Truth, to Obedience, to Him. For at the end of the day, it's not about *me*, but it's All about Him. May we find ourselves crying out to Him like the blind man did, and never be stopped by the voices of the world, even the religious world, around us for it's not visible acts that matter, but the fire and passion and flicker of life that only the Spirit brings. For as sure as the sun rises every morning, Jesus will hear our cry and will stop the noise of the crowd to call us to

Him. Incidentally, the price we pay for following Him is not of our own strength, but is in fact what He deposits in us by His Spirit to know and practice daily. He dwells within us because we dwell with Him; We keep coming to Him, because He keeps inviting us to abide "In Him". *(Tuesday, February 25, 2014 at 10:42A.M. CST)*

Praying Right
From my heart to yours

Oswald Chambers (author of My Utmost For His Highest) was so seriously committed to praying and receiving whatever the Lord wanted to provide, that when a wealthy friend once offered to completely endow the Bible College in 1911, Oswald responded, "No thank you – because, if you do that, the school might go on longer than God wants." The Bible school he founded in 1911 closed in 1915 because of the start of WWI. His promise to God was that he would never turn away any applicant because of need. In 1915, he had 106 students; 60 became missionaries around the world. He was so committed to prayer lifestyle that he was known to be unconventional, and was described as "The Apostle of the Haphazard". Chambers authored more than 35 books. His most well-known is "My Utmost For His Highest", read by millions, was translated to 39 languages, and has been in continuous publication since 1927. Chambers died at the ripe old age of --- 43. Yes, 43. He always prayed "Lord, please do not allow me to live one day beyond my usefulness to you". Makes me ask myself: "Does it really matter how long I live, just marking time on my life's odometer? Oswald Chamber's passion was to make Christ known. What's your passion? His sole desire was to be at the

Master's feet. What's your desire? His one thing in life he did early on, and made all the difference, was that he completely and deliberately surrendered to the control of the Holy Spirit in his life. The rest of his life was simply details that God filled in. Have you completely surrendered yet? Or, are you still in negotiations ? *(Thursday, March 6, 2014 at 5:10A.M. CST)*

SLEEPING WITH THE ENEMY
From my heart to yours

After a lovely evening of conversation and fellowship with dear friends in Knoxville, I woke up this morning with this thought. I submit it from my heart to yours: I cannot sleep with sin, even in separate rooms, and expect to have a clean house for Christ to dwell in and be Lord. When the Holy Spirit, whom Jesus promised to His followers, comes to abide in me, His plan is to take down all the walls. Why? So that Christ can shine out from inside to the world. And the Spirit is the only one able to make that happen. The question is: When I claim to be His follower, is my heartfelt desire to completely surrender to Him, or has Satan deceived me to think that I CAN negotiate? Is my life a negotiable saga of "territorial integrity", meaning: there is that which is mine, and there is that which is His, in my life? All who were useful to Him and practiced His Presence throughout history exercised complete surrender to Him daily. He is not with me to do what I want and bless me, but I am in Him to be what pleases Him, and bless and worship Him. My daily prayer is as the words from the song: "I surrender all, All to you my blessed Savior, I surrender all." *(Saturday, March 8, 2014 at 7:55A.M. CST)*

BEING REJECTED

From my heart to yours

It is only reasonable, as man rejected God who became man, that God would reject man who is always attempting to become god. The reason is simple. When God became man, He came down and humbled himself; He loved to the uttermost; and He gave His nature, His Spirit, and accepted us forever. Man has failed miserably on all counts. And, at best, man is continually discovering he's like an onion. All we have to do is start peelin'. Nothing appealin'! Jesus loved us enough to turn ashes to beauty, death to life, and hell to heaven through his sorrow, his death, and his taking on himself the full judgment of the holy God. And instead of us drinking the cup of wrath, He gave us the cup of salvation and joy. As He asked many when He walked our earth, He continually asks us: Do you believe? Do you? We dare not give Him what He did not give us first. Even our love, "we love Him because He first loved us". The question is not: how much; but, do we really love Him? For loving Him leads us to only one thing, and that is: "Worship". For from the fountain of worship, we serve, we love, and we accept even the unlovely. The psalmist said: (116:12-13) "What shall I return to the Lord for all his goodness to me? I will lift up the cup of salvation and call on the name of the Lord." *(Saturday, March 8, 2014 at 10:04A.M. CST)*

ONE MIND

From my heart to yours

The band of brothers and sisters simply calling out upon the only living God, who, by promise, hears our cries, is an irreplaceable gift, and grace. Thank you, one and all. Not because of who I am, But because of what He's done; Not because of what I've done, But because of Who You are! The God of ALL, adopted us, so that we can cry out to Him constantly, and call Him "Father"! *(Wednesday, March 19, 2014 at 6:11P.M. CDT)*

DYING TO LIVE

From my heart to yours

I woke up this morning, on the other side of the pond, with this thought in mind - from my heart to yours: Jesus said: "The seed must go into the ground and die; and when it dies, it brings forth fruit". Do I believe what He says? The answer can only be: Yes or No. We are most effective when we die to self. For the battle belongs to The Lord (meaning: not to us). Our lifeline, while dead, is the very Spirit of the ever living God. For His singular purpose is not the detail, but is to bring glory to the Eternal Son. The challenge to Christians is simply one. It is the challenge of dying a complete death to self. We'd rather negotiate to our last breath to retain control, even 1%. However, the fact remains that no death- no fruit. All else is noise. The question is: Do I believe? Do I trust Him? Do I love Him? For me, it's a Yes. For you? *(Friday, March 21, 2014 at 4:51P.M. CDT)*

"THY KINGDOM COME"
From my heart to yours

I woke up this morning (3/23) earlier than my alarm was set, and I really needed the extra sleep before leaving for the airport. Promptly, I was caught in the thought of the work of the Holy Spirit in the building of God's Kingdom. Some thoughts made me quite uncomfortable, which I will share. However, the Spirit quieted my heart, pressing gently on me to be still, not like cold water on fire, but like a mother's touch filled with compassion. I found myself saying with Peter: Lord, you know everything; you know that I love you". For what really mattered was whether I love Him with a pure heart. I realized that to truly love him does not mean I must understand all that He is doing, but just enough to sense His leading when it's my turn to do my part, as in a symphony where each musician has a turn for his instrument. My focus ought to be, not on playing the notes, but to play the music. There is a difference. For the one whose presence exclusively matters to the orchestra members is that of the conductor. So basically, each musician is playing to please only the conductor. I asked if my life is being lived for His pleasure alone. Is my love for Him conditional or unconditional? Meaning: must I know all that He does, even with my own life, or can I say, as the song says: "where He leads me, I will follow" --not question, not wonder, not hesitate, not look around to see who else is going with me; but simply Follow, not because of who I am but because of who He is.). That made me uncomfortable. Reason being, while words communicate thought, it always takes the Spirit of The Shepherd to give the sheep the sense of His Presence, in real time, for them to follow. The "understanding" the Scriptures refer to (e. g., many places in Psalms) is the understanding of His Word, enough to trust Him, and not to understand the details of my journey with Him beforehand. That's why I need His Spirit always. That's why even Jesus himself needed to be under the "full control" of the Holy Spirit in order to accomplish the will of the Father. Why? To demonstrate to us that, we too, in order for us to live a life of faith, pleasing Him alone, my life must be under the full domination of His Spirit. The question for the believer is not: "Do I have the Spirit of Christ" but, "Am I yielded completely to the Spirit of Christ in me, by faith, in order for Him to do His will in me". For I cannot ask Him: "where am I going, Lord?" Much better to say: "Lord, I'm ready, I'm all yours, "lead me oh thou gentle Savior", "Lead me on oh King Eternal". Then, my desire is one, and it's to abide in His Word, in Him who IS the Word, even through the valley of the shadows. *(Sunday, March 23, 2014 at 6:28A.M. CDT)*

GOD NOT IMPRESSED
From my heart to yours

God is never impressed with what I do, and for at least two reasons. The first is that His focus was, is, and will always be on what He does in the power of the Holy Spirit to the glory of the Son to reflect the full impact of the Father's love. The second reason is that He is the one doing any work worth mentioning. My life duty is to love Him and adore Him with all my heart, placing myself at His disposal to use me when it pleases Him. The rest of my time can be spent waiting upon the Spirit while I search my heart to be clean in His sight. *(Monday, March 31, 2014 at 5:16A.M. CDT)*

GOD'S PRIORITIES
From my heart to yours

I'm learning that God is not concerned about what I do in my life as much as how I answer three questions whenever His Spirit prompts me: (1) Do I love him with all my heart? (2) Do I love those who are members of His Body, the Church? (3) Do I love unlovely people the way He loves them? True and persistent love is manifest in that order: Him first, His people second. Then others will see how we love one another and give Him glory. Incidentally, since His love knows no geographical (or other) boundaries, "Disciples" and "Denominations" are not interchangeable. He teaches the first to love; while we manufacture the second to work. The first follow Him unto death for Christ's sake, while the second distracts many for no real purpose at all. *(Monday, March 31, 2014 at 10:08A.M. CDT)*

CALLING UPON HIS NAME
From my heart to yours

This morning (4/1), I was awakened, and the Lord brought to my mind a verse about which I've been thinking very often over the past several months. It's Genesis 4:26, which says: "And they began to call upon the Name of the Lord." We know a few things already by now: (1) creation, (2) fall of man, (3) Mr. and Mrs.

Adam are out seemingly on their own, (4) sin's impact was felt, (5) Cain killed his brother Abel and blood was spilt for the first time, (6) many generations were born, (7) music was invented, and that's no monkey business, (8) certain skills became known to man, (9) the burden of sin was felt repeatedly, (10) Adam and Eve had Seth marking a new beginning, (11) we have an up close view of Eve's take on things for she said "God has 'appointed' another seed in place of Abel", (12) she still remembers, how can she not?! (13) we have a glimpse of Eve's broken heart because of death, (14) we know of man's aching heart to go back "home" to God where fellowship and love existed and His voice was heard always, (15) despite the separation, there was hope and faith in God alone and an ache for Him again even after many generations. What triggered it? Was it a sudden self-awareness of a possibility for self-help? How can that be and man was clearly going further down, and fast? Something else had to be happening! Then Seth شيث had Enosh آنوش born to him. And now we learn that "they began to call upon the Name of God." Who were "they"? Adam and Eve? The last generation born ? Seth and Enosh? Or a certain group of people somewhere? We really don't know? But we do know that there was a shift, something unusual happened, and a new course of action was taken, SO very different from the day-to-day life that it captured even the mind of the Spirit to include it in the inspired Word. What we do know is that a group, somewhere (not sure of number), had an aching, a strong desire, a new kind of passion. It was not to sing, even though music and instruments were invented by then. It was not preaching or collecting a special donation that they thought of. Nor was it forming a committee for social change. It was a "climate change" (pun intended) of a different kind. It was not becoming groupies with differing doctrinal positions on God, creation, sin or whatever really happened-whether it was really Cain's fault or his parents' who didn't raise him well. Nor was it making a memorial for Abel and praying to him because he was such a good man who offered sacrifices and was a true believer. It was not being content enjoying the vast creation which God designed for man. The mind of man was corrupt enough that they didn't need to create the goddess of the Earth, a figment of their imagination. Something SO different happened, and it captured a certain group of people's attention - even captivated them and radically changed their lifestyle that they "began to call upon the Name of the Lord". Calling out to Him!... implying that if there was going to be an answer, it must come from only Him. We know for sure that Adam and Eve were still alive but not so well, especially that they still remember the Garden, the Presence, the fellowship, their contentment in God, that He was truly their sufficiency. Was the calling on God (a new kind of praying) because a few heard enough about the God of Adam and Eve and all that happened to them, that they just knew something really horrible went wrong? And that the only way to get it right was to call upon that Name they kept hearing about in the distance? Oh, the craving they had to go back, back to Eden, back to God, back home, back to His shelter and back to His love. No so easy a task. So, they began to cry out to Him! Would to God that the people today who are called by His Name would call upon Him - humble themselves and cry out to Him today, again! Oh, the awful crisis of hanging in the eternal balances, in the hands of God and

having no Exit, and finding none other to answer our cry!
(Monday, March 31, 2014 at 11:13P.M. CDT)

"SUFFICIENCY" ON MY MIND

From my heart to yours

This morning (4/2), I woke up with the word "Sufficiency" on my mind. People seek attention by never ending needs. Jesus attracted people while on earth with His never ending love. Accurate doctrine without Christ's love is very dead. Christ's love brings it to life. In other words, Jesus makes His love the air we breathe to learn His doctrine. Man makes doctrine the condition for love. A Pharisee begins with doctrine. A humble and contrite heart stays at the cross for love's sake. In his stillness there, man begins a new journey and writes a new story. For love's sake! There are at least four human needs. They are: The need for Identity to avoid loss of essence; the need for Control to avoid loss of orientation; the need for Pleasure to avoid Pain; and the need for Belonging to avoid loneliness. Identity, Control, Pleasure, and Belonging. From the beginning of time, man by his desire for control decided to define the criteria and has set himself as the standard for desired outcomes deriving unsustainable Authority from him/herself. Not much has changed. It is such a constant heavy burden! Now, the Invitation: Christ said: "Come unto me -- all with heavy burdens--and I will give you rest". And the Promise: "My God shall supplies all your needs according to His riches in glory [while on earth too] in Christ Jesus my Lord. Here's why: "...that in all things, He might have the

Preeminence". Religion is such a dead alternative! *(Wednesday, April 2, 2014 at 12:59A.M. CDT)*

CONFRONTING GOD
From my heart to yours

It is one thing for people to confront people. For what follows is damage control -- which usually fails, and each receives or gives the numbing "silent treatment". Jesus Christ is also in the business of confronting people, sooner or later. But He does not take the same approach at all. That's why He says "Learn from me, ... Follow me... Take my yoke...". Paul says "you did not learn Christ that way", and "Put on Christ". Peter was someone whom Jesus confronted but always loved, for His love was always actionable. He wasn't willing to leave Peter alone to his own ways. So, He confronted him at the right time. Confrontation time: (Mk 8:31-34 and Lk 22:31-34). Jesus said, very directly, in essence, "Peter, you will either have to deny yourself, or you WILL deny me." Peter was so full of Peter, filtering everything his senses experienced through his own perspective on things, and unwilling to surrender completely. He fell, and he fell hard. That's when Peter came to his end and Jesus began His work of grace. Think of it like the awesome work of grace when after Adam's fall, God kicked him out of the Garden. He did not "fall out of grace", but in fact he fell into the very lap of grace. Sad that he did not realize that! The awesomeness of Christ is not that Peter denied Him and He accepted Peter back. It is rather that Jesus prayed for Peter earnestly, while He knew all along that Peter was going to deny Him and never told Peter that, yet fully trusting the Father for a full restoration of Peter by faith. Jesus said to Peter "I prayed and asked on your behalf that your faith fails not; and when you are converted, strengthen your brethren." (Lk 22:31-34) What mattered was not the qualifications of Peter but the character of Christ. What matters today is not that we are better than Peter, but that we refuse to be like Christ. Yet we hide behind pithy cliché's and say "I'm a work of grace in progress". To Jesus, it was never a question of whether Peter deserved prayer. He loved Peter too much. It was what moved His own heart! Now, He calls us to go and do likewise. Simple, right? Think again. The only way we can succeed is to fully surrender to the dominance of the Holy Spirit in our life to make life-in-Christ possible, just like Jesus was always "in the Father". Reason? It's all about Him, not me. That's why :) *(Wednesday, April 2, 2014 at 8:28P.M. CDT)*

Let's Not Be Fooled
From my heart to yours

There is no such thing as Faith in Christ without Obedience to Christ. There is no such thing as being filled with the Spirit without being dominated by the Spirit. There is no such thing as following Christ without truly becoming like Him. There is no such thing as putting on Christ without taking off Self. There is no such thing as loving others without Christ showing me His true love. There is no such thing as loving God without being passionate about being in His Presence. There is no such thing as seeing God's holiness without seeing my sinfulness (Isa 6:1ff). There is no such thing as loving "the lost" without loving those who are found. There is no such thing as knowing Christ without reading what the Eternal Spirit of Christ took time to inspire the writers to write about Christ. There is no such thing as heaven without hell. There is no such thing as passionate toward Christ without being cold toward the "love of the world system". There is no such thing as scaling the heights of a Spirit-filled life without scaling the depths of my fallen-ness. There is no such thing as living for Christ without denying self. There is no such thing as "I do my part and God takes care of the rest". Moms pickup after their kids, after the kids make a wreck out of the house. However, God does it all and I rest in Him, for He works in me what pleases Him. What do I do? Nothing, For the Spirit changes me into His likeness in His Presence day by day and uses me according to His pleasure. God doesn't say "mi casa es tu casa". He says "My house is called the house of prayer". I hope He doesn't finish the verse -- again. There is no such thing as "Christ in you the hope of glory" without being in Christ the lover of my soul. There is no such thing as "Revival" without concerted prayer that precedes revival. There is no such thing as Holy Spirit anointing of programs, efforts, denominations, activities, locations, traditions, etc. But there IS such a thing as Holy Spirit anointing people. *(Wednesday, April 2, 2014 at 8:52P.M. CDT)*

FINGERPRINTS OF GOD
From my heart to yours

Life is not about how I Feel, but whether I clearly see the traces of what He's done in it, unaided by my religiously correct verbiage. Once a crime takes place, two things at least are sure to happen. The first is that People stand from a distance and observe, then give their opinion as to what might have happened with a high degree of certainty. The second is that fingerprint experts are certain to come in, and very quietly dust the crime scene with special identifying powder, and reconstruct the story of what actually happened. Are you able to see the fingerprints of the Almighty in your life? If Not, then STOP because He is not there. If Yes, then don't worry what people say from a distance. He's not impressed by what you accomplish, but by the fingerprints He leaves behind. Fingerprints tell, not where you've been or come from or done, but where God has been and what God has touched, and whom God has touched through your life--without our own input into the matter. We may be content with "hanging around Jesus" to see what we can get, like most people in His days. But only one woman felt His power. What was impressive is not that people noticed, but that Jesus noticed. The people who touch Him feel His power and get his attention. The people He touches are brought to life -- in Him. *(Wednesday, April 2, 2014 at 9:15P.M. CDT)*

DOES IT NOT SURPRISE US ?
From my heart to yours

Does it not surprise us that the first century church did not establish seminaries but were content with providing extended teaching on an As-Needed basis? Does it not surprise us that teachers were not hired by people but were sent by the Holy Spirit? Does it not surprise us that it was not the Holy Spirit who agreed to the will of the people but the people obeyed the Holy Spirit's command? Does it not surprise us that while the government of the United States during the nineties were debating where to erect one statue honoring Elvis Presley, the government of India decided to erect one statue honoring Gandhi and William Carey, the pioneer missionary to that country? Does it not surprise us that the church at Antioch, made up of converted Gentiles, The Novices, did not need the church at Jerusalem, The Establishment, to get it started because they were truly led by the Spirit of God? *(Wednesday, April 2, 2014 at 9:53P.M. CDT)*

Pain Is Universal
From my heart to yours

Like pain, there are few things that have a universal character! The UNIVERSAL heartfelt SADNESS at the loss of a loved one regardless of age affirms that, by design, we had to have been created to live forever. The Bible says: "In the beginning, God ..." The UNIVERSAL presence of DEATH, and its aftermath in human emotions, affirms regardless of human variations, that something went seriously wrong and applies to all without exception. The Bible says: "All have sinned" The UNIVERSAL desire and YEARNING with various expressions toward the experience of deep "cleansing and purification" of the soul and spirit affirms that there is a global desire to do right, even the proverbial "acts of kindness", and that we lost the way home. The Bible says "There is none that continually does the right thing, no not one." The UNIVERSAL sinking feeling that all human efforts may NOT be 100% assuring and accurate regarding eternal blessedness affirm that at the deepest levels of the human heart, man's search for meaning and belongingness remains a pressing passion. The UNIVERSAL and persistent REJECTION by man of any offer from God who sufficiently provided a way of salvation affirms the impossibility of a natural human tendency toward accepting the gift of God in Jesus Christ our Lord. The UNIVERSAL complication of any SOLUTION by man, though imperfect, to quiet a rebellious heart and a rioting conscience makes the simple Gospel of Jesus Christ a treasure that's out of this world. What is so awesome about Jesus Christ is not that "he helps those who help themselves" and are never sure, but that He reveals himself to anyone who asks, and can be sure, especially those who are beyond "helping themselves". WHAT does any man/woman have to pay? Nothing, Nada, ملّیم ولا, rien, niks, intet, هيچ, waxba, لا شيء, kitu, hiçbir şey, کچھ بھی نہیں, Nothing. WHY? "God demonstrated His love toward us ...., and -- Because HE PAID IT ALL; All to Him I owe. Sin has left a crimson stain; He washed it white as snow. *(Thursday, April 3, 2014 at 5:11A.M. CDT)*

ABOUT THE ONE WE LOVE
From my heart to yours

Somehow, time stands still when we are with the one we love. We talk about the one we love. We imitate the one we love. We act like, sound like, behave like the one we love. We do the pleasure of the one we love. We make every effort not to break the heart of the one we love. We give all the value to the one we love, for we discover that all else never had any value. The question from Jesus simply is: Do you love me more than these? The challenge is: To discover that nothing else has value when compared to Him. .... *(Thursday, April 3, 2014 at 5:29A.M. CDT)*

FINGERPRINTS OF GOD (PT. 1)
From my heart to yours

How can I know and tell where the fingerprints of God are in my life? Psalm 23:6 "Surely goodness and mercy shall follow me all the days of my life...". Q: If His goodness and mercy shall FOLLOW me, it means that they are behind me every time or any time I look. How do I know them and where they are? A: Notice first the central words: "me", "my", and "I shall" in the verse. Very personal, right? That means I can stop at any time and glance back over the recent or distant past. Flashing before my eyes, He reminds me of places (where I've been, where I've fallen, where I was lonely, where I was about to give up), persons (who hurt me, encouraged me, or whom I served), events (joyous or sad), trials (with me or others), challenges (in life), sickness (nagging, near death, tormenting, surgeries), life storms (death, physical or emotional or mental abuse, bankruptcy, debts of many kinds), or times when I fell from grace but God embraced me with HIS grace, rash judgments I made, struggles, meetings, quiet moments, conferences, work experiences. And through it all, I know that I have been spared many disasters and shown how immense His love for me has been. I fall at His feet, and often. Then I thank Him, I praise Him, I worship Him, I bow to the ground before Him for ALL His mercies and kindnesses toward me, totally undeserving, and confess that He is worthy of all honor and glory, majesty and blessing. And I plead with Him to keep me within the circle where I can sense His Holy Presence all the days of my life and know that it's Him -- here and there, and can see His incomparable fingerprints all my days. My friend, His Amazing Name is Jesus, my Lord and Savior. *(Thursday, April 3, 2014 at 6:07A.M. CDT)*

WALKING ALONE IN THE CROWD
From my heart to yours

"And as He prayed alone, His disciples were with Him". This verse is tucked in between the feeding of the 5000 - (the "ministry of abundance" which could have easily been a distraction from His singular purpose for which He came, which was not saving humanity but doing the will of the Father, abiding in the love of the Father, being daily under the full control of and in implicit obedience to the Holy Spirit) - , and the "ministry of suffering", rejection from men, and ultimate separation from the Father with whom He had been One before there was something called "time". We aspire for the ministry of abundance. He aspired for one thing while on earth that had nothing to do with "people" - the many - but with One - the Father. We may not be able to know "what" He prayed, but we can just imagine "why" He was praying constantly. I'm learning that true prayer begins when we run out of words. His effectiveness was not that He did on earth but that He was one with the Father. Being consumed by the love of the Father was not only the passion of His life, but the only ingredient in His spiritual diet that sustained Him during His earthly ministry A-Z. However, and not surprisingly, even He, Jesus, the Son of Man, could not have sustained Himself in that love had it not been for the dominant presence of the Eternal Spirit. Again, we see the Triune God in perfect and perpetual active harmony -

until the rending of the veil into two. What's on your agenda today? *(Monday, April 7, 2014 at 9:25P.M. CDT)*

ON PLEASING GOD
From my heart to yours

From heaven's perspective, we ask: Why was the Father so "pleased" in the Son? (Prophecy fulfilled in the Gospel: "This is my beloved son in whom I am well-pleased"). From earth's perspective, we describe it as the ministry of the "walking dead" (no pun intended). (Read what the Spirit of prophecy said in Isaiah 42) The journey of the Son can be described as: "Breaking down the gates of hell forever, by being obedient and crushed on the cross of Calvary for me". Stepping through the panorama of the Father's pleasure in the Son –

1. The objective determined, and the vessel found (vss. 1-4)
2. The character and resources of God declared (vss. 5-9)
3. The creation invited to take part (vss. 10-13)
4. The agonies of Calvary foretold as birthing screams in the hallways of heaven (vss. 14-17)
5. The single-mindedness and utter obedience of the Son as reason for complete pleasure (vss. 18-21)
6. The utter depravity and sinfulness of man (vss. 22-25).

In other words, The only way I can be pleasing unto God is by dying unto self and the world every day in all things, and by being made alive unto God everyday in all things...A summary of what a life of faith looks like. Dead and Alive at once ! (" I am crucified, but I live, Yet not I ") The only possible way for this to happen is through the Holy Spirit. "Complete Surrender" is what's for dinner. Unconditional, Real, Active, Implicit, Impactive. Why? Because it's all about Him, not me. Is my walk with Him still "optional" and based on my preferences, Or am I passionate enough to say: "Yes, Lord"? As someone said: "There is no such thing as 'No, Lord' ". *(Monday, April 7, 2014 at 10:35P.M. CDT)*

WALKING ALONE IN THE CROWD (PART 2)
From my heart to yours

Some of what it does NOT mean: "Alone" doesn't mean "I'm lonely", or that "I'm independent". "Walking Alone" doesn't mean that I chart my own course in life in my own strength; Or that I can rely on myself some and "God will do the rest". "Walking Alone" is not something I do to influence other people; nor is it a history of my ups and downs in life. "Walking" does not mean "moving from one point to another". In fact, "walking alone" has nothing to do with people or what I do in the midst of people. But it has everything to do with the One who is "walking" with me. He it is who enables me to "walk", for I am crucified (dead); Yet, I live, but not I. It is Christ who lives through me (alive). Being the "living dead" is what the Holy Spirit alone does in me day by day. Synonyms of the "the living dead" (from Isaiah 42) are: "the listening deaf", and "the seeing blind". Next, what does "Walking Alone" really Mean, then? *(Wednesday, April 9, 2014 at 8:19A.M. CDT)*

Losing To Win

From my heart to yours

> To wrap his arms around the cross, His union with the Heavenly Father had to be broken, so that I can say, when I pray, "Oh Father, Now I know that you love me because you did not withhold your Son from me." And to my Lord in gratitude, I can say, "The joy of heaven has become the joy of my heart. And the love of the Eternal Father has become the lover of my soul". (Saturday, April 12, 2014 at 4:11P.M. CDT)

On Reconciliation

From my heart to yours

> Man To God, First: Jesus came to earth not to reconcile man with man, but to reconcile man with God. That's worth coming for. The meeting place was not a conference room at the UN, but on an insignificant hill, at the Cross. So, He moved Heaven and earth to make that happen. Man To Man, Second: For man to reconcile with man, man has to reconcile with God -- First -- at the Cross. For at the cross, Satan was disarmed and crushed, and everyone who believes can now lay his arms too. True Disarmament: Both happened at the cross. No wonder Satan hates the cross with such passion that he wants to kill anyone who comes to the cross. For there, even Satan saw the full passion and love of God in Christ expressed towards us, and He paid it all. Man In Darkness: Since man began, man Always attempted reconciliation on his own, and Always failed. Not exactly a good track record! Actually, pathetic.

Man In Christ: God in Christ succeeded from the first and only time. Once is forever! His love was shown at the cross. And His glory radiates forever in that He desires for us -- by faith -- to be one with Him, for Christ's sake. Oh, the love that will not let me go! *(Sunday, April 13, 2014 at 12:00A.M. CDT)*

WHY IS IT LIKE THIS ? (3 PARTS, HERE'S PART 1)
From my heart to yours

I've been wondering for at least the past 15 years, and asking God a simple question: "Why, Lord, there is such an unacceptable rate of divisions, splits, and humdrum in our Arabic churches? Even within a church where splits and breakups haven't taken place, the spirit of "each to himself" -- lukewarmness -- is so rampant. With utmost respect to all that is taking place in the form of activities -- (pulpits, singing, conferences, seminars, training, etc. etc.), nothing is helping remedy and solve this epidemic. We pretend that our duty is to save the world. But the last one I can think of whose task was to save, died on a cross and accomplished it. Yet, we think in our cleverness that somehow we can come down from the cross and save others too. The more I see and hear and read, the more I see heartbreaks, hear of splits (some are "soft" meaning: agree to disagree then go in separate ways). Reading loads of material and reports, and tracking it over the years has led me to develop the distinct understanding and grouping thus: (1) there are many in our ranks who are ready to quit and walk away (and maybe they should; I know not); (2) others have settled to a life of despair while remaining in Kingdom work, and that for a variety of reasons; (3) those who decided to marginalize the church and strike out on their own under labels unfamiliar to NT record and spirit, building castles of their own making and trapped in long-term life of spinning wheels in the sands of western money, having dreams of grandeur in ministry saying "God gave me a dream of abundance", thinking that abundance of one sort or another surely implies that God is "walking among His people", when in fact as in Jeremiah 23 God never sent them nor given them holy dreams. As also in Isaiah, many are oblivious to the fact that God's ears are listening only to those who are "poor, of contrite spirit, and tremble at His word". *(Sunday, April 13, 2014 at 11:37A.M. CDT)*

WHY IS IT LIKE THIS ? (3 PARTS, HERE'S PART 2)
From my heart to yours

As I am still struggling trying to grasp what is happening, I am stunned at certain evident contradictions:

1. There are many gatherings and much singing in large numbers, but not much contrition, repentance, confessions, and forgiveness of one another. Even a surface review of many lyrics shows how little soundness they contain and much emotion and personal feelings they express. It has become almost competitive. And that's sad.
2. There are books written or translated but less and less love for The Book that matters and has life within its pages. There are books on "family and relationships", leadership and such, but families (so called Christian families) are breaking up and staying within the walls, becoming more

like the world, losing their children one by one, and pretending all is well, or at least content that it's a "shame" عيب to talk about such things. That's heartbreaking.

3. There are sermons in abundance, but not weeping in the pulpits and before the Holy of Holies. Pulpits have become platforms promoting certain denominational agendas, promoting self-help and riches, and making entrance into the Kingdom conditional on consent to a certain list of statements.

4. There is a passionate run after money (the god of money about which Jesus had something ominous to say). At the feet of this strange god many have bowed to the ground changing whatever it takes so we can have crumbs thrown to us, and there is little individual passion and presence (I dare say by us the pastors and church leaders), as if our very life depended on it, broken before Almighty God, crying out because of our sins and the sins of our people who claim to be Christians. Even Job was recognized for interceding daily on behalf of his 10 children, offering a sacrifice on behalf of each of them, and saying, "perhaps one of them sinned in his heart toward God".

5. There is NO conversation or even recognition of the Person and Work of the Holy Spirit in the Church, giving the impression that "we better not talk about that controversial subject", or "we do our part and he does His part and that's better for the unity of the believers". And I want to ask and plead: REALLY?

Acknowledging his person is one thing. Experiencing His power is a whole different idea. And many have chosen to postpone the discussion in their heart thinking that God will accept their offering, like Cain, without the fire of Mount Carmel or of Pentecost. *(Sunday, April 13, 2014 at 11:39A.M. CDT)*

WHY IS IT LIKE THIS ? (3 PARTS, HERE'S PART 3)
From my heart to yours

Other contradictions exist. But enough is mentioned here. This is not my soapbox by any means, but an agony of many years, a call, and a statement of desire ON OUR PART to cry out for mercy. Mercy..... :

1. that God would send a spirit of brokenness, hopelessness and helplessness among Arabic churches, then a refreshing Spirit in His time on all who are called by His Name, to stir scattered bones and allow many to discover the horror of being without Him and cry out for the hovering of His Holy Spirit on us;

2. that the Spirit who brought us to Calvary to obtain grace, mercy and forgiveness will pervade our churches and hover over the "angels" of our churches and stir us to our "first love"; that we declare Him our Lord even in public, and discipline our lives to belong to Him and Him alone, meaning, all is on the table and ready to change at His command. If we have the Spirit of Christ, we can one by one live in His Presence every day and experience that;

3. that seasons of prayers of confession and repentance would begin - to reflect cries from our hearts because we have gone after other gods, neglected the Living Word, and stepped on our sheep around us as we sought "higher grounds" of advancement. And in His Holy Presence wait, I say WAIT, on Him who hears and answers;
4. that we become jealous of those whom we deemed and described as "unqualified", "unrepentant", "undeserving", "unlike us in the established church", "unworthy rebels until they agree to our religiously suffocating terms".

I say "JEALOUS" because across our land God is doing a wonderful and marvelous thing we dare not take any credit for any part thereof. The people in darkness for centuries have seen the Light of our Awesome God and Savior, are coming in droves, wanting Him and none other, willing to die for Him at any time, passionate about His Word, praying with such daily fervency that puts the most dignified to shame. Their prayers breath life, their cries are cries of hopelessness without the cross, their thankful hearts reflect the thirst of centuries. But God in His infinite mercy came upon them across Africa and Western Asia as on a child about to be aborted and saved them, and is saving them one at a time, making a great army unto Himself of those who love Him with a pure heart and not counting their lives of any value for the sake of the Gospel, of Him who died and rose again. The outcome is causing tremors and aftershocks in false foundations of our own making, and rendering us a minority in the Kingdom of God. WE HAVE GOT TO REALIZE THAT BOTTOM LINE: NOTHING IS ABOUT ME, AND THAT ALL IS ABOUT HIM. He's my Lord, my Savior, the lover of my soul- His name is Jesus. *(Sunday, April 13, 2014 at 11:42A.M. CDT)*

THE HOLY SPIRIT OF GOD: HIS PERSON AND WORK - A BIRD'S EYE VIEW

From my heart to yours

Two Questions:

1. Who is He?

First, He represents Jesus Christ on earth in all that our Lord desires for His Church to be like and act like, for He knows "the deep things of God". The only functional difference is that He is not limited to a human body. He is, as Jesus said, the "other Comforter".

Second, His singular purpose is not earth-generated or motivated, but it is to bring glory to Jesus Christ, the Incarnate God, and Savior of mankind. And He often does that in the least likely places and through the least likely qualified candidates.

Third, His function is to deliver a perfect, holy, and complete Church as the Bride for her Bridegroom. His focus is impeccable. His deliberations are precise and with full authority.

Fourth, His loyalty remains implicitly and completely within the Godhead. He is neither owned nor manipulated by human schemes or words (regardless of how well-intended they may be).

Fifth, He moves with complete ease, without even acknowledging what we may call "obstructions", to bring glory to Him who loved us and died for us.

2. How does He accomplish all of that?
    a. He *governs* all the operations of the Church. Meaning, He decides, directs, empowers, grants, leads those who determined in their hearts (Dan 1:8), and have given up self for the sake of Christ and His Gospel.
    b. He *Facilitates* all the work of the ministry of the Church as He pleases by gifting persons of His choosing and for the duration He determined to accomplish what the Godhead has decided before the foundation of the world (Eph. 2:10).
    c. He *equips*, He *teaches*, He *convicts*, He *gives* gifts, and that's without human advice, effort, wisdom, qualifications, or pursuit.
    d. He *stands* for Jesus Christ among all people, redeemed and unredeemed. He is the "layer" through which God communicates to us, and He is that same "layer" through which we have access to God in Christ. As Jesus was with His disciples while on earth and they had need for nothing while with them, so is the Spirit of Christ with the Church. We gained with His Presence more than

the disciples lost at the ascension of our Lord. All this, and more, is very threatening to our "comfort zones", our fallen desire to control, even 1%. He comforts the disturbed and disturbs the comforted. But to the broken, fallen, contrite, and completely surrendered heart, this is welcomed news. For in our helplessness we discover that while we are suspended by the threads of faith, mercy, grace, and love, it is He, the Holy Spirit, who sustains, strengthens, enables, accomplishes and blesses to the glory of God the Son. No other desire is necessary or acceptable! Personal holiness and discipline, driven and completed dominated by that indwelling Spirit alone (Rom 8), engenders growth and purpose, and directs all eyes towards Him, toward "that Name" (Acts 4), toward "that city whose creator and maker is God Himself. In a summary snapshot, the Holy Spirit's objective is to take all that Jesus was in His earthly days (in whom dwelt the fullness of the Godhead bodily, and with whom the disciples needed nothing else), and distributes Him continually to every member of His Body, the Church, as He pleases (not to/through a particular denomination) to perfect us who are obedient and walk in Him with fear and trembling. *(Monday, April 14, 2014 at 4:24A.M. CDT)*

"NO" Is Clear Enough
From my heart to yours

No Cross, No Resurrection! No Jesus, No Heaven! No Death for Him, No Life for Us ! No Obedience in me, No Faith in Him! He said "Yes" to the Father, I say "Yes" to my Lord ! What do you say? "May the words of my mouth and the meditations of my hearts be acceptable unto You, Lord." *(Tuesday, April 15, 2014 at 11:18P.M. CDT)*

Two sides of A Coin
From my heart to yours

Side 1: True Faith in Him requires complete Obedience to Him. The rest is just talk and noise. Side 2: Since "without faith, it is impossible to please Him", He loved us so much that He also gave us His Spirit who make that possible. Then, Obedience is not because of what I do for Him, but because of what His Spirit continually changes in me to His glory. Summary: Complete and Unconditional surrender to Him is what His cross and Resurrection demand. *(Tuesday, April 15, 2014 at 11:38P.M. CDT)*

Thinking of Hell (in the shadow of the Cross)
From my heart to yours

Hell can tolerate Christians who sing, preach, work on projects, or do any activity in a regular church or ministry. However, hell has absolutely no tolerance for people who PRAY. So, hell's strategy is very simple. It intends to distract Christians - All Christians --

from the ministry of pray. For hell (Satan and his entire host) knows that when a church prays, things happen, things that can cause some serious damage to Satan and his kingdom. The first century church was a clear example. Hell does it through at least one of three ways: (1) External: through destroying the two organisms that God devised for mankind (marriage for saved and lost, and the Church for the redeemed); (2) Internal: through sins (of the flesh, of the mind, and of the heart); and, the most preferred way, (3) Organic: this is the most pernicious, and it is to engage Christians in any and all "good ministry work" so much that they have no time for serious praying. Praying that begins when there are no words to speak but groaning to see the Holy Spirit, work alone or through holy vessels. Distracting from prayer is hell's most successful strategy that brings the best results. The reasons it is such an evil strategy are: (1) it distracts the focus from heaven to earth; (2) it distracts the focus from what God is doing in the world to what people can do; (3) it distracts the focus from what the Holy Spirit demands to what work-by-consensus can make happen; (4) it distracts very easily the focus and center of all glory from the "Joy of Heaven", "that Name", "the One and Only One in whom the Father was pleased -- Jesus who died and rose again. And hell will settle for anything that can replace Him. A side-caveat to this picture is that Satan doesn't mind slithering in the shadows. According to Revelation, what drives Satan raving mad is a white-hot anger that Jesus is the love and joy of heaven and His Bride, and Satan was cast out. Are you blacklisted in hell? *(Thursday, April 17, 2014 at 1:49P.M. CDT)*

MY AMAZING LORD
From my heart to yours

What makes Jesus Preeminent, standing head and shoulder above all else? Stars and Dignitaries of the world in all ages live for a while only to be celebrated at their Death for whatever they did in life. And that remains to be tested by fire. That's it. How sad! That's why I call that a "Dead End". JESUS, on the other hand, died and rose again, and that's when LIFE happened; and all hell broke loose. Satan was crushed, Sinners were forgiven, Holy Spirit descended, Church was born, Comforted were disturbed, Disturbed were comforted, and All who believe, to The Lord may come. Trust and Obey! That's what I call a Good Start, Or is it : a God Start :) Now that's like Jesus. That's just like my Lord. And it's only the beginning. What's next? How about Heaven :) With them, I ask: What's next? With Jesus, I say: There is No Next :) *(Saturday, April 19, 2014 at 6:21A.M. CDT)*

HEAVEN IN SOUTH SUDAN
From my heart to yours

Worship is better in multicolor. This is one section in a funeral service that turned into pure worship and adoration of our Lord. Very sweet and tender moments, mixed with tears and praise. Spoke on: How It Is Better When we Serve from Weakness". Service lasted 3 hrs. Had a meal afterwards. They sang سوف ينتهي العذاب، نعبر وادي الدموع (All Our Suffering Shall End, And We'll Cross The Valley of Tears). It all felt like the great family of God. I had to tell them who wrote the lyrics and music. Made the worship time that much sweeter. What a Savior We Have ! *(Saturday, April 19, 2014 at 1:49P.M. CDT)*

FELLOWSHIP OF SUFFERING
From my heart to yours

I touched then held these hands. I held one then both, and wanted to kiss them for Christ's sake. Then my friend hugged me. It felt like the Master's embrace. His hands were tied above the wrist for 5 days during suffering time. Circulation stopped. Then torture began. I discovered that talk is just that, Until a price has to be paid. Then, nothing stands unless I look to Him who made, even the cross, beautiful. Why? Because Resurrection follows! It sounds different now every time I sing: "Oh, how I love Jesus... yes, because He first loved me". *(Saturday, April 19, 2014 at 1:58P.M. CDT)*

SHAKESPEARE ASKED: WHAT'S IN A NAME?
From my heart to yours

One Fascinating Attribute about Jesus that goes unnoticed at times is that He loved to call people by their name. But how can we call Him by His Name? Is it Wonderful, or Counselor, or the Mighty God, or Everlasting Father, or The Prince of Peace, or Jesus, or Lord, or Christ, or Master, or King, or King of Kings, or Lord, or Lord of Lords, or Lover of my Soul, or Fairest of ten thousand, or Angel of the Covenant, or Friend Closer than a Brother, or Son of God, or Son of Man, or Beloved of the Father, or Altogether Lovely? To Mary, the angel said: "And you shall call His Name: JESUS, for He shall save His people from their sins." Paul said: "For that reason, God also has highly exalted him, and given him a name which is above every name: That at the name of JESUS every knee should bow, of things in heaven (angelic beings and saints), and things in earth (redeemed and Unredeemed), and things under the earth; And that every tongue should confess that JESUS CHRIST is Lord, to the glory of God the Father." (Philippians 2:9-11) CHRIST IS RISEN! قام المسيح What binds us to Him forever is the name: JESUS. Normally people rejoice when a baby is born. But we know He was born to die; and that is sad. Normally people are saddened when someone dies. But we know He rose again and turned the tables on Satan forever. I call that: Altogether Lovely ! *(Saturday, April 19, 2014 at 9:57P.M. CDT)*

To Be All His
From my heart to yours

"Oh Jesus I love thee, I know thou art mine." - so goes the song. BUT, He cannot be all mine, unless I'm All his. He died, so I die. He lives, so I live. Fair is fair. In fact, He demands it. The Bible calls it "Obedience unto Faith" (Rom 1 and Rom 16). After all, He died for me and rose again. Is His demand unreasonable then that I live totally for Him? He prayed: "For their sake, I sanctify myself". Is His demand unreasonable then that I should say: "For His sake, I sanctify myself"? All of Him for me. All of me for Him. What makes it easy to happen in my daily life is to remind myself that "It's Not About Me (my, I, and mine), but about Him". Stickers on the fridge and mirrors might help :). But His Spirit is the One to actually make it happen in me. Key word: Obedience. *(Saturday, April 19, 2014 at 10:23P.M. CDT)*

THAT RESURRECTION MORNING, NEVER LIKE IT, BEFORE OR SINCE
From my heart to yours

The disciples were confused when He spoke of His "Resurrection". When He told them often that the Son of Man must be handed over, suffer, be rejected, be crucified and die, then rise again, they looked at Him very much like some of today's Sunday crowd who are mesmerized by teaching or announcements, but have a crying emptiness and desperately need fire, not fire of the tongue but tongues of fire - from the Holy Spirit. The only task they had until such time when the "promise of the Father" comes was to go to Jerusalem and wait. All they did there was PRAY. True Prayer is commensurate with its Purpose. Humanly speaking, to build a Church to reach the world, the disciples needed to recognize and reduce their dependencies to the absolute minimum that can accomplish the absolute maximum. All they came up with was: GOD. PRAYER led them to discover how hopeless and desperate they needed to be for God to accomplish His work. Today, there appears to be a tendency to find alternatives to expedite things, which maybe the reason why there is little prayer taking place. *(Sunday, April 20, 2014 at 4:04A.M. CDT)*

POWER OF PRAYER

From my heart to yours

PRAYER changes things like nothing else: 1. Unites believers. Nothing else does that. Not all the delicacies of the Mediterranean can even come close. Acts 1:14 "These (disciples) all continued with one accord in prayer and supplication, with the women, and Mary the mother of Jesus, and with his brethren." No one was special. All "continued in prayer", not as usual but with "supplication". Acts 2:1. "And when the day of Pentecost was fully come, they were all with one accord in one place." When people are UNITED, heaven moves. But people can never be united unless they PRAY. The early church did not have a seminar on Prayer. They just Obeyed and Prayed -- the two missing jewels in the churches today. Today's Christians find it easier to obey a person (which is not true obedience) than to obey the Holy Spirit of God. For when they PRAY, they discover His Presence which unites, and purifies, and sanctifies, and liberates and sets the stage for God to act. In other words, His Holy Presence empties us to be filled by only Him. The true "Acts of God" are not only moving nature, but moving people. To move nature, a mere angel can take care of that. But no one dare touch His Church except Him who died for His Church and rose again. *(Sunday, April 20, 2014 at 2:08P.M. CDT)*

HOW DOES THE FAMILY OF GOD WORK?
From my heart to yours

Here's a sample - After I shared with the church in Juba some of the more-than-just-clinical trials of recent years that Lily (my dear sister) went through, it was interesting how they responded by impulse. This choir of the first Baptist church in Juba, South Sudan wanted to sing a special song dedicated to her and what God has been doing in her life. They were scrambling earlier like they needed to practice, and turned out it was this Sudanese song they were practicing. One of the pastors was totally touched that he made his way to me and wanted few minutes. We sat where it was quiet and he told me how much her experiences have impacted his life. He comes from Muslim background, and said she encouraged him to press on in the faith and reach others with the powerful Gospel. He leads a church of some many converts who have seen torture like never before. Then a young lady came and said she was touched by her experiences, and wanted to sing a song and dedicate it to her for the blessing she was to her. The iPhone was ready. She sang with a very beautiful smile that I couldn't peel off her face. Then, before I spoke, the whole church sang سوف ينتهي العذاب and were enjoying it very much. Then I stood and thanked them for the song, and told them who wrote it. They about died and gone to heaven...started clapping hard. The special thing was that the service was supposed to be a funeral service :), but it was a very sweet tearful and blessed time. One more - A young lady who has been married for 7 years and hasn't been able to have a baby, came with the pastor who introduced us and said she wanted prayer for her to have a baby. It's a very negative stigma for a woman here who can't have children. We prayed. The interesting thing was that she asked me more than twice during the few minutes we spent what (Lily's) name was, and how to spell it. I didn't say anything more but have a feeling that if someone here has a baby girl, I know what the baby's name will be :). And God's family is growing by the minute! *(Sunday, April 20, 2014 at 11:21P.M. CDT)*

SEE YOU NEXT YEAR
From my heart to yours

Easter celebration is over. It's Monday. I've been to church, saw everyone I could see. I sang, prayed, even spoke. I caught myself really "feeling good", not that I celebrated Easter, but that I don't feel obligated to think of it again for another year. Then I wondered: Now, how heathenish is that? *(Monday, April 21, 2014 at 3:26P.M. CDT)*

UNTIL I GOT HOME
From my heart to yours

My heavenly Father had me shaking my head in total amazement until I got home on this trip. During the flight from Dubai to Atlanta, fatigue caught up with me, so I slept most of the 17-hr flight from before pulling back at the gate in Dubai. There were times I'd wake up for 15 minutes or so. I didn't pay attention to what was taking place during this flight until about an hour before we got to Atlanta. I was sitting on the aisle side of the middle 3-seat section of the Boeing 777. Beside me sat a couple with the lady in the middle beside me. From the eye mask, to the listening ear plugs, to the two meals and the snack in between, and the light breakfast before we got to Atlanta, this lady saved me one of each. And when I'd wake up, she would either be holding the flight refresher towelette in her hand saying "I saved this for you", or points to the breakfast that she kept one for me, and so on one thing after another. Toward the end of the trip, when she handed me the light breakfast, I was shaking my head from side to side with this big grin on my face. She goes: is everything ok? I said, "oh yes, Everything is just fine, thank you so much". One incident? I might say it's a coincidence. But the whole trip? Come on! :). As they say in the South, Ain't God good! I say, there ain't nobody anywhere near where he's at on the scale! Then Jonathan's "7000" hugs and my Sweetheart's smile-without-words at breakfast were just the icing on the cake. God was just too overwhelming to me on this trip. So undeserving! If you prayed, you share in everything He showed or did with me. And I thank you from the bottom of my heart. And I thank Him for you. "What shall I return to the Lord for all his goodness to me? I will lift up the cup of salvation and call on the name of the Lord. I will fulfill my vows to the Lord in the presence of all his people." (Ps 116) *(Wednesday, April 23, 2014 at 6:27P.M. CDT)*

THINKING CLEARLY ABOUT THE GOSPEL OF JESUS CHRIST
From my heart to yours

During this recent trip, I went through several time zones, met many "different" people, heard more than 15 languages, saw enough variations among people groups, sat on dirt floors and on marble, ate simple food and delicacies, and came back with one question. It's not a new question, but one that needed a fresher perspective in my mind. I'm not sure that what I learned is anything earth-shattering or comprehensive. But it is a start that keeps my heart worshipping and my mind surrendered to Him alone who is worthy. The question is: "What is the true nature of the Gospel of Jesus Christ"? The reason Jesus loved to sit with the lowly and felt at home with the dejected in their minds, broken in their hearts, possessed by demons, or rejected by almost all is because He came especially for them. His mission must be accomplished on target, on time, and on the Cross. So hear Him saying frequently, "the Son of Man MUST", 1. The Gospel of the Kingdom which He brought and spoke of was . . . even for them. 2. The Gospel of the Kingdom, if true, will remain accessible for all people. No one is Unqualified to hear it, and have an opportunity to respond to it. Jesus uniquely posed and personalized the question: "Do YOU believe" to many (like Mary, Martha, the blind man, etc.). Does it not surprise us that, all who came to Him, came...one at a time? 3. An "other gospel" that has conditions placed/imposed by language, culture, group, or doctrine is not the true, but the "other" gospel Paul speaks of in Galatians. It can be summarized in one word: "corrupt". And when believers, for one reason or another, demand that people follow a corrupted gospel, they have committed what Scripture calls "spiritual adultery"--synonymous with "straying after someone/something else". 4. No one denomination has "the religious corner" on the Gospel of the Kingdom, and that is so for one simple reason. If any denomination says that, to properly receive/have the Gospel of the Kingdom, one must belong to "that denomination specifically", then "that denomination" is under a moral obligation to tell the world, and nothing less is acceptable, that what only they teach/possess is in fact "the truth". The alternative is advocated by others, more lenient, who have been deceived and have taken the approach of "all roads lead to Rome". But, alas! all have been, without exception, one disappointment after another. 5. The Gospel of the Kingdom is not a book, philosophy, place, teaching, or lifeless doctrines or practices. All these are proven limited and limiting. 6. The Gospel of the Kingdom, in fact, is wrapped up completely in A PERSON. His Name is JESUS. He is timeless, priceless, matchless, and doubtless he is the Savior who paid the price and has power to save to the uttermost. He operates across time zone, in all generations, with all ages, in all places, languages, and powerfully in all people groups. His effect is always life-giving and life-changing in whoever comes to Him by faith. "To receive His Kingdom" IS "to receive Jesus Christ". To remain in the Kingdom is to remain in Jesus Christ. 7. To Him alone, I pray, we bow the knee and worship. He alone, I beg, that we present to people uncorrupted, for He said "when the Son of Man (specifically) is lifted up, He will draw all people unto Himself". 8. The ONLY condition to true faith in Him is: OBEDIENCE. Keeping it simple: No obedience - No faith. Always faith - Always Obedience. It's not about me, Never. It's about Him. Always has been, Always will be. So the Word says: "Jesus Christ (is) the same, yesterday, today, and forever". Q1: Do you love Him? (Yes / No) Q2: Do you love Him Alone? (Yes / No) Q3: Are you obedient to Him? "All you need to say is simply 'Yes' or 'No'; anything beyond this comes from the evil one." (Matthew 5:37 NIV) *(Thursday, April 24, 2014 at 5:01A.M. CDT)*

It's Only Reasonable
From my heart to yours

WALKING BY FAITH means that you and I begin a new life with God, and allow Him to blindfold you, and demand that we live the rest of our lives guided only by the voice of His Holy Spirit that dwells in our heart. What shocked me is not that He asks: Do you trust me?, but, Do you love me? This life of faith begins when you and I say: "Come into my heart, Lord Jesus. Save me. I want to belong to you." For at that moment, we do not belong to ourselves but to Him. We have chosen to deny ourselves, and surrendered to follow Him. Jesus says to every follower in His steps: "You are not your own. You have been bought with a price."- My blood. What happened here is that He emptied Himself for our sake. Therefore, if we choose to follow Him by faith, we must empty ourselves for His sake. For without faith it is impossible to follow and please Him. He became the Great Sacrifice on behalf of all humanity. So, now He asks us to be reasonable. He expects devotion. He asks us "to (continually) present your bodies a living sacrifice, holy, acceptable to God, And . . . be transformed by the renewing of your mind, and you may prove what is the good and acceptable and perfect will of God. (Romans 12:1, 2) His Spirit begins, from the start of my walk by faith, to transform me into Jesus' likeness. The only demand He makes is: to obey. 100% of my problems as I was with Him is that I'm substituting, bartering, trading, negotiating, or selfishly insisting that He accepts something else instead of my complete surrender and obedience to Him alone. I think we suffer from Misplaced Affections that render us useless in the Kingdom of God and our faith questionable. The only motivation I can have, is Love. Nothing else is acceptable as a pure motivation for devotion - except love. We love Him because He first loved us. He loved us and died for us. It's only reasonable for us to love Him and selflessly live for Him, and die. Jesus asked Peter (and you and me): "Do you love me"? The lyrics say: 1. My Jesus, I love Thee, I know Thou art mine; / For Thee all the follies of sin I resign; My gracious Redeemer, my Savior art Thou; / If ever I loved Thee, my Jesus, 'tis now. 2. I love Thee because Thou hast first loved me, / And purchased my pardon on Calvary's tree; I love Thee for wearing the thorns on Thy brow; / If ever I loved Thee, my Jesus, 'tis now. 3. I'll love Thee in life, I will love Thee in death, / And praise Thee as long as Thou lendest me breath; And say when the death dew lies cold on my brow, / If ever I loved Thee, my Jesus, 'tis now. 4. In mansions of glory and endless delight, / I'll ever adore Thee in heaven so bright; I'll sing with the glittering crown on my brow, / If ever I loved Thee, my Jesus, 'tis now. *(Friday, April 25, 2014 at 6:21A.M. CDT)*

IT IS ONLY REASONABLE - (SUMMARY)
From my heart to yours

WALKING BY FAITH means that you and I begin a new life with God, and allow Him to blindfold us, and demand that we live the rest of our lives guided only by the voice of His Holy Spirit that dwells in our heart. He said, "My sheep hear my voice and know me". (John 10) What shocked me is that Jesus did not ask: "Do you trust me?", but, "Do you love me?" For to trust only Him is to obey only Him, and to obey only Him is to love only Him. This life of faith begins when you and I say: "Come into my heart, Lord Jesus. Save me. I want to belong to you." For at that moment, we do not belong to ourselves anymore but to Him. We have chosen to deny ourselves, and surrendered to follow Him. That's our position. That's where our affections ought to be. *(Friday, April 25, 2014 at 6:53A.M. CDT)*

FACEBOOK NOT APPEALING
From my heart to yours

I am reasonably certain that if Jesus were still in the flesh on earth today, he would not touch Facebook with a ten foot pole. Here are some reasons: 1. He's not interested in "Requests to add Him as a friend" 2. He's not interested in people who just "Like" who He is or what He says 3. He is very transparent with nothing to hide. So he will delete all privacy settings 4. He doesn't have albums with 1000s of pictures 5. He wouldn't be interested in adding lots and lots of "friends" 6. He doesn't play "Games" and just "Attend" events. In fact He's known to crash events of His choosing. 7. He doesn't "Update" His info. He operates with an open Book 8. He doesn't just "Chat" or "Poke" anyone. That's rude. 9. He doesn't create "Groups" by areas of interest 10. He definitely doesn't "report any problem". He nailed every last one of them. 11. He doesn't dwell in "Nearby Places". He sits on "the circle of the earth" and His permanent address is Jesus@theCross.bomb (on Satan's head) 12. He doesn't make any

"Offers" for people to choose from. 13. The "Help Center" is CLOSED. His interest is: "All things are new" 14. His information is all up-to-date. 15. He has no nickname. His Real name is: JESUS Christ. In the list of heaven, He's the First and the Last. In all the alphabets of the world, He's the Alpha and Omega. He's the joy of heaven and earth, the Lover of my soul. DO YOU KNOW HIM ? And as for the invitation, He's not waiting on us, because He already sent an invitation out to the most comprehensive list that includes everyone that fits under the heading: "Whosoever". Btw, He has no password, but He gives the "Seal of the Holy Spirit" to all who come to Him by Faith and kneel at His Cross, and yield their hearts to Him. And that's good enough for Him. The most amazing thing about Him is that He doesn't have His own "social network" but He has a Tribe - where true fellowship takes place with true love and compassion. It's called: The Tribe of the REDEEMED. Its two-part logo is the Cross and empty Tomb. Its mascot is the Lamb and Lion in One. His colors are Red and Gold. Cheerleaders are all heavenly who are clueless about the salvation He brings but are still very excited. They don't whoop and holler, but they bow to the ground in absolute adoration and call out to each other and say: Holy, Holy, Holy. Of course you know who I'm talking about. He is the matchless King, my Savior and Lord, the Delight of His Eternal Father. JESUS!
(Friday, April 25, 2014 at 11:21A.M. CDT)

DO YOU KNOW WHAT DTR STANDS FOR?
From my heart to yours

I would like to recommend a book that made me uncomfortable, and i don't like to be left uncomfortable alone. So, I would like to encourage you to consider stepping outside your comfort zone too. The book is entitled: "Not A Fan", written by Kyle Idleman. The book addresses the character of a true follower of Jesus Christ. Reading it allows the reader to reconsider and renew his/her relationship. A statement in it that caught my attention was this: "Fans go to the stadium; Followers go to the sanctuary". The Table of Contents includes: 1. DTR 2. A decision or a commitment? 3. Is the relationship "About" or intimately "with"? 4. Is He "One of many", Or "The One and Only"? 5. Are you Following Jesus or Following Rules? 6. Are you Self-empowered or Spirit-empowered? The 224 pages are worth the $4.00 or less (used) . If you live in North America, you can get it from major retailer sites. *(Friday, April 25, 2014 at 11:56A.M. CDT)*

LOOKING FROM THE PEW
From my heart to yours

Here are some Questions the weekly audiences are thinking to ask of every speaker from a pulpit: 1. Do you, in your heart, BELIEVE what you preach? 2. Do you live by what you preach WHEN NO ONE is looking? 3. Do you have three points and a story, or do you POINT ME to Jesus Christ? 4. Do you tell me how to live BY FAITH, or just how to live better? 5. Are you yourself OBEDIENT to the Holy Spirit like you want me to be? 6. Do you trust me into the hands of the HOLY SPIRIT to live by what you preach? 7. Is Jesus on your mind, or you just want me to feel GUILTY? 8. Are you offering me REAL LIFE in your message, or wishful thinking? 9. Do you speak about Jesus, Or do you SPEAK JESUS to me? 10. Do you tell me THE STORY, or do you just tell me a story? Jeremiah 23. *(Sunday, April 27, 2014 at 11:55P.M. CDT)*

CALVARY SNAPSHOT
From my heart to yours

I find it strange, and not reasonable, that people flock to walk where Jesus walked, but don't want to die where Jesus died. *(Thursday, May 1, 2014 at 12:38P.M. CDT)*

PROBLEM SOLVED
From my heart to yours

The enigma of the cross of Christ is this: To the first Adam, God said (in effect) "If you obey me fully and always, and let my will be done in your life, I will always be with you. I will bless you. I will give you life." Adam disobeyed. As a consequence, he died. And all his descendants died also. To the last Adam, Jesus, God said (in effect) "If you obey me fully, if you live a life that is pleasing to me, and if you let my will be fully done in your life, I will crush you, I will humiliate you, I will let others ridicule you, I will nail you to a cross on behalf of all who disobeyed me and are related to the first Adam. I will give you death. And *only* then, the penalty can be satisfied in full, and they can have life." The horror of

Gethsemane was not the horror of man's sins but the terrifying horror of the unthinkable separation from the Heavenly Father with whom He had fellowship from eternity past. The Father, (in effect) passed the cup of wrath in front of Him in Gethsemane, He tasted it, He smelled it, and He saw evil staring him in the face. Jesus looked at his so-called "friends" sound asleep, and felt, not the loneliness on earth but the loss and total disconnect about to be felt from the Father. And the Father asked, in effect, "Do you love them so much that you're willing to pay the ultimate price?" Jesus was in shock that He said "if it be possible, let this cup pass from me. But let it not be my will but your will." His complete surrender of His will and obedience unto death made all the difference in the courts of heaven that he secured forgiveness of sin on our behalf, and a new covenant sealed forever on our behalf through his blood. So then, he says, "Therefore there is now no condemnation for those who are in Christ Jesus". So it is reasonable to ask: Why? Why did He go through all this for my sake? Why was He ridiculed and spat upon and died for me? The only answer I can find is: "Because He loved me so much!" Yes! Jesus loves me. The awesomeness of love is that no one can love with the true love of Christ, and have an ulterior motive, except for love's sake. It's only reasonable and fair to accept that He who died on my behalf and paid my debt of sin and was separated from the Heavenly Father, should receive all the blessings of heaven as well. So, if I'm "In Christ", I am covered from wrath, and am smothered with all the blessings of God forever, for Christ's sake. He died for me so I can live. I find it very reasonable then to live for Him, and even die for Him, because in the final analysis ... It's Not about Me, but it's about Him. *(Thursday, May 1, 2014 at 3:16P.M. CDT)*

WHY DO I LOVE HIM SO?
From my heart to yours

To the first Adam, God said (in effect) "If you obey me fully and always, and let my will be done in your life, I will always be with you. I will bless you. I will give you life." That's choice at its purest level. But, Adam disobeyed. As a consequence, he died. And all his descendants died in him. To the last Adam, Jesus, God said (in effect) "If you obey me fully, if you live a life that is pleasing to me, and if you let my will be fully done in your life, I will crush you, I will humiliate you, I will let others ridicule you, I will nail you to a cross on behalf of all who disobeyed me and are related to the first Adam. I will give you death. And Only then, the penalty can be satisfied in full, I will be pleased fully, and they can have life." The horror of Gethsemane was not the horror of man's sins but the terrifying shock of the unthinkable separation from the Heavenly Father with whom He had fellowship from eternity past. The Father's wrath on the Son's sacred head, for my sake, because He loved me so. *(Friday, May 2, 2014 at 9:52A.M. CDT)*

"ARE YOU GOING TO JUMP?"
From my heart to yours

The Spirit reminded me recently of an incident that took place during my first semester in college. It was spring of '71. Being my first term and I wanted to make a significant impact on humanity and impress my advisor, one of the courses I chose was "Swimming 101". I was impressed by the swimming pool in college, and I could just see this budding Lebanese "dolphin" weaving myself through the watery depths (mere 8' on the deep end), wanting to explore my Darwinian roots (ha!) when I slithered my slimy body from the water onto the beach with my human aspirations packed under my fins (oops! I forgot; No needs for wishful thinking, as the saga itself as I understand is merely chemical and biological adaptations, mutations and responses to natural selection of haphazard sort -- very much like weather predictions that were never 100% accurate since the flood when God told (not predicted to) Noah that it WILL rain 40 days and 40 nights). But this matter is for another day! Back to my first semester of my whipper-snapper college ingenuity in swimming class. The instructor, an Olympic champion himself, said that the course will be divided into two segments: first part is in class, and the second is actual swimming at the pool. My level of excitement was elevated suddenly. My heart raced for that moment when the first SPLASH! Will take place. I could just see the snapshot flashing on the billboards of Times Square. The one secret I never told anyone yet is that . . . I didn't know how to s-w-i-m at all. My level of expertise was limited to one visit to the Mediterranean in my younger years splashing water on my face, looking like I just came out of the water :). During the classroom segment of the course, I excelled like a champion; I understood all the swimming techniques, flapping my feet in rhythm with my arms; my head turning from side to side, breathing at the right moment, and learning how to keep water from entering my mouth. In the classroom, my test score was 100. That was a highlight of my academic life. It was also the last thing I recall of my joys and the thrills of victory. I knew that the agony of defeat was just around the corner. Then the instructor blurted, "Monday, we meet at the pool." That weekend was almost traumatic. My thinking thinker stopped. No person on earth could help me. No counseling session could slow down my anxiety and calm my soul. I almost started to pray, but one of the transport angels said, "Forget it. Not even a prayer will help." Monday came. The class planned to gather around the pool. I SO wished at that moment that I would be skilled like my Olympic class instructor. I imagined myself right beside him, an Olympic champion like him and many others. Medals clanging around my neck. Flowers! and all the rest. I could not wish it enough. The sweat beaded on my forehead, and my knees became weak. I SO wish I could fabricate an excuse from that class. The classroom grade of 100 flashed before my eyes, but faded very quickly. The real test of my skills was about to take place. Then the instructor at the pool said, "OK All, everyone step into the shallow section this first time." Oh my! Did I ever sing the Hallelujah chorus at that moment! My heart was filled with joy, ecstasy, glee, and all its cousins of human emotions. I am proud to announce that I was able to get into the shallow section, JUST like everyone else. I even practiced perfectly waving my arms under water, my face turning in sync, my eyes closed and opened, and my feet well-planted into the imaginary "ocean" floor. I looked around, and everyone else was doing the same pretty much. In comparison, I was an expert. My advisor knew I couldn't swim but he assured me that it's easy and I will learn in due course. But in my heart I knew that all the wisdom of Einstein and eastern mysticism could never infuse into me the skill and art of successful swimming. The instructor was pleased in general with everyone's performance. We practiced for a period of time. I could even swim across a corner of the deep section. I went back and forth, and as long as I knew I could get my feet on the bottom of the pool anytime I needed to, I was doing fine. Then he said to everyone, "Next time, you will apply what you learned in class about diving. At that moment, I knew that the Titanic experience was about to happen again (skip the iceberg). Somehow, time began to move faster. To my utter dismay, the hour and minute arms of the clock in my dorm room danced before my eyes in harmonic rotation. Oh the horror of betrayal right before my eyes. The "next time" came, but, Alas! It rained. Yes! I could breathe again! Needless to say, there was nothing in the world I could do to push THE MOMENT further into the future, and enjoy more peace of mind. The time arrived, and the class gathered, and it was time to jump. The instructor shouted, "Alright guys! Let's jump in the pool" (with a certain cadence in his voice with a crescendo toward the end of his call. Everyone jumped . . ., except me. The moment of truth came without delay. He saw me in my true self. He knew I had to jump. I knew I had to jump. But I also I realized that ALL my classroom knowledge could not help me at that moment. There weren't enough neurons in my head to process what I learned in class in a moment. I looked down, and I could see the watery abyss staring at me. I lifted my eyes toward heaven. That "angel" intercepted with a grin, waved his head side to side as if to say "Don't even think about it". The instructor walked toward me and said, "John, Are you going to jump?" "Yes, Sir, but you know I can't swim well. I don't know how to stay afloat in the deep". He said, "Apply what you learned in class. Remember, you did real well. Breathe right, flap your feet right. Raise your head up right after you dive. Move your arms correctly, and you will be fine." I said, "But, how do you do that?" He walked closer to me, and said, "If you don't jump, I will fail you in the course. I don't care how you do in the water after you dive, but you've got to jump. Are you going to jump? You didn't make a grade high enough in the course to pass if you don't jump". I gasped and said, "But I made 100". He said, "That wasn't good enough. That was intended to get you to where you're standing right now." Then he blurted out again, "Are going to jump?" Thank you for reading thus far. Except for the angel saying "Forget it" part, the rest did actually take place. I think many so-called followers of Christ have scored 100 in the classroom. Very few have jumped. Many, I dare say, are standing behind pulpits too. I wonder at times what Jesus meant when He said, "When the Son of Man comes, will He find the faith on earth?" Many, at one time or another, have slipped their spiritual toes into the water testing. Others stay in the shallow side making sure whenever they wanted, they can plant their feet on solid ground. Very few learn to jump. The fact is, that if jumping ever takes place, it cannot happen in part, but in whole. My entire body must move completely from a secure position on the ground into the water. Further, what guides me in the water is not the textbook or my note that I took profusely, but what I have truly acquired in my mind and heart. Somehow it translates into practice. Life in Christ is just as real. There aren't enough courses or classroom notes or seminars or sermons or speakers in the world who can make me a true follower of Christ.

Being impressed by one perspective or another regarding the swimming pool is frankly immaterial. It takes direct contact and immersion into Him. What the instructor told me before I jumped was, "John, after you jump, the water will carry you and keep you afloat. Don't be afraid." To whoever is reading this, and wondering, please be assured that once you jump into Christ (by faith), He will most assuredly carry you. He promised! Whatever attributes differentiate us, it matters not. Like with Mary, Martha, the blind man and a billion others, He asks, "Do You believe?" So, Are you going to jump today? *(Saturday, May 3, 2014 at 6:55A.M. CDT)*

On "Customizing" God
From my heart to yours

There is an increasing trend these days to "customize" everything, driven by a passion to set oneself as the standard for everything (judge, jury, prosecution, and defense). To "customize" means to modify something (call it: model B) out of something else that precedes it (call it: model A). Model A has to be there first; and someone makes it slightly different, hence, model B. To "customize" helps a person modify, and be comfortable with something to suit their preferences. Such preferences are determined by a person (one's comfort zone), or by a society (religious, social, or language), or by force of rule (e.g., a national religion). But How does one "customize" God, his attributes, his character, his actions, his likes and dislikes, expectations of him, etc.? And, by what standards? The penchant desire, in summary, is to come up with a version of God that we can place demands on, and he's required to deliver as with an order from china. And if he doesn't, then we beat him up with biting and demeaning words in whatever context or setting we choose. And even when we curse, we drag his name through the slime and mud of humanity coloring him with the holiness of cows to deviations of the actual name or trait, so as to imply something less threatening to our form of godliness that's more religiously and politically correct. Given the opportunity to "customize" God, we muse: How should God behave? Who should be the one or what entity is deemed most qualified to approve his behavior? Who will be his advisor, or the designer of such endeavor? What set of doctrines will surely lock God in a box of our own varied making? Which denomination has the corner on the more perfect set of doctrines? And, assuming one denomination succeeds in this task, how will they inform the world of their success in coming up with the "perfect custom" model of God? And all along, making sure that heaven is guaranteed for all. I suspect that God fits under the option called: "None of the above". Man's track record is of historically pathetic and dismal proportions at best. For God is God, has always been God and nothing less, for in Him is the less and the more, the center and circumference. For "In the beginning, God...". So, by what competence can such "quasi-engineer" formulate what might apply to God (or any part thereof)? And what about all these customization efforts across the human tapestry of cultures and social collaborations? I am inclined to believe that they are modern versions of what used to be called in yonder day as "idol worship", idolatry as described in John's first epistle. John, after an entire letter speaking about God's love, he concludes affirmatively with a warning by saying in 5:20-21: "... (20) This is the true God, and eternal life. (21) Little children, keep yourselves from idols." Why say "idols"? Why now, at this closing point of the letter? He is simply saying, at least in part, that if we think of God and His love that was manifest fully in our Lord Jesus Christ as LESS THAN WHAT IT OUGHT TO BE, then, we are committing the sin of idolatry. God help us! The only option we are left with is to repent, and let God be God. *(Monday, May 5, 2014 at 12:01A.M. CDT)*

LISTENING AND HEARING OVERLAP IN MEANING
From my heart to yours

Twenty five years ago, we moved to the city where we live now, into an apartment complex where we felt comfortable enough and within our means. Our next door neighbors were a medical doctor in his late eighties, in reasonably good health, and his lovely wife who took a liking to our family as newcomers. Her husband practiced medicine for many years with a good bit of success. The only thing that was getting weak with him was his hearing :) On a bright weekday morning, he got up for his daily walk. When he came back home, he said to his wife, "Honey, I'm going to the store. Do you need anything?" She said, "Yes, please bring a "dozen eggs". He was gone for a while. Here's the doctor going shopping. Upon his return, he had a rather small bag in hand with a tube of "Desenex" rash cream in it. His wife smiled. I call that ... True love. :) Listening ... A premium skill, and a lost art. The Bible says: "Listening is better than offering a sacrifice". *(Tuesday, May 6, 2014 at 2:39A.M. CDT)*

WHAT IS A "QUIET SPIRIT?"
From my heart to yours

A dear brother and friend asked: "What is a '*quiet spirit*'". One verse that uses it is 1Peter 3:3-4 . Here's what I said: Sometimes a concept can be understood (at least shed more light) by describing what it is NOT. What is not reflective of a "quiet spirit" is:

1. a fretful spirit
2. a fearful spirit
3. a distrustful spirit
4. a spirit that makes choices strictly based on emotions or fleeting passions
5. Trusting in one's abilities driven by love for power and control is not reflective of a "quiet spirit".
6. A "quiet spirit" does not "vent" emotions such as anger.

Toward a greater understanding of what a "quiet spirit" IS, here are some thoughts:

1. It's a spirit that has no problem trusting and submitting, because it's at peace with, and about, the object of trust.
2. It's a source of strength of character that matures in life.
3. It is a state of the heart that restrains stormy emotions and passions
4. A "quiet spirit" is a characteristic of a heart at rest, at peace, a teachable heart, that finds strength in submission.

I have a feeling that in today's world where sometimes excessive assertiveness is the name of the game, there is little tolerance for a "quiet spirit" This is a very beautiful character trait that can only be part of a maturing follower of Christ, because He said, "Come unto me all ye that are weary and heavy laden, and I will give you rest. Take my yoke upon you and learn from me for I am meek and lowly in heart, and you will find rest." Here lies yet another reason why I love Him so, because He is my sufficiency without doubt. *(Tuesday, May 6, 2014 at 8:57A.M. CDT)*

MY PRECIOUS FRIEND
From my hearts to yours

I may have to wait until I get to heaven to find out for sure. But, for now, I have two reasons to thank God from the bottom of my heart for my young friend Rana. First, before I left on my recent overseas trip she promised me that she will be praying for me the whole time. Half-way through the trip, she and her Mom and Dad assured me that she is still praying. Then when I got back, I asked her and she assured me that she prayed for me "the whole time". THANK YOU RANA. Second, she and her Mom came today and told me some GREAT news. With a big smile on her face, she told me that "she gave her heart to Jesus" to be her Savior. I asked: how old are you? She said: Nine. I told her that she put a BIG smile on my face because I was Nine too when I gave my heart to Jesus. But I had a smile in my heart because of the Awesome God who always hears prayers and has no problem reaching to the youngest and gentlest of hearts. To my young friend I want to say: May God bless you, Rana. May He keep watch over you and your beautiful family. May His face shine on you always and make you a blessing to many people for years to come. Here's my promise for heaven and earth to see: I will never stop praying for you! I love you. Amo John ("Amo" is Arabic for "Uncle") *(Wednesday, May 7, 2014 at 11:38P.M. CDT)*

TRUE IDENTITY NEEDS AN ANCHOR
From my heart to yours

The "fallen woman" and the "Samaritan woman" are labels that can be easily found in the archives of our memories, and may lead some to breathe with a certain sigh of relief, as if to say, "whew! I'm glad I'm not like that." Yet, both women found refuge, healing, and anchor in the person of Jesus Christ. Everyone else rejected them, including the religious community. But His love, gentleness, and the Holy Spirit that had full control of Him made it quite easy and simple to accept these women As-They-Were. Not only that, but one group of spectators who were ready to annihilate the "fallen woman", fully prepared to judge her according to the very Law God gave, just realized that they were being investigated and scrutinized by the same searching eyes of Him who knows the hearts and is able to judge. What spared them (and her) that time was that "the Son of Man did not come to judge the world (this time) but that the world through Him might be saved." They overlooked one simple truth. The Giver of that Law, who burned with His finger the very words He spoke at Sinai on tablets of stone, was Present and they didn't take notice. In the case of the "Samaritan woman", she was enslaved over the years by chains of society's and perhaps her own making too -- religious, familial, friends, neighbors, even perhaps of her own heart and stubbornness. Riddled with shame and guilt, trodden by every heavy foot in town, she found healing from Him who said, "Come unto me all ye heavy-laden . . . and I will give you rest." The lover of her soul won and faced the wolves that devoured their victim of the moment. She was clothed again. She found beauty from ashes. She found the One "who told her all things". She didn't realize though, and he didn't say a word, about the fact that He came in fact to take her shame and sin, her scars and brokenness, her numbing silence about her past, and to make her whole again. To be sure, in neither case did he give excuses for what happened in their lives for years. He did not debate "nature or nurture". He did not "sweep things under the carpet". He didn't say "forgive and forget". He didn't say "time will heal". He didn't try to lift up her self-esteem. He didn't "shame her into living a better life". He didn't refer her to a local support group. HE BECAME HER REFUGE, and even the disciples were stunned and said nothing. Thus, in the ministry of reconciliation He gave His followers, He asks us to stop thinking like the world and begin thinking Jesus, and speaking Jesus to all. What Love! What Forgiveness! What Life! What Peace! What joy! What Grace is this! The woman, who was caught, was set free, and those who were free, got caught. He said to both (in effect) "Go and stop living in sin as before for I give you newness of life." She accepted His offer. She was filled with joy unspeakable. She ran and told all the ones who looked previously with disdain upon her. They came; they believed; they followed, not her, but Him. They didn't change religion. He changed their hearts to become new. And the disciples just watched, and had no clue what just happened. Yet He loved them too, knowing that the time will come, and it is not far hence, when they become fishers of men too. He didn't believe in giving a second chance. He came to BE the second chance. The amazing thing about Christ is that when He enters a person's life, that person discovers very quickly that all else - ALL ELSE -- has suddenly become of lesser significance. Have you been to the well ? Has anyone lifted a rock to stone you with their looks or words? There is a Refuge. His name is: JESUS. *(Thursday, May 8, 2014 at 1:55A.M. CDT)*

WATER WALK
From my heart to yours

What made the difference in Peter's life when he walked on water was not the miracle but the hand of the Master that stood between his life and his death. It was not what Peter could do miraculously but what the Master does naturally. It's never about me, but it's about Him from start to finish. *(Saturday, May 10, 2014 at 12:57A.M. CDT)*

SINGLENESS OF HEART
From my heart to yours

Nothing is more devastating to a person than having a divided heart. A divided heart means divided allegiance, divided love, divided passion, divided mind, and a divided union. Divided allegiance leads to treason. Divided love yields absence of communion. Divided passion renders frustration and anger. Divided mind leads to indecision and quagmire existence. Divided union dissolves what was being held together. A double minded man is unstable in all his ways. (James 1:8) One thing removes all uncertainty, and it's LOVE. For love conquers all. *(Saturday, May 10, 2014 at 1:13A.M. CDT)*

TRUE LOVE
From my heart to yours

I am convinced when I think of Jesus that I cannot love Him right until he rights my love and brings me to union in Himself. My love for others, in the meantime, lingers and staggers like a drunk, content with societal variations and clamoring for prominence, not knowing that true love surrenders self to the object who captured it. Then, in One, love is wrapped and suspended; and in the same One, it is set free to reveal its true nature. "Nothing shall separate us from the love of God in Jesus Christ our Lord." (Romans 8) *(Saturday, May 10, 2014 at 1:21A.M. CDT)*

THE MASTER'S EARS
From my heart to yours

Jesus hears when we least expect it. Bartimaeus (in Mark 10), the blind man, the beggar, the nuisance of society, and the rebel against all tradition, stopped Jesus in His tracks to receive from Him something that ONLY Jesus can deliver. He needed a solution, not a debate. He demanded attention out of desperation from the only One who heard his cry. How did He succeed?

Although he was blind, he came in the right direction when he heard the Master's voice. He succeeded

1. When he recognized Jesus from the first chance he had that Jesus was his last hope;
2. When he recognized Jesus was His only hope;
3. When he acknowledged Jesus' kingship by right, and
4. When he cast himself humbly before the Master.

I call that the true audacity of hope. *(Saturday, May 10, 2014 at 1:42A.M. CDT)*

SINGING UNTO THE LORD
From my heart to yours

It is very enchanting to hear the beautiful sounds that different birds make. It is very rewarding also to guess which bird makes which sound. But it is very sad that birds cannot change their tune as they please. So God inhabits the praises of His people. Not birds! Why? God designed man and gave him the specific ability to communicate. That requires the ability in the vocal cords to change and modulate at will, and express the desire of the heart. So, now with the same cords, even the inexpressible groans that communicate deep pain and devastation are possible to express until the cords strain and get sore.

This morning, I woke up humming a tune I had on my mind since last night. I learned it back in youth choir days. Here are the words: (you can look up the music on YouTube) "I do not know the depth of Jesus' love, That brought him down to earth, from heav'n above, Nor why He bore the cross, up Calvary, And shed His precious blood, So willingly, But this one thing I know, that when the crimson flow, Dropped to the earth below, it fell on me; My eyes were open wide, and I saw Him crucified; I knew for me He died, on Calvary."

My heart quickly bows in worship, adoration, and communion when I think of how His amazing love engulfs us as His children, embraces us and draws us closer each time, desiring for us to bask in His love. And in my heart I wonder...I wonder and get teary-eyed... When I think of how He came so far from glory Came to dwell among the lowly such as I To suffer shame and such disgrace On Mount Calvary take my place Then I ask myself this question Who am I? Who am I that The King would bleed and die for? Who am I that He would pray not my will, Thine Lord? The answer I may never know Why He ever loved me so That to an old rugged cross He'd go For who am I? (You can look up the music on YouTube) And I ask Him, again and again, Why did you love me and us so much, Lord? From His lips, it was said that... "Jesus knowing that His hour had come that He would depart out of this world to the Father, having loved His own who were in the world, He loved them to the very end." (John 13:1) And Paul reassures us by the Spirit of inspiration and says, "Who shall separate us from the love of Christ? Shall trouble or hardship or persecution or famine or nakedness or danger or sword . . . For I am convinced that neither death nor life, neither angels nor demons, neither the present nor the future, nor any powers, neither height nor depth, nor anything else in all creation, will be able to separate us from the love of God that is in Christ Jesus our Lord." (Romans 8:35, 38-39)

Then my heart bursts out rejoicing in deep gratitude and says: "I love you, Lord, And I lift my voice To worship You, Oh, my soul, rejoice! Take joy my King, In what You hear Let it be a sweet, sweet sound In Your ear". (you can look up the music on YouTube) May this day be that of worship even in suffering, of thankfulness even in want, of thirst and hunger for Him who loved us even when we are content. *(Saturday, May 10, 2014 at 5:34A.M. CDT)*

HIS THOUGHTS AND OURS
From my heart to yours

How is it that His thoughts are *not* our thoughts? God doesn't "improve" anything. That's for those who start with "less"; so, improving becomes expected. "Less", with man, is in everything we have so long as we are without Him. But, with Him, it's "All that I Need". God doesn't run specials on what He provides. No such things as "buy one, get one Free". No "blue light" specials either. God does not "stock" shelves for me to take and pay for. He provides all my needs according to His riches in glory through Jesus Christ our Lord. But He expects me to appreciate what I receive from Him. And even when I don't, he still loves me, and waits for me to grow up. God doesn't have a parking lot or "valet parking" service expecting courtesy tipping. Whosoever will, to the Lord may come, ...anytime. God welcomes me at the door when I come wanting to see Him, and takes me to be cleaned up by His Spirit first before I go into His holy Presence. He takes His time on that one, because He doesn't compromise. The only difference is He doesn't call this cleanliness, but He calls it godliness. Then I come into His presence "in the Spirit". God is good all the time. But He "frowns" on those who take advantage of His goodness, even if they were His children. So, he sends them to the SOS (School of the Spirit), and they learn few lessons there on As-Need basis. God does not just dole out advice, nor make suggestions, or play games. In fact, He doesn't have time for that foolishness. He usually gets our attention first, one-on-one, then gives us the sense to understand Him. All we have to do is: Ask Him. God makes sure before we go back to work that we know that He loves us more than anything, for His Son's sake. Then he says to Go tell the world about His mercies and kindnesses, for they are fresh every day. *(Saturday, May 10, 2014 at 5:49A.M. CDT)*

A QUESTION OF FAITH AND AUTHORITY
From my heart to yours

A fine gentleman and friend asked if there is a contradiction in gospel records. Is there discrepancy between the two records of the same incident, that of healing the centurion's daughter? Here's what I said: "My apologies for the delay, not intended as disregard or disrespect. Looking at the centurion's daughter's healing incident, the centurion said: "just say a word". Very unique story because it brought two people of authority face to face (not literally). Jesus didn't address who's got more power because when there is humility, transparency, honesty, and absence of malice, pride, posturing, or political correctness, such discussion never comes up. This is a contrast that's good to keep in mind. Jesus always respected the humble, or weak and lowly and castaways. I dare say that he showed every individual he met (except the religious) more respect than we are able or willing to reciprocate. Nonetheless, a king will always be a king. Regarding the technical comparison and contrast between the two gospel records, two key concepts and words are necessary to keep in mind. And we can safely take that as a model in principle. First, the dilemma people face when communication is intended is the ability to convey "meaning", not just throwing out words, but what is the "meaning" intended. Sometimes we convey meaning by saying a lot, or little or no words but other expressions (such as fear, anger, concern, sadness, joy, etc.). Yet, other times we express in words what can carry in all honesty more than one meaning and still remain true. For example, if I call my wife who, I know, went to see the doctor and ask her the question: "where are you now?", she can give me a single answer which can carry multiple meanings, yet remain reasonable and true, and fairly accurate. (I can on the other hand be obsessive compulsive and a control freak and ask her back, "and how many steps are you away from his office?" :). However, she can reasonably answer "I'm at the doctor's" (without any additional elaboration), which can mean: - I'm in the parking lot at the doctor - I'm going up in the elevator - I'm in the hallway just outside the doctor's office - I'm in the waiting room at the doctor's office - I'm in the bathroom at the doctor's office - I'm in the exam room at the doctor's - I'm in his office at the doctor's. The amazing thing is that any and all are true answers and can be reasonably derived from the much shorter answer: "I'm at the doctor". Another answer she might give me which carries multiple meanings, and I would find no necessity to drill further, is: "I'm on my way", meaning/referring to any particular location, without exception, and I may accept within reason as sufficient. It's the "meaning" that I'm after, not laser precision of expression. Second, not having ALL the details in front of us sometimes calls for respect of absence of facts and not jumping to conclusions prematurely. This is in general a fairly "scientific" approach without any specific context. If you re-read both records, you will very likely see what I mean. Many gospel records are of similar nature. The New Testament Greek at times uses synonyms to refer specifically and precisely to a particular answer, IN DISTINCTION FROM another possible understanding, which may corrupt the meaning intended. Bottom line, the centurion had faith in his heart beyond comprehension and further experienced the power of Christ according to the record. Jesus never declined the request of anyone who asked believing. Such a gentleman! Such a Savior! (I beg your pardon for the lengthy reply.) *(Saturday, May 10, 2014 at 11:49A.M. CDT)*

FATHER-SON SPECIALS
From my heart to yours

Father-Son Specials are the Best! Since I returned from my overseas trip, I decided to make up for the "Father-Son Breakfast" tradition I missed with my Jonathan. So, as we drove aimlessly to start with, the plan became clear: Panera Bread for lunch then Starbucks for some fresh coffee and pretend the world has stopped turning. Dad: so what do you think of the plan? Son: I'm game for sure. Dad: I've missed our time. Son: believe me, me too Then it hit me when I wasn't paying attention. Spirit: if you with your son think like that and have this sweet transparent pure loving relationship as though you have all you can ever imagine, interacting in time about something meaningful to the two of you, how much more do you think the Father and Son love one another from eternity past? I couldn't close my eyes because I was driving. But I was swept off my feet in a moment of worship and gratitude, looked at Jonathan... Dad: I love you, Son. Son: I love you too, Dad. He smiled. I knew at that moment that he has all he needs. Praying you too may have a special bonding time today with the Father, the Son, and the Spirit Our Father who is in heaven, may your Name be hallowed...forever! *(Saturday, May 10, 2014 at 2:04P.M. CDT)*

MOM, LIKE ALL MOMS
From my heart to yours

My Mom, and the Mom of many has been a treasure and a blessing for many generations. All the gold and diamond of the world doesn't begin to measure her true worth. It's not even the right currency to use. That's at least one of the reasons it took God to prepare her at the beginning to be a mother by design. She came with no warranty except for the stamp on her designer on her heart. Her value is more than what the eye can see or the mind can imagine. Yes, it is very true: "She gets up while it is still night; she provides food for her family and portions for her female servants. She sees that her trading is profitable, and her lamp does not go out at night. She opens her arms to the poor and extends her hands to the needy. Her children arise and call her blessed." (Proverbs 31:15, 18, 20, 28) Yes, we "Honor her (and every Mother) for all that her hands have done." (Prov. 31: 31) We love you, Mom! Happy Mother's Day ! *(Sunday, May 11, 2014 at 3:22P.M. CDT)*

KEEPING IN MIND "OLDER" PARENTS (1 OF 2) -A NEW REALITY TO THE YOUNGER GENERATIONS

From my heart to yours

This note is only for those who do have much older parents, and face frustrations sometimes in "dealing" with them. I'm not sure there is a specific age at which things begin to change. We will assume any age after 75-80. Keeping certain facts in mind and in context, let us actively remind ourselves that the following is happening to them: 1. They are still living, but they are changing. We initially may not realize that they are really getting older, and assume that they are still young and are expected to "stay on top of things" as always. Truth is: they can't, and may not know yet that they can't. 2. They are easily shaken when any "change" takes place in the lives, especially the change that seems "trivial" to us. This can be relocating, or diet, or schedule, or medical, or social life events. 3. Change can happen slowly or quickly and in stages, and may vary from one parent to another even in the same house. The general stages may be from light to mild, to severe. Other categories that are more specific do exist. Use a scale, such as, from 1-10 to determine or ask about severity of the case. 4. Change can happen in the general areas of life all at once, one (or more than one) at a time; this may happen slowly or quickly too. Always show love with respect and unconditionally. 5. They may suddenly become conscious of their past episodes of life more than present episodes. You can expect them to recount past events, sometimes more than once. It may be events that they haven't resolved in their minds yet, or events that have been pleasant or unpleasant to them. 6. Certain negative emotions can be expected (and at times expressed) more readily than usual. These emotions include: frustration, sadness, anger, mellowness, gazing into the distance seemingly in thought, stress, sadness, fear, loneliness, resignation, disgust, distress, guilt, disappointment in self, desire to fight back, etc. 7. Certain positive emotions can be expected (and at times expressed) more readily than usual. These emotions include: excitement, friendliness, seriousness about life which can lead to desire to give advice more than usual (then comment that their advice will likely go unheeded), wishful thinking, and happiness over pleasant memories, tenderness, love, nostalgic, gratitude, hope, joy, forgiveness, pride in the younger generation, etc. With much love and appreciation for all the elderly parents, John (*Monday, May 12, 2014 at 3:19A.M. CDT*)

KEEPING IN MIND "OLDER" PARENTS (2 OF 2) - A NEW REALITY TO THE YOUNGER GENERATIONS
From my heart to yours

Here is a short list which the younger generation can keep in mind and practice (and improve upon with time): 1. Always show/express toward the older generation (and make a conscious, concerted and genuine effort to show) these attitudes: kindness, respect, love, admiration, hope, courage, confidence, relaxation, satisfaction even in little accomplishments, willingness to take a positive action expecting good outcome. They are looking for someone to "hope" with them. 2. It's always "better" to be tolerant and forgive, than to be frustrated and shun the older parents. Whether we realize it or not, they do appreciate it but may not have a way to express their appreciation because appreciation was never their style. 3. It's always "better" to bring up good memories and let the parents re-tell the stories (even for the 10th time). These are their strings of hope and relevance in life. 4. Have a plan in mind, and discuss and/or communicate, for sudden events if/when they happen. An example of such event is a fall and a damage caused such as broken bone, bruise, fainting, or other. Such situations are NOT time to be frustrated and walk away or get overly stressed and end up doing nothing. Such events require self-control and taking actions toward life, and very systematically, regardless of the response of the affected parent. The actions include having phone numbers readily available in multiple places (fridge, bedroom, kitchen, wallet, car, and maybe others). The phone numbers are more than just 9-1-1. They may include family members, doctor office, and maybe those of emergency, fire and police. 5. Use statements that are "conversation starters". These can help the parents going in a positive direction in their conversation. This may also bring good and sweet memories that they can share. It may also be about what they are worried about. Letting them express themselves does give some relief and comfort. For your part, you are showing unconditional love. 6. Parents relish the thought that someone still cares to listen to them talk. Be a good listener. Remember two things: you may discover that you never were a good listener and now is a good time to start, and also you may realize that your parents still deserve to be loved and listening is one way to show that. 7. Parents know, I think, that they are "on their way out", and just need every now and then to know and/or be assured that they can hold our hand like we used to hold theirs when crossing the street. Now, it's crossing a valley that's somewhat dark and unknown. Letting them know that "you're there for them", or that "you will never leave them alone", or highlighting how nicely they impacted the life of so-and-so, is useful to mention, without patronizing them. Remember they are still your parents and they can tell a fake :). 8. When you need to leave them to go elsewhere on a given day, assure them of how much you enjoyed the time, promise them you will come back to see them, express how special he/she is and will always be, and if you tell them a day/time when you will come back, keep that time like an official appointment if at all possible. If something changes and you can't come, respect them and call them and reschedule. They are your parents. During this stage in life of shifting sands of time, we as the children may unexpectedly discover a lot about ourselves, our character, thinking, attitudes, approach, etc., that we may not have been aware of, things we may like or dislike. Being honest and change will be worthwhile while it is day and while there is time. We may have often repressed certain negative attitudes that we may have seen in parents. But in fact we may discover during this stage of relating to them that we have those selfsame attitudes. Change for the better becomes in order. Christ can help. With much love and appreciation for all the elderly parents, John (Monday, May 12, 2014 at 3:21A.M. CDT)

Never Too Late

From my heart to yours

On Mother's Day, my sister said as she went to see Mom, that she found Dad combing Mom's hair in the back :). And I thought: Now I know that Miracles never cease to happen indeed :), even after 65 years of marriage. Then I thought: it's really never too late to encourage and to practice little expressions of care and affection. They speak louder than words, especially when words are about done. *(Monday, May 12, 2014 at 11:56A.M. CDT)*

Failure Is Not An Option

From my heart to yours

When my brother and I started working together, we adopted the principle that "Failure is NOT an option". We found that to be very useful on many occasions, but very critical to experience when it mattered most. First, I traced the origin of the statement, and came across its use in space craft missions to various destinations. I quote from an article I read where an interviewer asked an astronaut: "What are the people in Mission Control really like?' One of their questions was 'Weren't there times when everybody, or at least a few people, just panicked?' My answer was 'No, when bad things happened, we just calmly laid out all the options, and failure was not one of them. We never panicked, and we never gave up on finding a solution. Failure was not an option.'" Then I thought if in all human efforts, failure was intended consciously not to be an option, then it would seem reasonable that when God did His work also, failure was intentionally not an option. And each sought to accomplish that same principle based on His character, capacity, and power. Some observations: 1. In all human efforts and after millennia of examination and assessments, failure was a reality that keeps haunting the human journey and experience; and that could be due to entropy, but more likely due to something beyond human capacity to discover. And that's where in reality "no human has gone before." 2. When God planned for man's redemption, failure was not an option, for sure. So He put His seal in every human heart to accomplish what no human had the capacity to comprehend or accomplish on his own. 3. When God designed symbolically the Tabernacle in the OT, and showed a model of it to Moses on Mt. Sinai, with all its details (including material, workers, gifts, purposes, dimensions, colors, tools, design, etc., as recorded in Exodus), He clearly instructed Moses that he (Moses) is not to make any contribution in thought, suggestion, or action whatsoever to the plan, but to simply execute the plan [OBEDIENCE]. Principle: When God initiates anything and seeks to accomplish His purposes, he does not ask for ideas but for OBEDIENCE. The only thing man rebels against when it comes to God is: OBEDIENCE (Rom 3:23). Amazing! The only thing Jesus, the Son of Man, learned and practiced perfectly in His earthly life was nothing other than: OBEDIENCE (Heb. 5:8). Really Amazing! So Jesus died on our behalf the death we deserved, the Sinless for the sinners, and lived the life we should have lived but could not. Then he said, "I am the way, the truth, and the life", and "Come unto me ... and I will give you rest", and "If any man be in Christ, he is a new creation". Q: Why such offer and such path? A: Because failure, with Him, is not an option. Q: How can that be? A: It happens when I realize that nothing is about me, but everything is about Him. Q: What do I get out of all this? A: I have HIM, in all His wonders and His love, in all His sustaining power and life. I am His, and He is mine! That's perfect! Praying that you every day, with all its details, becomes a series of lessons in the school of OBEDIENCE, for His glory. *(Tuesday, May 13, 2014 at 6:00A.M. CDT)*

I EITHER WONDER OR I WANDER
From my heart to yours

George Beverly Shea died recently at the age of 104. He accompanied Billy Graham on his journeys for over 70 years. I call that "the journey of a lifetime." One of Shea's favorite songs that I learned in yonder years is entitled "The Wonder of It all". The words are: "There's the wonder of sunset at evening, The wonder of sunrise I see; But the wonder of wonders that thrills my soul, Is the wonder that God loves me." REFRAIN: "O, the wonder of it all! The wonder of it all! Just to think that God loves me." Oftentimes I go to NASA's website, and spend few minutes looking at pictures sent by the Hubble telescope of stars, galaxies, and our Milky Way which contains our solar system, in total and absolute amazement, and I worship the One who created it all. What I'm always in total wonderment at is that He is also my Father, my Papa, my Daddy, my Abba, and lover of my soul. I come away every time grateful that His grandeur and my insignificance form each time the proper context for true worship. And in total loving condescension He chose to come, to seek, and to save. The All-Significant and me (and you), the In-Significant, are on a journey of a lifetime, and of eternity. Oh the wonder of it all is that he reached down from His distant and absolutely self-contained and self-sufficient glory and touched me, and loved me, and accepted me. My growing passionate desire is to know Him more, and to worship Him forever. That's another reason why I love Him so. *(Tuesday, May 13, 2014 at 6:39A.M. CDT)*

BECKONING THE BROKEN
From my heart to yours

After reading afresh about the woman who touched the hem of His garment (Mt 9:20-22; Mk 5:21-34, Lk 8:41-56), I found the Spirit challenging my comfort zone - again. My sense is that Jesus genuinely seeks to convert charcoals into diamonds while we diligently attempt to cover our charcoal heart with a thin coating of fake and cheap diamond glaze. It has the luster but lacks the muster. The difference is that he's familiar with the crushing force of a wine or olive press, while we spin our lives wanting contentment in the mirage of religious affluence. For the religious crowd who "hang around church" and "do stuff", it is sobering to realize that the way "we look at Him" and "the way He looks at us" are NOT one and the same. The difference between being "pressed" and being "pursued" is like the difference between "transient company" and an "Audience of One". Being pressed is what throngs create, but being pursued is what a worshipper experiences alone. Man's Perspective: To us, if we (as in Lk 8) "throng him" (today's lingo: hang out 24/7 and chit chat and get in the groove), we think he's the hot ticket since sliced bread, and that gives us the feeling that "being with Jesus" surely is a good thing and makes us the 'IN' crowd" and "the qualified and the dignified". But when he is finished examining our heart's intentions, we become "the horrified and the petrified". Jesus' Perspective: To Jesus, he was never impressed with the crowd for He seeks the weak, lonely, hopeless, helpless, contrite and broken, the enslaved and the crushed. He also expects to be touched, more likely, by those whom no one cares to touch in return. He doesn't look for "connoisseurs of refined religious tastes", but He looks for the ones desperate to be embraced, hungry and know it, naked and yearn for a covering that gives wholeness and restores original dignity. We authorize who touches us, but Jesus was the honey whose seekers obtained without touching or stinging anyone else. The crowds "pressed him", but the woman "touched the hem" and He noticed only her. That's Jesus! May you and I be His faithful ambassadors for the rest of our lives, speaking Him, knowing Him, and settling for nothing less than Him. *(Tuesday, May 13, 2014 at 11:57P.M. CDT)*

DOCTRINES DEAD UNTIL

From my heart to yours

There may be power in doctrine, but there is no life. Doctrine gives order to the follower of Christ, and that's good and essential. But doctrine does not give life, and that's not good and very detrimental. Jesus gives life and sustains it, and that's wonderful and very promising. Then He organizes doctrine and everything else in life around Himself by the power of His Spirit. And that's better. In fact, that's AWESOME! *(Wednesday, May 14, 2014 at 3:25A.M. CDT)*

COMMENTS ON LUKE 8:45, 47, 48

1. "AND JESUS SAID, WHO TOUCHED ME?" - Jesus is a show-stopper when things matter to Him - Jesus alone knows what really matters most - Jesus is where the normal course of events becomes not the normal course of events - Jesus knows between "tagging along" and "holding on to Him for dear life".

2. "WHEN ALL DENIED," - No one is willing to assume responsibility and tell the truth . He gave everyone to respond, but none did - Denial may refer to ignorance of fact, or refusing to be held accountable

3. "PETER AND THEY THAT WERE WITH HIM SAID," - the spokesman opens his mouth with false sense of confidence - having a habit of being with Jesus and listening to His nice words gives a false sense of security - consensus-building is no guarantee of truth - unanimity is not synonymous with certainty

4. "MASTER," Being courteous and respectful is insufficient. Appeal to authority does make us acceptable - Calling Him by the highest label maybe "politically correct", but is not a bonus point to our credit - Saying "Master" doesn't make us humble servants automatically

5. "THE PEOPLE ARE CROWDING," the tone of their voice is offensive because it assumes that He doesn't realize that fact - it's an appeal for him to accept his popularity as indicative of his legitimacy (you got the crowd behind you) - appeal to status and influence by human standards

6. "AND PRESSING AGAINST YOU," strongly appealing as candidate to rule by "ad populum"- playing to the gallery- popular opinion and majority sentiment

7. "AND YOU SAY, "WHO TOUCHED ME?" - The audacity of questioning Jesus' awareness of any context we expect him to be in, is such a nasty lingering human habit!

8. "AND WHEN THE WOMAN" - she is one who was less than equal. - she is one who doesn't have the right to even approach Jesus - she is one who received less inheritance than male siblings - she is one who had genuine yearning for Him, and more than she loved life - she is one who lost with men but won with Jesus - she is the only one who fell at His feet - yet she is precisely the one who stopped Jesus in his tracks because no one but Him could get her back on track

9. "SAW THAT SHE COULD NOT GO UNNOTICED," - no one touches Jesus and goes unnoticed - no one loves Jesus and needs to hide - no one can avoid the principle of Christ's presence.

10. "CAME TREMBLING" - better to tremble in front of Him than anyone else - trembling, with Jesus, assures us that we are in His presence

11. "AND FELL AT HIS FEET." - it is the attitude of the weak in front of the All-Powerful - it is as high as we can see ourselves and be correct, because He meets us there and lifts us up - it is very becoming of one who loves Jesus.

12. "IN THE PRESENCE OF ALL THE PEOPLE," - What a testimony to His majesty in the presence of all. - there is their

presence and His Presence. He always wins hands down. - her motivation is that she gave Him His real worth in front of everyone - she marked the red line between what they did and what He did. That always takes place at His feet, and He takes it from there.

13. "SHE TOLD" - verbal confession - the recipient who was shut out for 12 years, now cries out with gratitude and told. - the woman can speak when it's all about Him. - She has no points to make because she wasn't even in the game, but now she is in Christ, and that's all she cares to talks about. - Her attitude is not something to work up a frenzy about with other women because there is no male or female in His presence .

14. "WHY SHE HAD TOUCHED HIM" - Can we tell the "Why" of approaching Jesus without being corrupted by people's expectations? Since He already knows, can we tell the "Why" in front of people, but not be afraid of people because we are so awed by Him? - the truth, nothing but the truth, because no one helped her but God there is always at least one reason why we touch Him, namely, the very intent of our heart. - the ones with the right intent are the ones who give Him all the glory because it's ALL about HIM .

15. "AND HOW SHE HAD BEEN INSTANTLY HEALED." - His impact and influence is always instant. - we know we are telling the truth when we tell just what happened ". - That's a good sign of a true witness - being healed is a fact that draws people's attention to Jesus Christ, and no one else. - the healing cannot be for sale because it's priceless and personal .

16. "THEN HE SAID TO HER," - Jesus listens when we speak truth about Him, but that's only one half of the picture. He takes His turn too . - Jesus expects us to listen when He speaks - Jesus wraps things up properly and gives closure. - Jesus always affirms His love and work in our lives .

17. "DAUGHTER," - in total sovereign condescension. - He gave her a relationship, a kinship, and a fellowship - He called her by the most sacred term of endearment. - NO yearning of a daughter's heart than to hear her own daddy calling her what no one else can - culture has its limit, Jesus cannot be controlled in what He says .

18. "YOUR FAITH" - she was aware of Jesus and no one exceeded him in awareness, "- she sought Jesus with all her heart. - She took steps in His direction risking everything because she had nothing left except Him يسوع ... . - she counted Him as her all-sufficiency even before she touched the hem of His garment " - It wasn't the shroud of his garment that healed her but the Presence of the Almighty stood unshrouded and unclouded, and all saw with their own eyes.

19. "HAS MADE YOU WHOLE;" - that's a condition and a status that takes place in time and immediately becomes past, but His presence will always be in the present. "I am with you always". He "IS" is what is always. - He brings healing and wholeness - He takes action with an end in mind - the outcome from His action is always better than the starting point. - With doctors, they left her with more questions. But with Jesus, she received answers. The answer is what He "does", not what he talks about. - Jesus always

speaks life, newness, peace, hope, healing, confidence, joy, forward movement, new order, and expectations.

20. "GO IN PEACE." - New commission - new lease on life because of His blood that was shed - the Prince of peace, gives real peace, in contrast to the wishful thinking the world gives. - the power of a new commission - the command is go ... and keep going; go tell it on the mountaintop that you've been in the valley but not anymore.

Questions?

1. Have you touched Him?

2. Are you awed by Him?

3. Has He captured your heart?

If Yes, then Life has happened, and no one can take that away. Now, Go and Tell, not what you got but what He did. You still got nothing more than Him. It's All About Him! *(Wednesday, May 14, 2014 at 9:51A.M. CDT)*

MY FUNNY MOM
From my heart to yours

There is the sunny side of life; and there is the funny side of Mom. I stopped by their house this morning to check on her. She has a bruise over her left eye and a bad headache from the slight concussion. But in general, she's doing Ok. Mom: I talked to The Lord this morning. John: I have too. You tell me what He said. Mom: He told me that He appointed a time for everything, a time to live and a time to die. John: But I have the distinct impression that you're trying to help Him change his schedule a bit. Mom: John (trying to pull a guilt trip), John, don't say that. John: well, your track record speaks for itself. Mom: I don't play with God like that :) John: Good, but I have to keep an eye on you. John: I love you Mom. Mom: I love you too, but I don't play with God. My Mom, a funny girl! *(Wednesday, May 14, 2014 at 11:25A.M. CDT)*

REVIVAL TAKES PLACE
From my heart to yours

- Not on the internet but through intercession;

- Not on the laptops but on the knee caps;

- Not in public agreement but in private agony;

- Not in a clean place but in a clean heart;

- Not in a heart burning with a plan but in a heart passionate for God alone;

- Not while we hold on to anything but when we hold on to nothing;

- Not with perfect grammar before people but in perfect communion with God;

- Not with more attendance but with full attention toward God;

- Not with open lips but with brokenness;

- Not with usual words but with crying hearts;

- Not with tears that people see but with agonizing that only God knows;

- Not in air-conditioned auditorium but in a musty barn;

- Not by bringing celebrity in but by divine power of the Spirit

- Not in comfort but in crisis;

- Not by a man who brings revival from God but by God who brings fire to man;

- Not from the east or west, but from the North, from the City of the Great King;

- Not by kinship, partnership, sponsorship, spectatorship, or relationship.

Revival takes place declaring His Lordship, despite all hardship, and in true worship, when the captain of the ship takes charge again in His time, in full power and regal majesty unexplainable by anything other than one calling to the other and saying: "The Master Is Here". May we clear the way, remove the trash of many years, wash our eyes with the salve of the Spirit, drink from the only well of living water, and let the new wine from on high shatter the old wineskins forever. *(Friday, May 16, 2014 at 5:04A.M. CDT)*

Doctrine and Life
From my heart to yours

The reason Jesus did not preach doctrine while on earth was because He was in fact the embodiment of all doctrine. So we have these key verses: "For God was pleased to have all his fullness dwell in him." (Col. 1:19). "For in Christ all the fullness of the Deity lives in bodily form." (Col. 2:9) When we focus on "doctrine", then the message is dry, ineffective, and does not yield life. When we present Christ as Savior and Lord, doctrine becomes, of necessity, an integral part. For this reason, the Holy Spirit is required, to bring glory to the Son. "In Him was life, and this life was the light of all people." *(Saturday, May 17, 2014 at 1:48A.M. CDT)*

Preeminence Snapshot
From my heart to yours

Don't make definite plans. God just might be at work. If you insist, then you will very likely lose. "In all your ways, give Him prominence." *(Saturday, May 17, 2014 at 1:59A.M. CDT)*

My Neighbor
From my heart to yours

In recent research, I learned that more than 94 million times people searched on line for an answer to the question: "Who is my neighbor". So do you think they are looking for something? Do you think there is a massive number of people whose heart is crying out for someone, anyone, who can help heal wounds left unattended? *(Saturday, May 17, 2014 at 2:14A.M. CDT)*

TRUE DISCIPLE
From my heart to yours

The ONLY word that held up around the world and across centuries of unpredictable human existence as the most representative and descriptive word of followers of Christ is the word: DISCIPLE. I doubt we need or can find another one until He comes. I suspect that Jesus knew that too well. So He said, "By this people will know that you are my _____, if you love one for another." "Disciple" and "Love" are all that Jesus Christ asks for, even today. Christianity is cluttered with unnecessary verbiage. True disciples need only love Him, because He loved first. True disciples are disciplined in Him and in His love, because the rest is detail. *(Saturday, May 17, 2014 at 2:30A.M. CDT)*

TIME FOR SPARROWS
From my heart to yours

I'm learning that God does not "wait" on people and that for two reasons. First, is that waiting requires time, and God has no time. Second, is that God is at work. However, His eye is also on the sparrow, and I know He watches me. So He demands that His disciples do the waiting, and, in due season, He promised that He will make a way. *(Saturday, May 17, 2014 at 2:37A.M. CDT)*

NO SPECIALS
From my heart to yours

Whenever we see a price tag, we are inclined to think something like this: 1. I want it, and NOW! or, 2. I need to shop this, or, 3. I'm free to get this elsewhere for less, or, 4. I can make payments, can't I? or, 5. I'm going to negotiate, or, 6. I can always walk away and exercise all my rights, or, 7. They're so unreasonable. Then we are stunned and shocked why we think the same way about being a disciple of Jesus Christ. He begins to turn up the heat more by saying that to be a true follower of Jesus Christ: 1. I have to lay down all my weapons 2. I have to depend on Him 100% 3. I can't do a single thing on my own 4. I must submit and obey with a smile on my face 5. I need to be willing to go as far as I can in NOT depending on myself 6. The only one motivation acceptable to Him in service is: Love 7. I need to change everything in my life 8. I must be the best I can be for the sake of someone else to succeed. *(Saturday, May 17, 2014 at 2:33P.M. CDT)*

BUILDING RELATIONSHIPS
From my heart to yours

Buildings have no relationship to the nature of the church that Jesus is building, and that is for one simple reason. Historically, and with no exception, whether in the Old or New Testament, God never sought man's input about anything He is building. God already knows how to beautify from within the place in which He dwells. If a group of believers has a building and another group does not, does God dwell with the first but not with the second? And if the first burns down, does God get upset and walks away or does he dwell less now? Not fair any way we look at it. So, He said, "Don't you know that you are the temple of God, and the Spirit of God dwells in you?" Some people, I wonder about :), but a fact is a fact. I suspect that some are a masterpiece car "In-Process", but still act like junk :). But that's for another day. Show me a true follower of Jesus Christ, and I'll show you someone who is a beautiful person, because God dwells in him, and he/she reflects the character of Jesus Christ. About the ones acting like junk, I need to change so I can love them more as Jesus did. *(Saturday, May 17, 2014 at 5:01P.M. CDT)*

LOOKING AT A WOMAN THE JESUS WAY
From my heart to yours

I am still learning, and am increasingly amazed about the real possibility of loving the wife "... just as Christ loved the Church and gave Himself up for her". And, with his followers in mind, He prayed (John 17), "for their sake I sanctify myself." So God gave us wives...Hallelujah!, but not to have babies and a quiet dinner. We don't need marriage for that. Certain ones of the male species think that one of the by-products of having a woman (convention calls her "wife") is to raise her and train her subtly or directly, by granting or withholding approval, to be "in their image" and to serve them for years to come, better than Timex or Japanese cars. But in fact, God gave us wives so that we, men, can sanctify ourselves and change for their sake. What do I mean? Meaning:

(1) I need to change so I can see her inner beauty like no other woman because she is in a class by herself. It's a farce and a bad bill of sale that "love is blind". (2) I need to change my character and be holy in my heart so I can see her wholly (as a whole) as a person. The only way this can happen is to see how desperate I am for God's help, not because of her, but because of me. (3) I need to reflect the true character of Christ before her eyes daily so she can truly "feel at home" and not just settle for "living in the same house". (4) I need to seriously recognize that it is self-destructive to view the woman as simply a body in constant motion designed at the factory for service, with lifetime warranty, can be discarded for a newer model, always as a means to an end, as someone who can cook and wash my clothes, as someone who is magically endowed with "energizer bunny" powers to carry babies, go through convolutions of gestation, carry on house duties, host the guests I invite (often without regard to her), take care of the other kids, raising them, tending to every domestic need, and I on one hand stare daggers and knives into her if she falters or fails or not live up to my expectations, and on the other hand bask in the conquest I achieved by having her and flip the remote in my hand through channels of utter nonsense. Recent studies have shown that men have gone into depression and anxiety when they were given by simulation to carry the weight of a baby around their bellies. Yet, some don't mind carrying the belly nonetheless, and don't hesitate to lecture on childbirth. The audacity!! (5) I need to discern her as a gift, a sheer gift from God. For when there is a gift, there is always a giver. If I reject God in my heart, then I have taken into my own hands the gift He gave, and have decided to dictate how to view her and how to relate to

her. And of necessity, I have determined then the criteria for her evaluation. Logically then, we conclude on this line of reasoning that since cultures are different, none is better than the other, and that's what man has settled for - a draw. Maybe that's why there is increasing distortion today of this business we call "marriage". We are glad that the rate of divorces is down. However, we are sad when we realize that marriage has been replaced with mutually-agreed upon cohabitation that flips like tv channels almost on a whim or momentary disenchantment, and how pernicious the substitute has become. (6) I need to realize, and quickly, that changing my character to be like Christ is the diligent work of the Holy Spirit, because I really don't even know where to begin. Furthermore, waiting till old age is a bad proposition. What does He expect of me? OBEDIENCE TO HIM. How often does he work on me? DAILY. Why ME? A thousand reasons, but suffice it to say: so that my sons and daughters can have a role model of unity, fellowship, and love; so that they can see demonstrated how to converse, listen, help, laugh, cry, cooperate, facilitate, ensure success, endure hardships, learn faith and hope, hospitality and discernment, bear all burdens together, and if need be, be crushed for her sake so God can make me a better vessel for His glory. That's for starters! To be fair, next will be: TREATING the wives the Jesus Way. And next will be: LOOKING at Husbands the Jesus Way. And last will be: TREATING the Husbands the Jesus Way. *(Saturday, May 17, 2014 at 6:39P.M. CDT)*

A CHARACTER TRAIT OF A JESUS FOLLOWER
From my heart to yours

"Not quarrelsome" is mentioned in 2 Ti 2:24. The follower of Jesus is not "quarrelsome". It means: 1. He recognizes that spewing of anger from his mouth has worse consequences than the original cause of his anger. 2. This attitude of heart and trait in character renders as worthless any established service and fellowship. 3. Such person ceases to see anyone else's perspective in the conversation. 4. He/she kindles many unquenchable fires in his/her heart, with vast repercussions. 5. He loses any sense of direction or clear thought. 6. He/she as a follower of Jesus is not looking to the Master, and is sure to grieve the Holy Spirit. 7. His service and effectiveness, regardless of how insignificant, are rendered as worthless. 8. His engagement in a "war of words" will be like a hurricane, intent on leveling or removing everything of value in its path. His favorite vegetable is "squash" (pun intended) 9. Such attitude is combative, intensive, and bitter, seeking to assert ownership, rights, or possession. 10. Recognize that the fighting with others reflects the war within, and we may not be aware. The purpose within is always to do that which pleases self. YIKES !!! TREATMENT - (This can apply in general, but specifically to a true follower of Jesus Christ): 1. Stop the attitude 2. Submit to His Lordship 3. Recognize the reality 4. Settle the war within 5. Confess the sin 6. Rebuild proper heart attitude 7. Restore damaged relationship 8. Focus on His pleasure not yours 9. Acknowledge the Presence of God's Spirit in you 10. Replace wrong with right attitude 11. Move forward in humility and meekness Rebuilding always takes longer; so, don't start :) His promise: "God in you is able to grant the will to do what pleases

Him", and has the ability "to do immeasurably more than all we ask or imagine, according to his power that is at work within us." That power is the power of the Holy Spirit who dwells in the follower of Jesus Christ. *(Sunday, May 18, 2014 at 5:45A.M. CDT)*

PURE CALLING OUT TO GOD
From my heart to yours

"With all who call upon God from a 'PURE' heart " (2 Ti 2:22) The word 'pure' is from the Greek original "katharsis". (From it, the word "catheter" is derived). It means:

1. To be continually "cleansed", drained of any impurities (here, impure emotions) that tend to compromise and bring the standard of measurements down. How far down? That's the compromise after all-- it doesn't matter how far down. It's heading in the wrong direction.
2. The result of "catharsis" is true healing. Sometimes, lust trumps discernment, but 'catharsis' is best treatment. Preventive prescription is Phil 4:8.
3. The refusal of "catharsis" is the hardening (i.e., refusal to change), which results in searing of conscience.
4. True catharsis leads to true obedience as first step.
5. True catharsis leads to a sense of (a) heart-break and sadness for the price that had to be paid, and (b) fear of ever wanting to have that attitude or go in that direction again.
6. This state of cleansing results in renewal of relationship with God and restoration of true fellowship.

David: "Restore unto me the JOY of your salvation." Q: How is the heart "cleansed" continually"? A: "the blood ... cleanses us from all unrighteousness (any 'not-rightness') (1 John 1:7). 7. The state of 'cleansing' takes place after actionable confessing. 8. Katharsis, cleansing, enables the true follower of Jesus to call out to God, and expect to be heard. 9. Katharsis, cleansing. A heart condition toward God that is built on four pillars toward men : (a) righteousness - sure rightness (b) faith - implicit trust (c) love - unconditional position (d) peace - unbroken relation 10. True catharsis is completely based on the great and precious promises of God. *(Sunday, May 18, 2014 at 7:25A.M. CDT)*

Sunday, May 18, 2014 at 1:32P.M. CDT

Being on a first-name basis with God causes us to lose the necessary sense of awe in His Presence. God help us!

Unction: An Old Word

From my heart to yours

Power of Unction leads to the Power of Function. But lack of unction results in doubts, ineffectiveness, and quenching of the Spirit. My prayer is that the Spirit of God keep all who name the Name of Christ from a pure heart. *(Thursday, May 22, 2014 at 7:06A.M. CDT)*

THE POWER OF THE GOSPEL (1)
From my heart to yours

When the result is Obedience to the Master, the power of the Gospel is made manifest. When the result is end to self and start of Christ in the life, that's the power of the Gospel. When the result is glory to His Name, that's the power of the Gospel. When the result is reconciliation with God, that's the power of the Gospel. When the result is confession of sin, that's the power of the Gospel. When the result is a clean conscience, that's the power of the Gospel. When the result is light and salt, that's the power of the Gospel. And, That's another reason why I love Him so. *(Sunday, May 25, 2014 at 1:41A.M. CDT)*

THE POWER OF THE GOSPEL (2)
From my heart to yours

When I'm in a fight with God and He captures my heart, that's the power of the Gospel. When I obey God and I capture His heart, that's the power of the Gospel. When Jesus Christ is my "One and Only", that's the power of the Gospel. When I am molded daily in His image, that's when I experience the power of the Gospel. When He gives me understanding, that's the power of the Gospel. When I grasp what He did on the cross for me, that's the power of the Gospel. When I die and He lives in me, that's the power of the Gospel. And, That's another reason why I love Him so. *(Sunday, May 25, 2014 at 1:48A.M. CDT)*

MY LIFE IN CHRIST
From my heart to yours

When my life is hid in Him, so He is shown to the world, that's my life in Christ. When my heart totally belongs to Him, that my life in Christ. When I hide His word in my heart, that's my life in Christ. When I yield to His gentle tug at my heart, that's my life in Christ. When I love the unlovely, that's my life in Christ. When His Spirit moves me to tears for a lost world, that's my life in Christ. When my debt of love to Him breaks me and re-makes me, that's my life in Christ. I'm sure there is more, but... *(Sunday, May 25, 2014 at 1:56A.M. CDT)*

TO BUILD OR TO DESTROY
From my heart to yours

It's part of the daily human experience, and that's the question we face. Few thoughts: - It's always easier to destroy than to build - It doesn't take a genius to destroy - A builder takes ownership. Destruction takes an excuse. - It requires no resources to destroy but much to build. - He who seeks to destroy doesn't have much invested that's of any real value to begin with. - Building and Destruction begin with "words". - Building requires effort and sometimes tears. Destruction takes only a fool. - Jesus said: "I will build my Church". In His case, he did not die in the process, but he died as a requirement. And His separation from the Father was so that we may never be separated again, Ever! So, He raised the bar, yet again, beyond human comprehension. And That's another reason why I love Him so. *(Monday, May 26, 2014 at 9:26A.M. CDT)*

LOVING THE JESUS WAY
From my heart to yours

Fully aware of 1Cor 13 (the Love chapter), Jesus preceded the Acts and Letters, and that's where all began. So I must ask a few questions: - How did He love when no one was chosen yet to love? - When, as the Son of Man, did He begin to love, or was it on hold until there were people in the picture? - Was He putting on a front when Peter came along? - Was He ratcheting up His stamina and intestinal fortitude in preparation for Judas Iscariot? - Was He caught by surprise when the disciples were afraid and went back and left him? - What kind of disciples were they? - Did they really love Him like He wanted them to, but they just slipped and fell back because of political pressures? - Did He not have any of the "other" emotions and feelings ever, such as "envy", "hatred", "fear", "jealousy", "doubt", "anger", "pride in his accomplishments", "low self-esteem", "assertiveness", etc. etc.? More to come, but suffice it to say that He refused to fall back on his other title, as Son of God, to which He was fully entitled but he intentionally set aside (Phil 2) One thing for sure. It is that He took upon Himself the death and full punishment of Almighty God that should have fallen upon us and we deserved but He did not deserve. At the same time, He lived the life that we should have lived but no one did or could. Period! The one thing that sustained Him was Love. *(Monday, May 26, 2014 at 2:24P.M. CDT)*

BETTER USE OF TIME
From my heart to yours

So we all have cell phones with loads of pictures of people, places, and events. Each of them, to us, is a "Kodak moment". Each of them, to us, has a story. We like to peruse them once in a while, or rush to show one to a friend with euphoric excitement. Knowing some details about each picture, have we considered in our idle times to browse slowly through them, pause at some, and PRAY? PRAY for everything that we already know about each picture. And we will find our prayers colored with gratitude, smiles and tears, requests, intercessions, pleadings, and perhaps confessions. We may even begin by saying "Our Father who is in heaven, I'm sorry for not praying as I should, but I do want to say 'hallowed be your Name, your Kingdom come, your will be done on earth as it is in heaven". If a picture you have is from a particular country, pray for God's mercy on the turmoil in that country, the leaders of that country, etc. If it's a picture of a few people, pray with thanksgiving for the joy they bring to your heart, for peace in their lives, for hope to have, for confidence in doubts, for forgiveness when needed, for grace all the time. Pray for their life circumstances, homes, children, parents, spouses, and what you know of challenges, struggles, illnesses, and anything else you can think of. Pray that they have wisdom and discernment in decision-making, that they not rush into errors and temptations, that they be protected from the evil one, that they find grace in time of need, that are reminded of God in their life, that when they fail they don't despair, that trials don't crush them, that they find refuge under the wings of the One who said 'Come unto me all you who are heavy-laden and I give you rest". We all know and have people who are looking for someone, anyone, to PRAY for them and lift them up. Oh, and about idle time? How about while riding in a car, bus, train, etc. How about while we are relaxing with a cup of coffee or glass of tea? How about during "quiet time", or while waiting in line somewhere -- at the gas pump, at the red light, at the doctor's office, in a drive-through, or for Mr. Sandman. Just imagine: Studies have shown that in a lifetime we spend 11 years in front of the TV, 5 months complaining, 38 thousand hours eating, 11 hours surfing the net each month (Nielsen research), 5.5 years doing house work, and we moan 8 minutes every day about bad service. And for the ones we love, how much time we pray?! Just imagine! Is it fair? You get the picture! Now. Do we have any excuse not to pray? Really and honestly! It's a good life habit to have. You'll have a change of heart attitude about the ones you pray for, about the One you pray to, and even about the one who is praying :). God is listening. You can start even now. *(Wednesday, May 28, 2014 at 5:40A.M. CDT)*

REALITY OF CHRIST
From my heart to yours

What matters in the entire matter of self-knowledge is whether Jesus Christ is, in fact, present effectively in the life of a person. For Jesus Christ does not twirl around in the orbit of each individual's life according to personal whims and preferences, but He is the very force and dominating Presence in the life of a person, if in fact he/she is a true follower of His, making demands that seek categorical obedience. He learned, and was perfected in learning, obedience. Hence, it is sufficient that the disciple/follower be likewise obedient. The question of true "faith" is equally and simultaneously a question of true "obedience", not to another human being but to Christ Himself. And obviously, I'm distinguishing between the obedience of a slave who operates on fear and ignorance of the person in charge, and the obedience the follower of Christ. For Christ desires us to know Him and to love Him, and then our deep-seated desire becomes obedience to Him. *(Friday, May 30, 2014 at 4:02A.M. CDT)*

THE FUNNY THING
From my heart to yours

It struck me somewhat odd this morning that we have no problem when it comes to describing what God can, and should, do for us; and so much trouble when it comes to discerning what God demands of us. And yet, He loves us and sends His rain on the righteous and unrighteousness. One sees the fingerprints of God, and the other one does not. *(Friday, May 30, 2014 at 6:00A.M. CDT)*

SKELETON AND MUSCLES DON'T
From my heart to yours

Just as a skeleton is not the body, so doctrines don't make up a true follower of Jesus Christ. Although necessary, a skeleton needs more than crackling bones to make a functioning body. So we add tendons and muscles. But even then, doctrines with prayers and good works don't make up a true vibrant follower of Christ. What makes skeleton + muscles + tendons add up to a living vibrant active and interactive human being is the breath of life. Likewise, what triggers doctrines + good works + ministry to become life in a true meaningful vibrant interactive and fruitful follower of Jesus Christ is the Spirit of life, the Spirit of Christ Himself, and nothing less. Then we may behold His glory as that of the only begotten Son of God. And that's another reason why I love Him so. *(Saturday, May 31, 2014 at 3:14P.M. CDT)*

IMMATERIAL DISTANCES
From my heart to yours

It is very possible to be dead and very far or very near to the cross of Jesus. Distance is immaterial. But to be dead on the cross with Jesus is much better, because He died for me, and now I am able to be alive in Him. " I have been crucified with Christ and I no longer live, but Christ lives in me. The life I now live in the body, I live by faith in the Son of God, who loved me and gave himself for me. (Galatians 2:20 NIV) *(Saturday, May 31, 2014 at 11:44P.M. CDT)*

KEEPING THINGS SIMPLE
From my heart to yours

Life is complicated as it is. I propose that we keep it simple. And we can. Here's how: Jesus Christ calls us: 1. To FAITH that He gives, because "without faith it's impossible to please Him". 2. To OBEDIENCE which He demonstrated, because "being perfected,

(He) became to all those who obey Him the cause of eternal salvation". 3. To LOVE like He did - the unlovely despised confused and the worthless, because as such we once were. The only question left to ask is: Will I obey? What do you say? *(Sunday, June 1, 2014 at 6:15A.M. CDT)*

MASTERS DEMAND
From my heart to yours

Jesus Christ makes demands on my life, not suggestions. The difference between His demands and Satan's demands is that His are out of unconditional love, while Satan's are out of passion to control us from the shadows. Both will succeed. The difference is that I will also win with the first, but will experience sure defeat with the second. What'll it be? *(Sunday, June 1, 2014 at 6:25A.M. CDT)*

WONDERING WHY WORTHLESS WORKS
From my heart to yours

Jesus Christ never calls anyone to perform better works. It is a mere "guilt trip", a trap and temptation, to think that by "working harder" God will be more pleased with my life. That is man-thinking. God-thinking is better. Here's why: 1. Jesus Christ calls us - not to live for Him the best we can, but to die with Him, and He will live in us. 2. Jesus Christ calls us - not to work and stay busy for Him, but to obey, and He will perform just what needs to be done without being late or disappointed. 3. Jesus Christ calls us - not to take charge of our life, but to completely surrender, and through His Spirit He will accomplish His desire. 4. Jesus Christ calls us to listen, not to talk, and He will speak through us. 5. Jesus Christ calls us - not to enjoy Him among everything else we call "blessings", but He calls us to enjoy Him alone, and "all these things - that He thinks we will need -- shall be added unto you". His ways in and goals for my life are always better, because all will lead to His glory and to my delight in Him. Only a fool thinks differently. *(Sunday, June 1, 2014 at 6:29A.M. CDT)*

TOUCHING THE INVISIBLE
From my heart to yours

Laying on of hands is a church coming together in agreement with the Spirit of God to bless and dedicate. Prayer prepares pleading and praising partners permanently. *(Monday, June 2, 2014 at 6:40P.M. CDT)*

AS SHEEP AMONG WOLVES
From my heart to yours

Certainly the picture of sheep among wolves is not a pretty one; not readily sure looking from the outside who's who because there is always the scenario of wolves in sheep clothing, surely not encouraging to be sheep, not 'smart' to be in such situation, and very likely not safe. And to be sure, the wolves will always seek to devour the sheep, and the reverse will never happen. Sheep are "among", not "away from", wolves. That's how Jesus described the reality of the true followers. It will never change as long as we are on earth. The sheep will always be sheep, and the wolves will be wolves. Wolves are not bothered by what sheep think of them. They are not interested in a leadership role among sheep. They prefer the kitchen to the living room in the house of sheep. Aside from the obvious differences, Jesus is speaking about two distinct natures, two distinct attitudes or mindsets, two distinct purposes in life, and a constant risk of which He's fully aware. We are sure to discuss or think of the two groups, sheep and wolves, and advise profusely how sheep ought to conduct themselves. But Jesus is alerting His followers not so much to the reality of their context (wolves and sheep), but primarily desires to impress upon them that there is a Presence that will always sustain them where they are, and they have no alternative but to practice being in that Presence. It is the Presence of the Shepherd. The question is not of the shepherd protecting the sheep wherever they go, but whether the sheep are staying in the presence of the shepherd. Jesus said, "I am the good shepherd." Are you and I practicing His Presence? *(Wednesday, June 4, 2014 at 8:35A.M. CDT)*

WHY PERSECUTION?
From my heart to yours

From Matthew 5:44 and Acts 4, followers of Jesus Christ knew that they don't have to seek persecution or ask for it, but they should expect it if two essential factors exist: (1) if people know that the follower of Jesus has been with Him; and, (2) if the follower of Jesus Christ introduces others to Him. Someone may ask, "But, Why?" The only answer I can come with is that it's all about Him, His wonderful Name, His majestic character, His unbelievable act of unconditional love expressed on the cross, His desire for all to come to Him, His precious blood that was shed, His awesome resurrection from the dead, His forgiveness that sets the captive free, His healing of broken hearts, His precious promises, and so much more. For it is truly about Him, and Him alone. In contrast, no one is left even to hold a candle to the light of the Sun of Righteousness. Some lash back, persecute, destroy, kill, steal, and attempt to silence. But life is always the better option. That's why the captives desire freedom, the drowning desire rescue, and the crushed desire re-creation from nothing. And all can come to Him who said, "Come unto me all who hunger and thirst." *(Thursday, June 5, 2014 at 10:37A.M. CDT)*

PRAYING FOR THE PERSECUTED
From my heart to yours

Praying for the Persecuted church: It was sobering to learn that approximately 80% of followers of Jesus Christ around the world are persecuted regularly. Peter said (Acts 4) that they could not "NOT" talk (double negative showing force of the declarative statement) about what they heard and what they saw. John (in 1Jn 1) sums up what they saw and heard, touched and gazed at, that it was JESUS, the Word of life, and Him alone. We can say that the true follower is truly and totally captivated by the Person of Jesus Christ for the rest of his life. Therefore, he/she can expect persecution. But how can we pray for the persecuted church around the world? For myself, understanding that I need not seek persecution, I can no longer pray that God keep and protect me from being persecuted. Coming, it shall, if indeed I'm known by

Him and by being in His company, that like the disciples, I belong to Him. So, praying would more likely be heard in heaven if we pray: 1. That His Name be made known 2. That He may enable us to love and pray for those who persecute us 3. That He may forgive us our sins BECAUSE we forgave those who persecute us already 4. That He be glorified 5. That He may grant us to rejoice in all things, and look to Him 6. That we continue to bear testimony to His Matchless Name 7. That the Gospel, who IS Jesus Christ, be made known around the world. The truth of the matter is that carbon when crushed yields diamond, grapes when crushed yield wine, olives when crushed yield oil. It's not about me; it's about Him. And that's another reason why I love Him so. *(Thursday, June 5, 2014 at 11:00A.M. CDT)*

PERSECUTION

From my heart to yours

Persecution is worldwide. Prayer should be too. Here's a snapshot. And you can find out more at www[dot]persecution[dot]org. *(Thursday, June 5, 2014 at 11:47A.M. CDT)*

JESUS ALONE

From my heart to yours

Throughout human history, there have been people of all types of experiences. Do you know any such as: The fearful, the broken, the haters, the mockers, the doubters, the anxious, the abused, the lonely, the distant, the fatherless, the homeless and hopeless, the crushed, the proud, the selfish, the desperate, the reprobate, the degenerate, the angry, the combative, the deceptive, the conniving, the abusers, the murderers, the ashamed, the unforgiven and unforgiving, the captive, the poor and live in misery every day. Have you met such people? Then, There is JESUS, who stands out and cries out and says: "I AM". He said, "I am the bread of life, I am the living water, I am the way the truth and the life, I am the good shepherd, I am the resurrection." He said, "Come unto me and take...". He is the Savior, the Comforter, the peace-maker, covenant-maker, the high priest, the door, the light of the world, the hope of the nations, the rose of Sharon, the bright and morning star, the joy of the whole earth, the wisdom of God, the power of God, the central figure of the Gospel, the covering for our sins, the thrice blessed in heaven and earth... And SO much more. And that's another reason why I love Him so. Any alternative? Really! :) *(Thursday, June 5, 2014 at 12:20P.M. CDT)*

A MEMBER OR A FOLLOWER?
From my heart to yours

People get confused at times and assume that a member in an earthly local church is the same as being a follower of Jesus Christ. Some clarification may help. *Becoming* a member is instant; but *becoming* a follower is life-long. Becoming a member is what the Holy Spirit does in me; but *becoming* a follower is what I do in Him. Becoming a member cost the death Jesus Christ on the cross; but Becoming a follower costs me to be crucified with Him. Becoming a member means life; but *becoming* a follower means death. Becoming a member gives me family; but *becoming* a follower gives me Christ. Becoming a member is positional; but *becoming* a follower is continual. Becoming a member means I become one with Him; but Becoming a follower means He becomes the Only One in my heart. Becoming a member demonstrated the passion of Christ for me; but *becoming* a follower reflects my passion for Him. Becoming a member required His complete surrender; but *becoming* a follower requires my complete surrender. These descriptive statements are not comprehensive but are intended to clarify the meaning and differences. However, the fact remains that *becoming* a member of the Body of Christ and Becoming a follower of the Person of Jesus Christ are two sides of the same coin. Membership in a local body of believers is the second act of obedience. *(Saturday, June 7, 2014 at 9:56A.M. CDT)*

WALKING

From my heart to yours

Following Jesus is no cakewalk. It's definitely not a sleepwalk or spacewalk either. Some may think it's a ropewalk or casual sidewalk. But I doubt it. That's why following Him is no advice He gives, but a demand He makes of everyone who was made alive. The reason is that there is no such thing anywhere in Scripture that says Faith is possible without Obedience. And the reason for the reason mentioned is that Christ, by His obedience unto the death of the cross, became the "author" and fountainhead of our faith. *(Saturday, June 7, 2014 at 10:13A.M. CDT)*

THE HOUSE OF GOD

From my heart to yours

Worship takes place between Genesis 28:17 and Acts 17:28. The house of God has nothing to do with human utterance but has everything to do with divine Presence. God always takes the first step toward us in revealing himself. An example is Genesis 28. Jacob was afraid and said, "How awesome is this place! This is none other than the house of God; this is the gate of heaven." (Gen 28:17 NIV) ... Not that Jacob went to heaven but that heaven came to him. And where God is, is the starting point. So it's true that "in the beginning, God..." So when Jacob saw a ladder in a dream, the story goes that the angels were "ascending and descending", which should be, at first assessment, that the angels come from and go to heaven. But, that's not the order of the words and Jesus referred to the same incident correctly too. The reason is that the angels are always in the Presence of God, and that's always their "starting point". And where God is, there is ... Worship. And from worship springs service. And from service springs gratitude. And from gratitude springs glory and praise, and continual worship again. It's always about Him. Recognizing the AWESOMENESS comes first, followed by the CONFESSION. Now it makes sense that '... in him we live and move and have our being.' (Acts 17:28 NIV) *(Monday, June 9, 2014 at 11:51A.M. CDT)*

HELPING, NOT ENOUGH

From my heart to yours

The Holy Spirit does not need our help but our obedience. For by so doing, we yield to His hand that shapes us in the likeness of Christ and to His glory. Obedience from the heart is complete, especially when we don't understand. For in obeying I understand, not His mind, but His love. It's His love that flows through his followers, and reaches the world. *(Sunday, June 15, 2014 at 2:34P.M. CDT)*

BROKENNESS SNAPSHOT

From my heart to yours

Healing, after brokenness, is always better with God than with people. For, though He crushes, He, without fail, makes a better vessel to His glory. *(Sunday, June 15, 2014 at 9:13P.M. CDT)*

ON BEING ACCEPTED

From my heart to yours

What makes Jesus Christ stand out from the crowd is that all He offered, commanded, or expected is universal in nature. Meaning, His Gospel message, its application, and its demands cross all barriers, generations, languages, and genders (all two of them). And He discriminates against no one. Furthermore, His love is sought after by all who hunger and thirst for true love because no one offered anything comparable, and accepting us as we are is what takes the cake. And that's another reason why I love Him so. *(Sunday, June 15, 2014 at 9:54P.M. CDT)*

THE MEANING OF THE CROSS
From my heart to yours

Being broken has many reasons which most can never comprehend. Getting broken has many paths that take their shape with time and leave timeless scars. Feeling broken has many expressions, most are silent and deep. But brokenness, still, find its complete meaning in the cross. For at the cross I did not make a U-turn, but all my brokenness found its rest in Him who, for love's sake, was broken and crushed for me. Therefore, coming to Christ and being one with Him is like coming home. So, He had to speak with a loud voice and say, "Let anyone who is thirsty come to me and drink. Whoever believes in me, as Scripture has said, rivers of living water will flow from within them." (John 7:37, 38 NIV) Do you believe? *(Sunday, June 15, 2014 at 10:04P.M. CDT)*

BUILDING THE CHURCH
From my heart to yours

It seems that there is a general trend of relinquishing any connection or affiliation to a local church and settling for the kind where the individual manages the relationship by remote control and precise scheduled events and productions. The reasons are many and most, in my view, come under the category of "Shame on the local church leaders and wannabe's". For many, if not most, have reduced the church to what can be compared to beer: lite, less-filling, and cheap. Too many conditions, straitjackets, and man-made structures, ad nauseam, left the church to the mockery of the multitudes, and an excellent target practice range from and toward the pulpit. The repeated scene of fallen TV stars did not help either, and has seemingly left the midnight sky of Christendom quite empty and riddled with chaos and disappointment. In the midst of this field of 'Christianese', Jesus said, "I will build my Church, and the gates of hell will not prevail against it." How can He accomplish His objective? Is it possible? The answer, I think, lies where we are not looking. *(Sunday, June 15, 2014 at 10:33P.M. CDT)*

ON BEING CALLED BY HIS NAME
From my heart to yours

"If my people who are called by my name" (2 Chr. 7) is a very formidable statement. The awesome force of meaning in the words: "my", "called", and "Name" leaves little room for guesswork. Immediately, I find myself arrested but without fear of retribution; invaded but without force; and separated but not leaving me with a sense of isolation. The first "my" seems to indicate a covenant relationship. The last "my" seems to indicate the basis of that covenant relationship. While on the human level each is given a name at birth, that holy Name seems to resonate with singularity, eternity, and affectionate attachment. *(Sunday, June 15, 2014 at 10:44P.M. CDT)*

"HALLOWED BE THY NAME"
From my heart to yours

To ask, "What does Jesus have to offer me", to be fair, needs to be met by and contrasted with the other question, which is, "What do I have to offer Him." Since He has become a fair and free target for all to practice with, the above pair of questions still remains for the most part unanswered. So the world ups the ante against Him by taking words such as "holy", "Jesus", and "Jesus Christ" among others, and attached them to what is demeaning and derogatory, and "wasted" thinking. I always wondered why people don't use someone else's name, like Buddha, or the other guy whose name starts with 'M', or Hari Krishna. Oh, I'm not blaming the world for such practices at all, for that's to be expected. I am definitely wondering, however, about those who call themselves "Christians" and their verbal practices. And a bar of soap won't do the job at all. *(Sunday, June 15, 2014 at 11:17P.M. CDT)*

THINKING ABOUT THE WOMAN WHO WAS "CAUGHT"
From my heart to yours

Unlike today's churches with the "refined" facade, Jesus seemed to always attract the fallen, lonely, abused, suspect, hated, shattered, lowly, dirty, pathetic, sick, demon-possessed, thirsty, hungry, distant, ashamed, and the rest of those who aren't allowed to enter without a name brand attached to them. Was He hungry for attention or fame? Was He deluded somehow? Did He

not attend the seminar called "How to Make Friends and Influence People"? Was He suffering from some social stigma that associated Him with such crowd of societal rejects? In fact, that's exactly the crowd for whom He came. For they had no meaning in life and He gave them one. Others came to Him because no one else would receive them unconditionally. And others were shunned by the in-crowd and the social elite that He became their refuge from the human storms that raged against them and decimated their very soul. But, Why would He take such risk? Why would he shun the high and mighty? Why would He stop the show at the touch of the hem of His garment? Why would He seek no one's affection or attention to feel "complete"? Why did He not cow down to the Pharisaic enticements? Was He blind or deaf? The answer is in fact a resounding "YES". That's exactly His state of being while on earth. This is what Isaiah's prophecy said: "Who is blind but my servant, and deaf like the messenger I send? Who is blind like the one in covenant with me, blind like the servant of the Lord? You have seen many things, but you pay no attention; your ears are open, but you do not listen." (Isaiah 42:19, 20 NIV) What does this mean? It means that a true follower of Jesus Christ is someone who categorically turns a deaf ear to the ways and system of the world, and has a passionate single-mindedness to doing the pleasure of Him who died and rose again for me, for us, for anyone who has an ear to hear. Caught by "them", but set free by "Him". And that's another reason why I love Him so.
(Monday, June 16, 2014 at 12:03A.M. CDT)

OBEDIENCE, NOT SLAVERY
From my heart to yours

Obedience is the twin sister of faith. It's a paradox and all too true. Faith without Obedience is emotionalism. Obedience without faith is legalism. Both lack life when alone. Neither can happen without the administration of the Holy Spirit and the attraction of Jesus Christ. But when they come together in the heart of the true follower of Jesus Christ, some amazing things begin to happen. Things ... - like: "being free indeed"; - like: "loving Him from a pure heart"; - like: "loving one another unconditionally"; - like: "keeping his commandments that give life and discernment"; - like: "learning and having the mind of Christ"; - like: "facing evil with good"; - like: "passionate love for His Word"; - like: "longing to spend time with Him"; - like: "doing my utmost for His highest"; - like: "standing alone without being lonely"; - like: "learning to fly when life is nothing but dark". Like I said, some amazing things happen when faith and obedience come together in Him. Why? Because it's All about Him. And that's another reason why I love Him so! *(Monday, June 16, 2014 at 12:19A.M. CDT)*

OBEDIENCE (UN)LIKE REBELLION
From my heart to yours

An obedient heart is like (and unlike) a rebellious heart. Here's how: 1. Both impact the person's life to the point of losing control. The obedient gives up control to the Holy Spirit in their life who leads, because of a promise, into all truth and to the glory of God

(John 14:26). The rebel heart gives up control to a devastating mindset that leaves behind summarily in the heart and mind a trail of total chaos without any sense of compass. 2. Both are directed toward God in their action, not people. The obedient heart says, "Yes my Lord, because I know you love me and desire to set me free" The rebel however says, "No God, you're trying to be my master to enslave me" (Rom. 1:21, 28). 3. Both are detectable. The obedient heart has an aroma and fragrance that is broadcast to all (Rom 16:19). The rebellious heart rejects God and invites others by example to do likewise (Rom. 1:32). 4. Both maintain inseparable friendships. An obedient heart is obedient to the Word of God and has fellowship that brings fruit and joy (Rom. 16:19), peace and communion (John 14). A rebellious heart causes divisions and is self-serving (Rom. 16:18). It leads to futility, foolishness of heart, sexual impurity, lies, deception, unnatural conduct, greed, envy, murder, strife, conceit, malice, gossip, slander, disobedience to parents, no true mercy, and no capacity for love of God (Rom. 1). 5. Both impact the character of a person indefinitely. An obedient heart is not satisfied with the relevance, but seeks after excellence of Jesus Christ. The rebellious heart knows and intentionally dismisses and rejects the significance and preeminence of Jesus Christ (Rom. 1:21). 6. Both target the truth, not people. The obedient heart wants to know it in real life practically. The rebellious heart attempts to "lock up" the truth and build barriers to knowing it. (Rom. 1:18). 7. Both impact a wider circle. Not an exhaustive list but a starter: the self-life, relationships, home, children, marriage, society, and culture with increasing darkness and chaos with time. But, God can make a way for the rebel heart to come home, and He did. Jesus said, "I am the way, the truth, even the life." *(Monday, June 16, 2014 at 9:39A.M. CDT)*

COMMISSION SNAPSHOT
From my heart to yours

He did not say, "You will come back" when He said, "Go" *(Tuesday, June 17, 2014 at 12:26A.M. CDT)*

LOVE HELD BACK
From my heart to yours

Even Jesus could not have accomplished anything, or shown his love toward us if He was not willing to obey. But He intentionally chose to yield and surrender His will. His obedience became the door through which all the love of the Father flowed toward us in all its glory on the cross of Calvary. None compares or comes close! John said "Behold what manner of love the Father has bestowed upon us ..." (1Jn 4:1) So, when Paul said "I have been crucified with Christ", he was simply saying "I have submitted myself wholeheartedly to His will, and determined to obey for His love to flow through me to everyone around me and to the world". Amazing love! Amazing Savior! And that's another reason why I love Him so. *(Tuesday, June 17, 2014 at 10:41A.M. CDT)*

WE DON'T REALLY BELIEVE
From my heart to yours

Although we know better, we often stay busy with religious activity thinking it's a sufficient substitute to these five anchors. We may offer lip service, but we really don't believe in their power almost whatsoever. These five things are: 1. The Power of the Living Word of God - that it is so alive that it speaks to the heart directly when the person reads or hears it. It is so alive that the Holy Spirit can give spiritual understanding and show the person what to do and how to live and respond. We Christians don't put too much confidence in that and feel we need to explain for the person to understand. But the fact is that without the Spirit giving illumination, the person remains in total spiritual darkness regardless. He maybe all dressed up and smelling good, but the heart is darkened. 2. The Power of the Holy Spirit - His Person, His Presence, and His Working. The fact IS that without the clear working of the Holy Spirit nothing, nada, can be accomplished or even started without Him. Nothing can bring glory to Christ without Him. No understanding or direction without Him. No unity or fellowship without Him. No prayer or song is heard or acceptable before the throne of grace without Him. And so much more. We don't believe in the absolute and sovereign movement of the Holy Spirit. 3. The Power of Prayer - the missing jewel in the church. It was Prayer that brought about revivals throughout church history. It was Prayer that brought sinners to their knees before God in true confession and repentance. It was Prayer that united the church and "the place shook" when the Spirit descended in response. It was Prayer that moved heaven to respond to the people of God. We don't believe in that Prayer. 4.

The Power of Spiritual Warfare - as if the church is so totally oblivious to this reality. Jesus lived in this reality. The early church lived in this reality. Discernment was cultivated and all hell broke loose attempting to destroy the church, but failed and The Gospel of Christ was preached throughout the known world in less than 60 years. We don't believe in such power, and prefer a watered down version where only self-confidence will do, and having the right positive attitude is good enough. 5. The Power of Sin - it's not mistake or fault. It's not error or slip-up. It's not failure or misrepresentation. It's not lapse of judgment. It's called SIN. To us it may not matter much, but it was the very thing that drilled the nails into the hands of the Son of God, the very thing that brought Him to earth, the very thing that shattered everything from man toward God for time and forever. It brings down the high and mighty, the rich and poor, and throughout history its casualties cover the landscape. And if it were not for the very power of the Spirit of God, even Jesus the Son of Man would have fallen as well. But Thank God that Jesus surrendered His will and His whole being into the hands of Him who is all-powerful, and through Him we now have through our complete surrender the only possibility of reconciliation with God, and confidence to live for Him and do His pleasure. So He calls upon us to "present our bodies a living sacrifice..." It's All about Him! It's heartbreaking when the church is not awake enough to these realities, and lacks insight into what really matters. *(Tuesday, June 17, 2014 at 11:58P.M. CDT)*

My Funny Mom, My Praying Mom
From my heart to yours

While sitting at the doctor's office, she asked me how I was, if I'm getting tired, if anything is hurting, if my head was ok, and a host of questions. So I said, I think I'm losing my mind slowly because I feel my brain is getting less and less. She laughed and cautioned me not to joke like that. She assured me that much praying is being done on my behalf. She said, literally translated, "what would you do with all the prayers chasing you?! My Mom has become so skilled that she leaves imprints without even noticing. And I thought, with a sense of urgency, of passing the same question to you, "Do you have someone in your life whose prayers are chasing you?" If not, pray, Pray, that you have one. For the prayer of even one avails much. I'm learning that I can almost do without everything. But prayer is desperately needed without ceasing! The Right prayer gets the right attention of the right person! The rest is simply details. May we always pray saying, "Father, I surrender my will completely because my desire is that "Thy will be done on earth as it is in heaven." *(Thursday, June 19, 2014 at 2:50P.M. CDT)*

Bearable Burdens
From my heart to yours

"Take my yoke upon you and learn from me ... For my yoke is easy and my burden is light." (Matt 11) As statements of fact: 1. Burdens are to be expected. 2. There is no "No Burdens" option for anyone. 3. "Prosperity thinking" and "you-don't-get-because

of-little-faith" thinking is a flat lie. God doesn't play games. 4. Burdens are certain to come, and are individualized. 5. Some burdens come because of the nature of things. Other burdens we ask for (as if we don't have enough). But, first things first. The key word in Matt. 11 is not "burdens" or "yoke" or "take". The central word that really matters is the pronoun "MY", repeated three times. Jesus wishes to distinguish for His followers between "HIS" burden and ALL other sources of burden. The yoke is placed over the necks of animals who are plowing a field; i.e., animals who are being useful. Carrying, pulling loads of responsibility to finish the course, holding things steady for the duration, are all part of the yoke over the neck. The yoke requires submissive attitude of the heart, readiness to serve regardless, whole-hearted willingness, cooperation in teams, focused until accomplished, and stamina/endurance/tenacity in service is the nature of the light burden of Jesus Christ. The other burdens/yokes, though cautioned against, are not covered under the "light burden" category. But even then, when a person yields to the Lordship of Christ, his/her burdens take on a different character and become covered by Him who "bore our sins on a tree". And the same burdens become the anvil on which He bends us and shapes us to be instruments of mercy and grace to His glory alone. And that's another reason why I love Him so.
(Thursday, June 19, 2014 at 5:20P.M. CDT)

MY MOM WHEN SHE HURTS
From my heart to yours

We grow up in life universally somehow with the conviction demonstrated again and again that mothers don't experience pain in any form. They are invincible, indefatigable, indestructible, a cross between the Energizer Bunny (who keeps going and going) and Timex (that takes a licking and keeps on ticking). They don't need hardly any sleep or slumber, all-knowing in matters of life, relations, language, etiquette, and illness, allergies, good cooking, and all the social graces that qualify them for high diplomatic positions. They somehow intuitively and genetically acquired negotiation skills, and have the capacity to communicate even with children when children don't say a word. They know the intentions of their children's hearts and can tell what troubles them from hearing a sample of their vocal inflection. Moms are amazing indeed. However, yesterday I had to take my Mom urgently to the doctor because of excruciating pain all over her back, so much so that the pain brought tears to her eyes and consistent audible groans with little explanation as to the cause. Strangely enough, my first thought was: "This is so unlike her. She's not supposed to feel pain!" After obtaining proper medication and started taking it right away, she fell sound asleep, not sure if from fatigue or hurting too much or the meds taking effect. This morning, not expecting much improvement so quickly, I walked into her room. She was sitting on the side of her bed, looking like she just finished a triathlon, totally wiped out and not much better since the day before. I sat beside her without a word, and wrapped my arm around her shoulder and tucked her in. She laid her head on my chest and with muffled tone she mumbled something that was several syllables and words but I didn't understand any of it, and didn't ask, but I knew she was really hurting. Then she stayed there for few minutes. And suddenly two thoughts slipped into my conscious mind unnoticed. The first was that our roles have been reversed, and at 88, understandably so. But the second thought gripped me deep in my soul. And it's that we have a Heavenly Father to whom we can go anytime, lay our head on his chest and mumble all we want and need. Our painful expressions can be as unintelligible as we please; yet He will stay right there with us. For "the Spirit helps our infirmities with groaning that cannot be uttered." (Rom 8) And when we pray, the admonition from the Lord was to go into our private room (space), and "close the door and pray to the Father (not the creator so as to highlight awesomeness) - but to 'our Father' and He will provide an answer." I always wondered about the details: why "close the door"? Why 'Father'? Why "your room"? Could it be the PRESENCE? Could it be the INTIMACY? Could be the PERSONAL part that no one else comprehends? As the line from a song says: *"No one understands like Jesus When the days are dark and grim. No one is so near, so dear as Jesus; Cast Your every care on Him."* I cherish more today the simple reality of God as Father who wraps his arm around my shoulder and lets me come close, to listen to his heartbeat, and lets me mumble and mumble away. Ps 27:10 "Even when my father and mother forsake me, The Lord holds me close and takes me in." And that's another reason why I love Him so. *(Friday, June 20, 2014 at 12:13P.M. CDT)*

Seven things that Impress and move God
From my heart to yours

- Serving the insignificant (Mt 10:42)

- Pure and faultless religion (Jas 1:27)

- Those who bless His holy Name (Lk 19:38-40)

- Someone who approaches Him with a pure heart (Mt 19:14)

- A sinner who places his glory at Jesus' feet (Mt 26:6-13)

- Spending quiet time in the Presence of One who knows everything (Mt 6:6)

- A broken spirit and a contrite heart (Ps 51:17) *(Saturday, June 21, 2014 at 9:40A.M. CDT)*

On Knowing God
From my heart to yours

Knowing God so well and His closeness being so real make the miraculous look normal, and not a priority at all. For He's always been the audience of One, and what the heart is fixed upon. *(Saturday, June 21, 2014 at 10:32A.M. CDT)*

TAKING A SIESTA
From my heart to yours

It irks me when I think of the disciples irked by the Master for being asleep during the storm, and they were asleep when the Master was in labor in Gethsemane...until I look in the mirror and realize that many times I did the same thing they did. Practicing His Presence teaches me when to hush when He's quiet, and when to scream steadfastly toward Him who hears during agony. For in quietness He speaks louder and during agony he's in full control because He surrendered completely and had nothing to lose any longer. *(Saturday, June 21, 2014 at 10:42A.M. CDT)*

CONFUSED ABOUT VISIONS
From my heart to yours

I was wondering before laying my head down to sleep, in light of Acts 13:1-6, why Paul and Barnabas while serving with the Church at Antioch, didn't have a plethora of creative visions similar to what we hear about these days in abundance. Could it be that they obeyed the Jerusalem church leaders and went (first class ground transportation) to Antioch to "encourage the brethren"? Could it be that they were so busy when they got to Antioch in "ministering and fasting together" that they had no time for so-called "visions" a la the too commonly heard talked about these days -- "God gave me a great vision" crowd? Could it be that Paul and Barnabas were working together at the local level first before going global? Could it be that they didn't have their sights on the distant and better attention-getter projects? Could it be that they were training their inner ears to really listen to the whispering voice of the Holy Spirit of God first? Could it be that they practiced yielding to one another? Could it be that they were making sure they were learning to serve in one accord, first? The burden to take the Gospel message was so strong and heavy, in fact, that on two occasions at least they looked outside their local border, and desired genuinely to go to Galatia and elsewhere, but "the Spirit forbade them" and, Alas! they recognized the voice of the Spirit and obeyed, and did not go. They obeyed and did NOT take the Gospel message to whom they thought needed to hear it. Why? Perhaps they knew the part of discerning the voice of the Holy Spirit and the fact that "to obey the Lord is more important than sacrificial service to Him." In other words, listening to the Lord was of greater and of paramount value and worth than the proverbially pithy notion of "needing to share the gospel with someone lost", or "reaching the lost for Jesus", as if Jesus needs us to really "reach the lost", as if His incarnation wasn't enough, and forgetting that even if someone rose from the dead they won't believe if they refused the inspired and living and powerful Word that they can read or hear. I have a hunch that we got a few things backwards. God help us! How did Paul and Barnabas, and the church at Antioch, accomplish their mission so successfully? It is very likely that they simply took the "vision" that Jesus had and immersed their whole being in it! And it is very likely that they were consistently bowing at the true altar of God, and were counted among "the 7000 who did not bow a knee to Baal", and definitely did not bow at the altar of mammon (more affectionately known today as "money"). Thanks to the workout and carry-out service offered by brother Ananias and sparkling

Sister Sapphira! Even Jesus knew the danger, and warned saying, "No one can serve two masters, God and Mammon." Visions were few back then. They surely had plenty of persecution which scattered them like fanning the flames of revival and the Gospel spread naturally. Maybe, just maybe, that's why they reached the known world back then with the powerful Gospel of Jesus Christ, and without Facebook, I might add :). Maybe, just maybe, persecution is what the church needs today, even in America and other comfort zones. *(Sunday, June 22, 2014 at 12:38A.M. CDT)*

THE GOOD DENOMINATION
From my heart to yours

I wonder which denomination Jesus would join these days and be voted as President of. I have a hunch that some may not want Him to get His hands dirty in the day-to-day business, so they will likely nominate Him to be "ex-officio" president. Btw, the independence declared by the "Independents" group doesn't qualify them to be any different, because by thinking that they are separate and different, they have become just another group, just like the rest. *(Sunday, June 22, 2014 at 12:57A.M. CDT)*

GPS NOT NECESSARY
From my heart to yours

Heaven is a destination by invitation for life. Hell is a "Dead End" destination, not of but by choice. Q: Does a person go to heaven or hell? A: Yes Q: Is there a third option? A: No GPS in that direction. *(Monday, June 23, 2014 at 6:43A.M. CDT)*

Forgiveness Snapshot
From my heart to yours

True forgiveness always has a price, and it's always paid by the one forgiving. Even when God forgives, God pays. *(Monday, June 23, 2014 at 6:44A.M. CDT)*

All-Sufficient
From my heart to yours

The word of God is the only true and sure foundation for life, whether it is personal life, family life, or church life. That is why it was inspired; It was empowered; and it is alive. It speaks life; It leads to maturity; and it has no alternative. *(Monday, June 23, 2014 at 7:14A.M. CDT)*

Smart Praying
From my heart to yours

If you have ever wondered how you can easily spend hours in prayer, here is a thought. Most everyone who has a smartphone has pictures and video clips on them. Most if not all are of people you know and places where you have been. While you are waiting at a red light or standing in line somewhere, or taking a break with a cup of coffee, consider browsing through the pictures you have one at a time very slowly and praying for each one because they are of people you know and care about and love. Consider thanking God for them individually and praying that God would bless them. Pray for them that God would strengthen them in difficulty, comfort them in sadness, use them to his glory, guide them when they are confused, open their eyes to see him, give them understanding of this word, protect them from evil in the world, protect them from the evil one, and give you an opportunity to share the love of Christ with them, and grant them discernment when they have a choice to make. If it is a family, pray that they will have healthy relationships within the family and with those outside, pray that they will look to him in difficulties or challenges, pray that God will have mercy on them when they fall in temptation, that they will have a listening ear and an obedient heart, and that God will make them a blessing to others. You love them, right? Pray for the marriage relationship to be strong and that the home will be protected from the evil one. Pray that the children will not be affected by the evil that is in the world, that God will protect them from wrong friendships, and that they will come to the knowledge of Jesus Christ as Savior and Lord. We spend hours and days and weeks and years over a lifetime waiting and waiting and waiting. Can we take advantage of the time we are waiting and pray for the loved ones that we have in these pictures that we carry? The question is, do we love them enough to pray for them with our whole heart? We will discover that our anxiety and stress level is down and that we are doing the right thing. Let's love them by praying for them. God replies to all wireless and tireless communications from His children. I always wondered what's so smart about taking pictures! *(Monday, June 23, 2014 at 8:45A.M. CDT)*

THERE IS NO SUCH THING (1 OF 4)
From my heart to yours

There is a deceptive tendency that seeps into my conscious mind that tricks me into thinking after simply attending an uplifting spiritual event, or spending a weekend at what has been labeled "A Spiritual Retreat", that I AM (have suddenly and instantly become) a mature believer. THERE IS NO SUCH THING. To have such thoughts is one of the most insidious illusions from Satan's pernicious warehouse of deceptive fallacies. He intends in all actions to be ambiguous, delusive, cunning, and desiring to lead Christians onto a slippery slope of self-righteous sanctification, seducing some, and if possible, all. No wonder why more than one finding point to 72% of so-called "evangelical Christians" have doubts and questions about their faith, and 76% among the 20-something evangelical crowd. God Help and have mercy on us ! Paul said: "But you did not learn Christ like that." How do we counter that mindset and serpentine deception? That's coming up in part 2. *(Tuesday, June 24, 2014 at 3:19A.M. CDT)*

"I'M BLESSED". REALLY?
From my heart to yours

Here's what I mean by that oft' abused affirmation: 1. I cultivate a perpetually grateful lifestyle and attitude. 2. I must decrease and

He must increase. So I acknowledge Him always. His name is Jesus Christ. He has no Facebook page but There is glory in His Face and sheer Awesomeness in His Book. He is very personable when one gets to know Him. His address is: 1 Mount Calvary, Grace Toll Road (its toll is His blood, Prepaid). 3. I seek to become a blessing to others, especially the annoying ones. He always wins. 4. I forget pursuing pleasing people and pursue Christ. People can be unintentionally deceptive but Christ will always be receptive. 5. I steadily look for God's fingerprints in my life. If they're not there, He ain't there either. 6. I passionately share what He means to me all the days of my life. 7. I longingly wait for His appearing. I really miss Him, and can't wait to see Him again. The first time He stole my heart away. Now, "He restores my soul". Next time I see Him, as the song says: "What a day that will be, When my Jesus I shall see, And I look upon His face, The One who saved my by His grace, And forever I will be, With the One who died for me, What a day, glorious day, that will be." Are you waiting for Him? What do you mean when you say that you are blessed? *(Tuesday, June 24, 2014 at 4:10A.M. CDT)*

THERE IS NO SUCH THING (2 OF 4)
From my heart to yours
(Kindly read part 1 first to get the complete picture.)

Living a life of seemingly satisfactory but actually Wishful-Thinking-Christianity will bring down such life every time, and will decimate beautiful lives intended to worship and adore a wonderful Savior and Lord. The Holy Spirit does not desire for things to be so at any time. Here is some evidence: 1. Eph. 4:20.

Ongoing learning of Christ is expected of every true follower of Christ. 2. Eph. 6:11. Spiritual warfare is dangerous, difficult, demanding, and at times daunting and draining to the best of the best. 3. Gen 3:4-5. Satan offers counterfeit promises to rule the masses outside the will of God. 4. 1 Peter 5:8. We're called upon to be vigilant continually. 5. James 4:7-10. We are to continually resist Satan. So, what should I do? How can I really live such "life in Christ"? Paul said, "For you died, and your life is now hidden with Christ in God." (Colossians 3:3). How can that be a true daily reality in my life? Is there such a thing? Emphatically, YES. (Please go to part 3). *(Tuesday, June 24, 2014 at 4:21A.M. CDT)*

STRADDLING A FENCE OF OUR OWN MAKING
From my heart to yours

John the Apostle admonished followers of Jesus Christ saying, "Do not love the world or anything in the world. If anyone loves the world, love for the Father is not in them." (1 John 2:15) The lines are clearly drawn in the sand stating position and consequences. No doubt or question as to intent! Attempting to love the Father without hating the world (not people, but system and mindset, principles and practices) is the "Modus Operandi" (method of operation) of a confused and fruitless life, presumed to be "in Christ" but is more like "in trouble", presumed by a person to be "in the Spirit" but confused as to which spirit is in control, because it straddles a fence of our own making, and casting a shadow that grows with time as the sun sets. The fact remains that only the Spirit of Christ has the capacity to enable us to live the balanced life of loving people with the love of God without hesitation or doubt. The question is not "What kind of person I ought to love" but "Am I being loved daily by Him who died for me so I can love others, even the enemies"? *(Tuesday, June 24, 2014 at 5:12A.M. CDT)*

THERE IS NO SUCH THING (3 OF 4)
From my heart to yours
(Kindly read parts 1 and 2 first to get the complete picture.)

The heartbeat of a true follower of Christ is OBEDIENCE. It's the norm of living in His Kingdom. It sustains a balanced life as we, as Paul said, "put on Christ" (Rom 13:14 and Gal 3:27). A true believer is characterized as a "child of obedience" (1 Peter 1:14-15; John 14:15). So, simply put: If No Obedience, Forget It ! The "balanced life" is two-fold, and like a coin has indispensable two sides. It is internal and external, one pertains to my person and the other pertains to others. It crowds Satan Out, and passionately yields to the Spirit of Christ exclusively. I am to practice both, and cannot do one without the other. That is living in the reality of what has been variously described as: 1. "walking with God" 2. "Learning Christ" 3. "Standing firm" 4. "Walking in the Spirit" . . . and other such expressions that, in principle, are saying the same thing. Such life experiences practically what Jesus prayed saying: "Now this is eternal life: that they know you, the only true God, and Jesus Christ, whom you have sent. (John 17:3 NIV) Such life enables every follower of Jesus to experience the Unity, Fellowship, and Love found in the Father, Son, and Spirit (John 17:20-23, 26 NIV) While the list below is not exhaustive, it is a good start. If never done before, taking one item per week, cultivates a life and gives the Holy Spirit and me the time to experience and yield to Him more each day. Here are a few items:

1. Spending time alone in the presence of God, and no one else. Dedicating silent time away from noise and asking God to speak to your heart. If need be, this can be in a crowd, speaking less and listening more.
2. Serving God behind the scenes by discerning areas of need and by serving others with the fewest people knowing, if any.
3. Living frugally and fasting frequently. Depriving self of excesses makes room for discipline to be the norm in life.
4. Living sacrificially beyond giving normally. Giving self to God is first prerequisite before sacrificial giving to others.
5. Voluntarily, as couples, agree to abstain from intimate pleasures for a season to spend more time and grow deeper in affection to God alone in purity and adoration of His majesty and glory.
6. Delighting and meditating in the Word of God, and discovering its value and significance to my life. It gives needed daily nourishment and strength to the soul and mind, and keeps the heart longing for more.
7. Practice the art of worship in the Presence of the King of kings by reading psalms, and singing songs from the hymnal, by keeping praise on your lips and in your heart, by delighting in Him with words of joy and honor to the Majesty on high, by speaking before Him words of thankfulness for his ever presence in your life and how gracious and merciful He has been, by declaring his

governorship and sovereignty on your life, your home, and all details of your existence.

8. Praying without ceasing. Speaking with and listening to God, seeking His guidance and wisdom in all areas of your life, interceding on behalf of others especially whom you love unconditionally, and whom you have difficulty loving.

9. Confessing and Repenting! Agreeing with God's Spirit what He revealed to your obedient heart, hating sin passionately, acknowledging His sacrifice on the cross that keeps on cleansing and purifying my heart. Ask God without delay to reveal any hidden sin in your life for He alone is able to show it and to hide it underneath the blood of Calvary.

10. Forgiving without delay. If we don't forgive others, God will withhold fellowship from me and my daily life shrivels to nothingness. Holding grudge is a vicious monster that creeps in later years when life's restraints are lax and objectivity becomes just a dictionary word.

11. Experiencing the true "one-another-ness". True fellowship is the dynamic, true, interactive, and targeted caring and sharing in the Body of Christ, the Church. As there is no substitute to a real human encounter in person, there can never be completeness in service to others in the Church. (Please go to part 4). *(Tuesday, June 24, 2014 at 6:27A.M. CDT)*

THERE IS NO SUCH THING (4 OF 4)
From my heart to yours
(Kindly read parts 1, 2, and 3 first to get the complete picture.)

It's very important to keep things in perspective and balanced. The balance in the universe around us or the universe within us (the macro and the micro) resonate with balance. Here's an example: If you can imagine the entire interstate system, from California to Maine to Florida, the major and minor highways, the exits and businesses on the sides of the roads, the trucks loaded with various goods they carry. Now think of accidents here and there with goods that don't make it to destinations or worse yet they get deposited at wrong locations, follow the systematic deliveries or chaos that takes place few times. Think of the laws and rules that govern trucks and weights and quality of goods, and how they are designed for different types of content and how they travel exact distances before making a turn and then another to reach correct destination. Think of the machinery and mechanisms regulating cargo and deliveries like clock-work, taking exact loads specific distances and handing them over to someone else. Get the Picture? NOW....... Shrink this WHOLE picture to fit - not inside one region or state or one city or even inside one person, but inside the cells of the human body to be exact, and you will have what's been called the "Vesicle Transport System" that's been characterized by scientists as "a major and essential transport system in our cells". It operates round the clock transporting proteins and other items specific distances and making proper turns along the highways inside each cell, making room for each other to pass without crashing, and depositing specific amounts in their proper respective locations to provide proper balanced growth at the macro and micro levels, and keep the body balanced. They carry correct instructions for the major systems of the body (nervous system, digestive system, etc.) to communicate and allow passage of the cargo being carried. An example of the cargo is insulin that keeps the sugar balanced. If the destination gets an overload then there is too much sugar and diabetes kicks in and requires treatment. And so on, and so on. Likewise is our spiritual life and relationship with God on a personal level or within the church, which is interestingly called, Alas! "The Body" of Christ. Shall we worship now or later, or all our life, Him who is too awesome to comprehend, yet loving enough to desire to reveal Himself to us and love us so. Isn't He awesome? Rejecting God's perspective on things in matters of growth and usefulness leaves us to experience chaos day after day and at all levels. His desire is to bring order and realignment with His purpose behind creating us. So, He took it upon Himself to recreate us in the image of His Son, My Lord, My Savior, My Jesus. William Featherston in 1864 at the age of 16 penned these words: 'My Jesus, I love Thee, I know Thou art mine; For Thee all the follies of sin I resign; My gracious Redeemer, my Saviour art Thou; If ever I loved Thee, my Jesus, 'tis now.' I urge you to gain or regain perspective, balance, and maturity day by day actionable steps toward Him. Paul said, So Christ himself gave ..., to equip his people for works of service, so that the body of Christ may be built up until we all reach unity in the faith and in the knowledge of the Son of God and become mature, attaining to the whole measure of the fullness of Christ. (Ephesians 4:11ff). Believe me when I say that this is yet another reason why I love Him so. *(Tuesday, June 24, 2014 at 12:32P.M. CDT)*

GLOBAL DESIRE

From my heart to yours

Millions around the world feel compelled to go somewhere for CLEANSING. But they have to go back again and again. They call it a ceremony, and are never sure they are cleansed until the day they die. That's sad! But, There is a fountain filled with blood Drawn from Emmanuel's veins; and sinners plunged beneath that flood Lose all their guilty stains. His name is Jesus. He came so we can be sure. He died so we can live. He tired so we can rest. He satisfied our hunger and quenched our thirst. He left heaven so we can have a home. He lost so we can gain. He walked alone so we can never be alone again. He emptied Himself so we can be filled forever! That's another reason why I love Him so! Precious Name, Oh how sweet! Hope of earth, and joy of heav'n. *(Wednesday, June 25, 2014 at 4:22A.M. CDT)*

AMAZING SAVIOR

From my heart to yours

She may have touched his feet totally broken, humiliated, alone, filthy, and filled with despair. But, He washed her clean, adopted her, mended her broken spirit, lifted her face, joined her into His family as many from every tribe and nation, clothed her with His righteousness, and..... For the first time, she felt whole again. His name is Jesus! *(Wednesday, June 25, 2014 at 4:28A.M. CDT)*

Faithful Unknown
From my heart to yours

Everyone knows Oswald Chambers, claimed by many to have written MY UTMOST FOR HIS HIGHEST, and 35+ other books. But in fact, he did not write any of them. Gertrude, his wife, who was skilled with exceptional shorthand ability of 275 words per minute, sat at the back of the room for their seven years of marriage and transcribed every single word that came out of mouth, before he died of appendicitis at 43. After mourning her husband's death, she spent the following 45+ years compiling her beloved husband's books that blessed millions around the world. She agreed to compile the books on the condition that her name will never appear on any, giving all glory to God. She said, as sure as she was that God called her husband to his years in ministry, God called her too to this ministry. She just had to wait a few years. The devotional book that blessed millions is still in publication since 1927; has been translated to 39 languages; and it's all because one person was willing to place herself on the altar and fade away so that the glory of Christ is shown, and His Wonderful name is made known. Are you willing to wait for God to use you when He gets ready? Are you willing to remain an "unknown" for the rest of your life, but known to God? Are you willing to place all you have on the altar for Him? The real question is: Do you love Him? His name is Jesus! *(Wednesday, June 25, 2014 at 4:45A.M. CDT)*

RELEVANCE RELATIVE TO RELATIONSHIP
From my heart to yours

Serving social causes deserves dedication of a lifetime because there are so many ailments at every level in society, and more surfacing daily. Did Christ fail then? Or He had his "agenda" and we have ours today. Many in evangelical circle are really confused, not about issues of religion but about relevance of Jesus Christ. It's the relevance of Jesus Christ that's being questioned not in the "main air-conditioned building" but in the street and coffee shop and home, so much so that statistics over the past few years have vacillated between 70-72% of adults and 74-76% of 20-something having serious questions about faith. While the religious establishment got it down to a science -- meeting at certain traditional times, being dismissed with decorum after precisely 60 programming minutes, relaxing on comfy seats, and getting lulled into religious oblivion with routine clichés and calm objectivity -- the number of those asking for more is definitely on the rise, more that gives the person reasons why he/she should even remotely consider Jesus Christ even an a viable option. The reaction of a growing number is bordering on violent. More ex-church attenders are categorically opposed to this face-value acceptance of religion, verbally abusive in their attacks against what they classified as "established religion", relationally dismissive to those who hold on to religion and religious practices for no apparent reason than a presumed eternal fire policy. And the church and its congregants seem to take the attitude of "oh well, I'm here and they're there." But Jesus was clearly labeled by the establishment as "lover of publicans and sinners." They may have been dismissed out of heaven, and it appears in Jesus that heaven came down to look seriously into this matter. Without flinching, he (Jesus) had it figured out quick-like, and decided to scribble on the ground when needed, and to sit in the modest coffee shops of the rejects and the riffraff of society and speak life to them. He said, "if anyone desires to be my disciple and follow me, he must deny himself." His impact was not that he didn't know the routine or the program, for he most certainly did. It was that he came to remind the establishment that HE is, and is above, the program itself, and no one can graduate if he/she does not have love. Real relevance is what Jesus is all about. The opposite of relevance is not "religion", but Tolerance. So the question is not whether I accept everyone else, but whether I accept Him, who He really is and claims to be. *(Thursday, June 26, 2014 at 2:54P.M. CDT)*

Long Overdue Debt
From my heart to yours

I'm finding in my life that I'm regularly behind on paying debts of gratitude. Here is one: Lauren Swindle, a very dear sister who in recent years has been coming to our church conference and volunteering to help out. I'm deeply thankful to God for her impeccably transparent attitude to serve from a pure heart; ready to serve wherever she is asked, redefining the term "flexibility". Her smile is genuine and infectious, her gentle spirit is precious, discerning opportunities to step in and help, serving alone if asked and also works with teams beautifully, a true ambassador for Christ with different age groups and willing to learn what can be done to serve Christ better. In a recent post on her FB page, a friend of hers expressed gratitude for Lauren's walking with her through many experiences as her friend was in graduate school. I had to pause for a moment because I realized that Lauren is like that whenever and wherever, which is true Christlikeness indeed. Thank you Lauren SO much. You are an honorary member of our Birmingham church, but we're already members in His Family into which He adopted us. Please know that many in our church expressed how thankful they are as well for your selfless serving attitude. We love you! I want to invite others as well to wish you every blessing on your major life decision and for the rest of your life. *(Thursday, June 26, 2014 at 8:45P.M. CDT)*

TRUE PASSION
From my heart to yours

The passion of Christ was to do the will of the Father. His success at the end was because He lived daily a surrendered life from the beginning. Thus, He had nothing to lose and everything to gain. What made this a reality in His life was the effective full domination of the eternal Spirit in His life, through whom He cried out day and night, and birthed us according to the Father's heart, and was able to truly love us unto the end. Likewise, those who cultivate a passion to do His will, can succeed by complete surrender and realize that by losing all we stand to gain all in Christ. And by means of the eternal Spirit we too can cry out now and say, "Abba, Father", for His Father was made ours forever through Him. Passion cannot be measured with a cup. It does not come in units, like the filling of the Holy Spirit. (John 3:34). *(Friday, June 27, 2014 at 3:26A.M. CDT)*

Pain and Suffering
From my heart to yours

Prosecuting attorneys file lawsuits, and demand at times very large sums of money from the guilty party to compensate for "pain and suffering". Then they extract up to 50% of that amount to themselves at times "for services rendered", and relieve the client instantly up to 50% of their pain and suffering too. Oh, that doesn't sound right for some reason. It must be because it's a mere business transaction. I'm eternally thankful that Christ did not do business with us like that. Though I walk through the valley...thou art with me...all the days of my life...and I shall dwell in the house...of my defense attorney forever. Hallelujah! *(Friday, June 27, 2014 at 3:41A.M. CDT)*

Feeling Shame Is Not Good Enough
From my heart to yours

Imagine Jesus leaning close to the woman who was caught and brought to Him by the religious vultures of the day, and whispering in her ear, "How do you feel?". I'm inclined to think that He scribbled in the sand what was carved in His heart toward her...and us. Perhaps he scribbled...her new name He's going to give her soon. Perhaps he scribbled...glancing at the sands of time and affirmed His unflinching passion and obedience to the Father to finish the course. Perhaps, he scribbled "Father, I thank you for the love we have, and I desire to pour out that love toward her, exactly as you have loved me from the beginning." "I have made you known to them, and will continue to make you known in order that the love you have for me may be in them and that I myself may be in them." (John 17:26 NIV) He taught her heart to sing a new song. The words go something like this: "Oh, how I love Jesus, Oh how I love Jesus, Oh how I love Jesus, Because He first loved me." Do you know it?   *(Friday, June 27, 2014 at 4:14A.M. CDT)*

COMMUNITY IN MISERY
From my heart to yours

Looking on the brighter side, some the words that come to mind are: Individuality, Independence, Differentiating lines clearly drawn, Self-preservation, Despair, Life cycle, Circles of love, Family, Fear, Tunnels going nowhere, Stunning silence, Traditions, and others. There is room for more. There is Humanity in community, in misery, in need .... of a Savior. *(Friday, June 27, 2014 at 4:33A.M. CDT)*

SPIRITUAL "TERMS OF ENDEARMENT"
From my heart to yours

As I was having a delightful conversation with a dear friend one morning, this female voice behind me said, "Good morning, Baby Doll. Are you having a good morning? Will it be just two, Sweetheart?" I had to do a double take in total amazement at how silky the words slithered from her lips, and said, "Yes, two". She proceeded to seat us. We settled in our seats and continued our conversation, ignoring the smooth language we heard. She kept that artificial smile she plastered on her face earlier and said, "Wanna start with coffee and water, Babe?" And again, I turned looking at her in total shock at the smoothness and ease with which she communicated what, at best, I would label as definitely meaningless verbiage of what otherwise would naturally be intimate terms of endearment. Yet, with an air of familiarity, she continued with words that I kept very special for only one. Now I find that someone stole them and is using them to make her patrons comfortable and at home. I had to concede the quiet of a cemetery is friendlier than any meaning she attached to what she said. Then from a distance, I heard her again greet another guest of the restaurant saying, "oh, good morning, Baby doll. Will it be three for breakfast this morning?" And I concluded in my mind that intimate terms of endearment normally reserved for two who are passionate about each other, now have become tools, just tools, free to use to make people feel at home, and enjoy the offerings, but mean nothing whatsoever. Words that normally carry deep meaning, and reflect intimacy of the most sacred kind, yet while they flow just as easily, they indeed mean nothing, simply nothing at all. I had a sinking feeling and mused with my friend, how often we sing songs, repeat clichés intended for worship and adoration, containing intimate words of affection to our precious Lord and Savior, I wondered how often these words glide from our lips with almost profane glamour, slithery and smooth, giving a good impression and retaining a form of godliness but totally oblivious to the power and depth of meaning they carry. Next time we glance at a song book, Errrr, I meant the PowerPoint splashing with gorgeous religious scenes and inspirational colors blending me in a moment of euphoria, you will know what I mean. Yes, Jesus is the lover of my soul. The question is: "Does He know He's my "One and Only"? What'll it be for breakfast, Baby Doll?! "May the words of my mouth and this meditations of my heart be pleasing in your sight, LORD, my Rock and my Redeemer." (Ps 19:14). *(Saturday, June 28, 2014 at 7:35A.M. CDT)*

REVIVAL AND WORSHIP MISSING JEWELS
From my heart to yours

True revival, is not a timed event. It is a God-visitation of His people. While the lost are affected, the intended audience behind both is His people who are called by His Holy Name. True worship, simply put, is a lifestyle - always has been and always will be. There were and are attempts to corrupt it, but the followers of Christ are reminded of the real worship. And those who know not Christ are invited to it. Both groups are told whenever it happens that it happens in Spirit and truth. For the Spirit knows the deep things of both God and man, and makes a way in person and through the Person of Jesus Christ. So in the cross He reconciled us to God, and in His Person He enabled us to simply worship. I doubt there is anything else worth mentioning. So, in the cross I knew the immensity and ugliness of my sin, and in Christ I knew the immensity and glory of His love for me. And, that's another reason why I love Him so. *(Monday, June 30, 2014 at 11:20A.M. CDT)*

Passionate Living
From my heart to yours

Living a life that's passionate about Christ and His Church is not a daily decision and cannot be measured by deeds; nor is it assessed by any man-made units of measurement. So is the filling of the Holy Spirit. (John 3:34) Being passionate about us led Him to the cross. Being passionate about Him will very likely lead us to the same destination. A line from an old song says: "The way of the cross leads home / It is sweet to know, As I onward go / The way of the cross leads home". Assessing the world situation, I say, I'd rather be home with Him anytime than in any man-made mansion or superhighway. So, I pray as some have before, "Lord, don't let me remain here one day past my usefulness to you." *(Tuesday, July 1, 2014 at 2:08P.M. CDT)*

One Pure Passion Needed
From my heart to yours

Being passionate about people is no affirmation that I am passionate about Christ. It may, in fact, be a corrupted passion at times as it vacillates with my mood. But, I cannot be passionate about Christ without conveying that to people I come in contact with. For His love finds a way. The question is not: "Do I love people". The question is, "Do I love Him." And if He's the One asking me, I shouldn't be surprised if He asks it three times. He did it before, right? *(Tuesday, July 1, 2014 at 4:09P.M. CDT)*

VERY SPECIAL

From my heart to yours

What made the disciples of Jesus anything "special" was simply that "they were with Jesus". Even His enemies recognized them as such (Acts 4). To be anything else, even today, causes a shift in the center of gravity, which leads to a fall sooner or later. Praying today that our center of gravity never change. It's all about Him. *(Wednesday, July 2, 2014 at 8:39A.M. CDT)*

LOVE SUFFERS

From my heart to yours

I was arrested this morning and brought back to reality by the thought that I'm always tempted to love Him less. May it never ever be so ! *(Wednesday, July 2, 2014 at 9:00A.M. CDT)*

LIGHT TRANSMISSION

From my heart to yours

Satellites, regardless of brand, can be abbreviated as SAT. Just "SAT". They capture signals and relay signals, and always need maintenance then at times come crashing down. But the Light of the world can never be abbreviated or dimmed or blocked or slowed or interfered with or jammed or disrupted. His name is Jesus! And He is the same. (Isa 59:1). *(Wednesday, July 2, 2014 at 9:10A.M. CDT)*

NOT NETS
From my heart to yours

To leave fishing nets is not a real qualification to be a follower of Jesus. But to leave the nets that snare the heart and soul and mind of a person, now THAT's worth the mention and will definitely qualify anyone to be the follower of Jesus Christ, because it is the working of the Spirit of Christ. Why is that so critical? It is simply because the Spirit will enable a true follower of Christ then to love Him with his whole heart and mind and soul. And that is the first commandment. But it's not a commandment for people to enforce with people, but for the Spirit to lift us above human capabilities to realize as a possibility for everyone. Peter indeed left the nets, and made sure Jesus knew it. Peter had to leave ... uh... Peter. And that's what he was incapable of until he was filled with the Holy Spirit. To love Him is the essence of worship, and the sum total of the life of true pursuit of Christ. Peter had audacity. But Jesus had class ! And that's another reason why I love Him so. *(Wednesday, July 2, 2014 at 12:58P.M. CDT)*

WORD AND WORDS
From my heart to yours

John the beloved disciple introduced Jesus as the 'logos', meaning "Word". Then he writes, "The 'Word' became flesh" (John 1) When many disciples had second thoughts and left Him, Jesus asked His remaining disciples, "Will you go away too?" Peter replied, "To whom shall we go, Lord; you have the 'words' of eternal life" (the kind of life that never gets old, archaic, or needs upgrading or maintenance with time). (John 6:68-69) Word and words -- not singular and plural. Both, 'Word' and 'words', have become inextricably and permanently bonded into ONE. The Word is far beyond the parts. The parts are ever renewed to continually and eternally express the whole. So Jesus prayed, "And this is eternal life, that they may know you, the only true God, and Jesus Christ whom you have sent." (John 17:3) The words are contained in the Word. The details are within the bounds of the preeminent expression. So Paul says, "that in all things, He might have the preeminence" (Col. 1:18). The German word 'gestalt' refers to the 'whole' which is uniquely "more than the sum of its individual parts." All religions without exception had the impossible task of conveying the 'Word' with 'words'. That's man-made, and without exception, they failed. The reason is one: They could not get to the 'Word' on their own. So the 'Word' had to reveal Himself. No angel or archangel could comprehend. . . . . . Until, "the Word became flesh, and "tabernacled" among us, and we beheld his glory as the one-of-a-kind glory of the Son of God, full of grace and truth. And for the first time ever, Jesus came, and became ON EARTH the full expression ('Whole') in whom we have the compounded effects of life + eternality + truth + grace + humanity + Godhead + fullness + glory + majesty. And He is far more than the sum of the individual parts. To the jailed disciples, after the angel set them free, the angel said, "Go and tell all the 'words' of life". John combined the two concepts of the 'Word' and 'words' and said, (1 John 1:1) "That which was from the beginning, which we have heard, which we have seen with our eyes, and have gazed upon, and our hands have touched - this we proclaim ('words') concerning the 'Word' of life." In 1917, Frederick Lehman penned these words as he tried to describe only the "love of God": محبّة الله سَمَتْ "Could we with ink the ocean fill, And were the skies of parchment made, Were every stalk on earth a quill, And every man a scribe by trade; To write the love of God above Would drain the ocean dry; Nor could the scroll contain the whole, Though stretched from sky to sky." So, I bow in humble adoration, worship and sing: "I love you, Lord And I lift my voice To worship You Oh, my soul rejoice Take joy, my King In what You hear Let it be a sweet, sweet sound in Your ear". (*Wednesday, July 2, 2014 at 11:58P.M. CDT*)

TRUE POWER
From my heart to yours

What made the disciples of Jesus so "special" was not that they held on to Him by their might or power (self-righteousness), but that He was holding them up in prayer constantly before His Father. He said, "Holy Father, keep through your name those you have given me. . . I pray not for them alone but I pray for those who will believe in me through their word." (Jn 17). (*Thursday, July 3, 2014 at 12:10A.M. CDT*)

FIRE OR ICE

From my heart to yours

The actual prayer is, "Deliver us from temptation" NOT "Deliver us from persecution". In fact, the prayer for God to deliver someone from persecution could very well be inconsistent with His purposes. Hell is always uncomfortable. The prayer "Deliver us from persecution" has zero chance of being heard. In fact, Jesus promised his followers that persecution is one of the clear marks of being a true follower, and coming it will come. Fire is always the preferred method to purify gold. The question is not how hot the fire is, but rather what kind of metal we are made out of. *(Thursday, July 3, 2014 at 3:49A.M. CDT)*

BEARING WITNESS

From my heart to yours

Being a true witness to Jesus Christ is more important than being delivered from persecution. Hell will always file a complaint in the courts of heaven whenever one of its tenants gets ready to leave. Jesus said that He will build His Church, and the gates of hell shall not prevail against it. Hell tenants need not bother find a way out on their own. Jesus promised to get them out himself. He said, "I have other sheep that are not of this fold. I must bring them also." The true follower of Jesus thinks of other followers as equals. One flock, One Shepherd. *(Thursday, July 3, 2014 at 4:06A.M. CDT)*

ADJUSTING THE LENS
From my heart to yours

In countries where there IS persecution: - MORE people are becoming followers of Jesus Christ - MORE people are interested in becoming followers of Jesus Christ - MORE scriptures are distributed and sought after - MORE people want to know what the scriptures teach - MORE people are willing to risk their life for Jesus Christ DTR - Define The Relationship (Kyle Idleman). *(Thursday, July 3, 2014 at 4:12A.M. CDT)*

WHAT RELATIONSHIP
From my heart to yours

Questions that help define the relationship with Jesus Christ:

1. Am I a user or a vessel of His grace?
2. Am I prepared to pay or negotiate the price?
3. Do I want faith in Him but not obedience to Him?
4. Do I know the meaning of complete surrender?
5. Do I know His expectations?   *(Thursday, July 3, 2014 at 4:48A.M. CDT)*

SILO VS. CONDUIT THINKING
From my heart to yours

The silo is tall and wide, stationary and round. Always in holding mode. Never thinks of giving, and it's always someone else's fault if I don't have an opportunity to share what I have acquired.

When needed, people always go to the silo. Gets rusted even when full. The conduit, to be useful, needs to be clean and prepared to be used. Never calls anything its own but always prepared to let something flow through. It can never take credit for giving. It's mobile to wherever there is need. Gets rusted only when not in use. *(Thursday, July 3, 2014 at 5:03A.M. CDT)*

TWO ARE TOO MANY
From my heart to yours

The passion of Christ was to do the will of the Father. His success at the end was because He lived daily a surrendered life from the beginning. Thus, He had nothing to lose and everything to gain. What made this a reality in His life was the effective full domination of the eternal Spirit in His life, through whom He cried out day and night, and birthed us according to the Father's heart, and was able to truly love us unto the end. Likewise, those who cultivate a passion to do His will, can succeed by complete surrender, and realize that by losing all we stand to gain all in Christ. And by means of the eternal Spirit we too can cry out now and say, "Abba, Father", for His Father was made ours forever through Him. *(Friday, July 4, 2014 at 12:54A.M. CDT)*

AT WHAT PRICE?
From my heart to yours

I'm yet to find someone who began praying for the salvation of a family member, without ceasing, and God did not hear from heaven and answer such prayer. I know several who prayed for over 20 years before God answered. I heard the testimony of one who stopped after 5 years, and gave up. Few years later, this person committed to start praying again. I don't have any right to talk to people about God if I don't talk to God about people. Talking in prayer is cheap. Agonizing in prayer costs. Talking in prayer bring a person to the throne. Agonizing in prayer brings one down with his face to the ground. *(Saturday, July 5, 2014 at 7:17A.M. CDT)*

PRAYER SNAPSHOT
From my heart to yours

Knowing that praying is according to the Father's will is good, because it begins with silence and emptying from any known selfish motives. In many instances, that takes time. *(Saturday, July 5, 2014 at 7:36A.M. CDT)*

DEATH SNAPSHOT
From my heart to yours

Death brings an end to everyone. But Jesus Christ on the cross brought an end to death. And with His resurrection, He made it possible for anyone to live again. It's a promise with confirmation. May we always claim it and live for Him alone. He is worthy. And that's why I love Him so! *(Saturday, July 5, 2014 at 7:54A.M. CDT)*

STARTING RIGHT
From my heart to yours

> One of the first mistakes we make when we pray is that we right away bring earthly concerns to the Father in heaven as if He doesn't know, when we ought to begin in heaven and stay a while, the thing that makes earthly concerns easier to express and the heavenly reply more believable and understandable. One of the first blessings of prayer that we discover is that He is more impressed with our brokenness than with our words. *(Saturday, July 5, 2014 at 11:13A.M. CDT)*

WHAT DOES IT MEAN
From my heart to yours

> "If any man be IN Christ", he/she should plan to leave outside the following: 1. Any Cultural preferences that lift you above your siblings 2. Any Personal preferences that separate you from your family members 3. Any Relational dictates that don't show Christ's "better way" for the family 4. Shoes. They stink; and besides, being barefoot reminds you to remain humble and prepares to worship 5. False sense of guilt and shame, because satan loves to load you with unnecessary luggage And, oh, in case you're wondering, these are few things to keep in mind. The good news is that since you belong to Him now, Jesus embedded the Holy Spirit in your heart to work with your pure conscience and your quickened spirit, and guide you into all truth so you can do the right thing. You'll find Him asking you sometimes: "Are you

listening"?" Isn't Jesus Wonderful ! ?   *(Monday, July 7, 2014 at 10:47P.M. CDT)*

VISITORS AND MEMBERS

From my heart to yours

I received a spam email this morning with the question: "Would you like to increase the number of church visitors you have?" My spontaneous response was NO, because visitors go to:

1. Parks where there are hired hands who do the clean-ups; or a ...
2. Zoo - now that's a thought - where some want to be the lion king; or a ...
3. Museum - where some have their assigned seats and always need spraying for bugs; or a ...
4. Car lot where used cars squeak and are polished to hide engine trouble; or a ...
5. Stadium with spectators and concessions and cheers and boos abound.

But, the church that's really the church is where genuine life and unconditional love and selfless service can be found. It has a name. It's the Church of Jesus Christ of Everyday Saints ! *(Tuesday, July 8, 2014 at 10:39A.M. CDT)*

Why No Membership Rush?
From my heart to yours

The ideal candidates for church membership are people who were hated, ignored, disregard, creeps, low-life, marginalized, discounted, discredited, disenfranchised, broken, fallen, crushed, disqualified, demon-possessed, tax collectors, and all those who are sure that they are nothing. But in Jesus Christ, they are all loved, redeemed, washed clean, and become beautiful in Him. The difficulty is with us who don't know what to do with their past, don't know how to view them in the present, and cannot see them at all useful in the future. Jesus asked Peter, "Do you love me?" The same question is directed to us. For Jesus insists on being: EVERYTHING and ALWAYS, or Nothing at all. That's why He reduces the "Some things" down to nothing, and He creates something beautiful out of the "Nothings", so that "in ALL things He has the Preeminence." (Col 1:18) Pure Awesomeness is He. His name is Jesus. The old song says: "Something beautiful, Something good; All my confusion, He understood; All I had to offer Him was brokenness and strife; But He made something, beautiful, of my life". So, someone may say, "But what about all the good people out there?" My reply is simply this: "When is the good not good enough? What good is the real good? When is the good dead?" *(Tuesday, July 8, 2014 at 6:38P.M. CDT)*

Kingdom Snapshot
From my heart to yours

There are no acceptable human criteria to evaluate who qualifies into the Kingdom of God. For it is His Kingdom, not ours. So, the woman who touched the hem of His garment stopped Him in his tracks, while His own disciples were clueless. Her only criterion was FAITH for she was bankrupt otherwise. *(Wednesday, July 9, 2014 at 3:59A.M. CDT)*

Saying and Being
From my heart to yours

Saying I am His disciple alone is an example in self-deception, until He in fact becomes my Lord. Then I can truly worship, for worship is not an act that I do but a lifestyle that I live. *(Wednesday, July 9, 2014 at 4:06A.M. CDT)*

Some Hard Facts
From my heart to yours

There are no acceptable human criteria to evaluate who qualifies into the Kingdom of God. For it is His Kingdom, not ours. So, the woman who touched the hem of His garment stopped Him in his tracks, while His own disciples were clueless. Her only criterion was FAITH for she was bankrupt otherwise. Saying I am His disciple alone is an example in self-deception, until He in fact becomes my Lord. Then I can truly worship, for worship is not an act that I do but a lifestyle that I live. *(Wednesday, July 9, 2014 at 4:07A.M. CDT)*

NO SUCH THING
From my heart to yours

There is no such thing as Being a follower of Jesus Christ without taking these to heart together: 1. Cost of discipleship; 2. Change in lifestyle; 3. Compassion toward others; 4. Communion with the Holy Spirit; 5. Commitment to Christ without question. His followers are Real and genuine, Obedient and attentive, Loving without question, Caring toward the undeserving, yielded to the Master with their whole heart. *(Wednesday, July 9, 2014 at 4:23A.M. CDT)*

NOT FOR SALE
From my heart to yours

Jesus Christ is NOT : 1. FOR SALE. That was attempted before, and it backfired. 2. DENOMINATIONAL. Corinth church acted like the world, like fools. 3. MADE KING. They attempted that, but He wasn't impressed. 4. MADE LORD. He IS Lord, and we just need to realize it. 5. CUSTOMIZABLE. He changes all, and remains changeless. "There is no other name under heaven by which we can be saved." His name is Jesus and He is my Lord. *(Wednesday, July 9, 2014 at 4:33A.M. CDT)*

Owner's Manual
From my heart to yours

> Since marriages don't come with "Owner's Manual", it would be wise to talk to whoever came up with the idea first. No? And better before than after, and sooner than later, and slowly than rush into it, and openly and transparently if at all possible. Otherwise, it's going to be painful and confusing and filled with unwanted surprises. And cultures that have things "figured out" completely, maybe they need to go first. Know of any? :). *(Wednesday, July 9, 2014 at 11:58A.M. CDT)*

Proper Loving
From my heart to yours

> I cannot love the church properly if I don't love my family first. It was Jesus who died for the church so that my family doesn't have to. Jesus was the right sacrifice offered to please God. Regardless of how many times I offer my family, even the people will never be pleased...which doesn't count in the first place. To love my family properly, I must adore the one whom He gave me, and for His sake. For loving the wife equips me to love the children, and loving the family equips me to love the church. *(Friday, July 11, 2014 at 8:15P.M. CDT)*

WHO ARE THESE?
From my heart to yours

The Church of Jesus Christ of Everyday Saints consists of: 1. Humbly bold, daily obedient, and completely surrendered men and women 2. Who are filled with His Holy Spirit, and... 3. Count their lives worthless for His sake, 4. Living a pure life, not loaded with the "STUFF" of this world, 5. Burdened to see the worthless of this world become worthy in His sight. In summary, A. They have nothing but the Gospel of Jesus Christ in their heart and mind, and in their character and behavior, B. Totally sold out to the Holy Spirit of God to accomplish what God intended before the foundation of the world. C. And all is to His glory and honor because He is worthy and, D. Because He redeemed His Church with His own blood and owns it lock, stock, and barrel. The rest of what's going on is simply corruption that feeds on itself, and uses many covers including "religion" to accomplish its objectives. And to flow toward us with His love through Jesus Christ on the cross is simply beyond my comprehension! But that's powerful enough to bring me to my knees in absolute adoration for all He's done. Absolute Wonder! *(Saturday, July 12, 2014 at 11:15P.M. CDT)*

OBEDIENCE: A SERIOUS BUSINESS
From my heart to yours

OBEDIENCE is not a word to peddle, but a lifestyle that reduces me willingly to nothing so that Christ becomes everything. And only by the power of the Holy Spirit this can take place.

OBEDIENCE is rejected by humans from earthly birth, but welcomed by humans through supernatural rebirth. That's why there is no such thing in Scripture as "Faith" without Obedience with it. It's simply a lie to think that just faith will do it. Obedience is inherent to the character of a true follower of Jesus Christ.

True OBEDIENCE has no part in it that's proverbially "Made in China", nor "Manufactured in one country and Assembled elsewhere". It's all "Made in Heaven" from concept to delivery. That's why its by-products are out of this world.

True OBEDIENCE disciplines the heart to love Christ for He alone is really all that matters. It disciplines the mind to be "Under New Management". It disciplines the will to be totally yielded to His will, even when things don't make any sense. *(Saturday, July 12, 2014 at 11:18P.M. CDT)*

OBEDIENT CHURCH

From my heart to yours

What really matters in the local church is simply this: How obedient are its leaders to the Word of God for others will know it? Those in its membership who are true followers of Christ will recognize true leadership and follow, not because of who the leader is but because of the leader's obedience to the Holy Spirit. Otherwise, whatever song and pony show is going on, it's only a circus. *(Saturday, July 12, 2014 at 11:48P.M. CDT)*

OBEDIENT LEADERSHIP

From my heart to yours

Obedient leadership in the local church is a MUST. Obedient membership thereafter is a natural consequence. Broken leaders before God stand tall even in the face of the enemy. *(Saturday, July 12, 2014 at 11:51P.M. CDT)*

SERIOUS WITH GOD

From my heart to yours

PRAYER refines the character of the local church. Otherwise, it's useless to God. God always surprises us when only one person in the local church gets serious with Him and prays. *(Saturday, July 12, 2014 at 11:24P.M. CDT)*

CHARACTER LEAST DISCUSSED

From my heart to yours

PRAYER refines the character of the local church. Otherwise, it's useless to God. Having said that, God always surprises us when only one person in the local church gets serious with Him and prays. The best thing these days that a local church can do is: PRAY; and that's for many reasons, but here's a few : 1. If "Prayer" was a measure of many a local church's standard of spiritual living, that church is not only below the poverty level, but it's in crisis mode. The sad part is that that church's "spiritual stomach" looks fat and pudgy, full of contaminants, and essential nutrients. 2. Lack of real praying in the local church has invited the world to join, instead of being a deterrent to the world. The NT church was known for being a "praying" church, nothing else. 3. Jesus said, "My house is called the house of prayer", not of preaching or music, not a hospital inviting the sick but there are no doctors nor medicine. 4. Prayer is something that the world cannot do driven by passion and love, but by fear and shame, refusing to repent. 5. Prayer, not notable persons, was what brought the world to Jesus Christ. *(Sunday, July 13, 2014 at 12:04A.M. CDT)*

ANEMIC AND DISCONTENTED
From my heart to yours

"Anemic" refers to being malnourished and in serious need of essential ingredients. "Discontented" refers to someone who is very unhappy with the status quo, with the situation, and wishes something seriously can be done about it. When those two characteristics come together in a person, usually it's someone who knows that things can be better and doesn't want to be idle. He/she is someone who the Holy Spirit has been disturbing and burdening for a period of time, and pressing upon his/her heart the need for change to glorify God. Such person speaks and shares what the burden is, and asks for concerted prayer that God would step in and change things. The request for prayer is not casual but serious, not only once but continual, not patronizing but genuine. All the while, agonizing in prayer, purifying self at the individual level from what doesn't please God, and waiting on God goes on. *(Sunday, July 13, 2014 at 12:15A.M. CDT)*

Indispensable Spirit
From my heart to yours

The Holy Spirit to the local church is simply indispensable. And contrary to popular opinion, the Pentecostals don't have the corner on the Holy Spirit. He in fact owns everything. Although we like to think that the Holy Spirit is a good "life support system" and we love to live indefinitely in the ICU with everybody taking good care of us, the Holy Spirit is likened in the Scripture to dynamite (which is His true character).....not exactly what was bargained for. *(Sunday, July 13, 2014 at 12:15A.M. CDT)*

Visions Snapshot
From my heart to yours

Visions driven by money are driven by numbers (the proverbial "just do the numbers"), like when David counted the people, and sinned. God help us! *(Sunday, July 13, 2014 at 9:34A.M. CDT)*

Holy, Holy, Holy
From my heart to yours

I've wondered for a while now why the western world indiscriminately uses the word "holy" in abusive and offensive expressions to describe what appears to persons of the world as shocking, while angels in heaven dare open their mouth with the same word only with their faces down and their bodies fully covered with their wings. Is it because the church ceased to be "shocked" at the horrors taking place in the world? Ceased to be "shocked" at the horror of God's judgment that filled that Gethsemane cup? Could it be that satan, the ruler of this world, has so imposed that thought on the fallen mind in the world to "mock" such sacred term by lowering its value beyond recognition? Did that really lower the inherent value of the term "holy"? NO. It rather reflects the gradual dismantling of the very fabric of a so-called "Christian society", one thread at a time, not realizing at all the real Church is built and established "ONE FOLLOWER AT A TIME". *(Sunday, July 13, 2014 at 10:23A.M. CDT)*

Servant-Leader Snapshot
From my heart to yours

How can I recognize a true "servant-leader" in a church regardless of his area of ministry? I look, not to his eyes, but to his life to find nail prints that were used to nail him with Christ in real obedience and complete surrender to Him. *(Sunday, July 13, 2014 at 10:27A.M. CDT)*

Fingerprints of God (2)
From my heart to yours

Recognizing the fingerprints of God in my life doesn't require brains, but genuine lifestyle in Him and transparent communion with Him. To know how that can happen, he said, "Ask and you will receive, seek and you will find, knock and it will be opened to you." God doesn't work well or use "induced spiritual coma transfusion". *(Sunday, July 13, 2014 at 11:07A.M. CDT)*

RESISTANCE: GOOD AND BAD
From my heart to yours

RESISTING can be good, and can be bad. This is BAD: Resisting the Holy Spirit in the invisible world (what people cannot see) takes place over a period of time in my heart, and manifests itself by persistent disobedience in the visible world (day to do living and attempted ministry). Disobedience in the invisible world manifests itself in holding on to what's in my heart that I got from worldly sources. Transformation to His image takes place by placing my heart in the hands of the Holy Spirit. Then he begins to dismantle any idol I attached my heart to or any altar I bowed and worshipped at. Then He rebuilds my character day by day to be like Christ's. To think that we humans can do any of that transformation on our own is a futile exercise in pride mixed with stubbornness and sprinkled with an "all spice" of greed, envy, and seductive evil that appears as acceptable but in fact it's very counterproductive to the purposes of God. This is GOOD: "Submit yourselves, then, to God. RESIST the devil, and he will flee from you. (James 4:7 NIV) My Resistance of the Spirit is BAD because its fruit is disobedience. My Resistance of satan is GOOD because it reminds me how desperate I ought to be to practice the Presence of God. *(Sunday, July 13, 2014 at 1:05P.M. CDT)*

WISDOM AND KNOWLEDGE
From my heart to yours

"Wisdom" is conduit-thinking, while "knowledge" is silo-thinking. Having a lot does not mean that I am more useful to Christ, because He relies, not on me, but on His Spirit to use the gift He gave. It would be such waste to have a lot of unusable stuff. Remember the five loaves and two fishes? *(Monday, July 14, 2014 at 4:08A.M. CDT)*

TRANSPARENT AND PURE
From my heart to yours

Q: How do I know that others see Jesus in me?

A: It is when nothing else in my life is distracting them. NOTHING! *(Monday, July 14, 2014 at 4:45A.M. CDT)*

BEAUTY OF HOLINESS
From my heart to yours

I cannot worship "in the beauty of His holiness" if I don't have His beauty and His holiness in my heart. Beauty is best seen when He changes my ashes. Holiness is best seen when He changes my sinfulness. *(Monday, July 14, 2014 at 4:09A.M. CDT)*

Living Contradictions
From my heart to yours

> Does it not surprise us, while the city of Laodicea was well-known for its ability to manufacture clothes, have medicinal capabilities, and function as the financial center, that the Holy Spirit said that the church there was naked, blind, and poor?!! *(Tuesday, July 15, 2014 at 12:13A.M. CDT)*

Not Funny
From my heart to yours

> If satan can get me to laugh about holy things, they will cease to be holy in my eyes. And suddenly I am not able to say a word about holy things, and mean it with my whole being. And what does Hollywood do so successfully? Not only that, but if I ever attempt to talk about them, it will come across as fake, and people will know it. The sacred hush loses its essence and glow. Nothing can repair the damage until I learn to practice the Presence again. I may not have another chance to speak of holy things but I will learn to be content when someone else speaks, and I discover afresh that it's been about Him since day one! God help us to find our contentment in you at all times. *(Tuesday, July 15, 2014 at 12:21A.M. CDT)*

REASONABLE RECIPROCITY
From my heart to yours

Is it even reasonable for man to expect anything from God and not reciprocate the expectation? But then again, since when has man been even remotely reasonable!! *(Tuesday, July 15, 2014 at 7:14A.M. CDT)*

LIFE OF HATRED, NO LIFE AT ALL
From my heart to yours

The reason hatred is such a serious matter is this: 1. While the object of hate is alive, hatred stirs up conflict (Prov. 10: 12) and hides behind lying lips (Prov. 10:18). 2. Then when the object of hatred dies, and this matter of hatred is NOT settled yet, it gets worse because the heart becomes empty, very lonely, and dies as well because there is no one to hate any longer. But when the object of love lives forever, even in hatred, he wins the one who hates over because he/she forgives and because LOVE NEVER FAILS! His name is Jesus. He said, "If you love me, keep my commandment." And "this is my commandment, that you love one another." Shedding more light on "Hatred", he who hates: 1. Is a murderer and has no eternal life in him (1John 3:15) 2. Is a liar (1John 4:20) 3. Is behaving in darkness, has a lifestyle of darkness, and has no sense of direction in his life (1John 2:11) 4. Has no capacity to love God (1John 4:20) 5. Hatred is in the same category with idolatry, jealousy, rage, witchcraft, selfish ambitions, and factions (Gal 5:20). *(Tuesday, July 15, 2014 at 11:13P.M. CDT)*

FORGIVENESS IS NO FORGIVENESS IF

From my heart to yours

We may think that what we did, or what we said in response, qualifies to be labeled as "FORGIVENESS". But, NOT SO FAST! It is NO forgiveness yet when: 1. We say, "Let's just forget what happened". Really? And what will that accomplish? And can we really expect either side to just ... forget?? 2. We just wait, let time go by, and simply do nothing. But wait for how long when it's like a nagging toothache?? 3. We interpret forgiveness based on different societal values. That's not consistent or fair, and it changes constantly. 4. We apply the "silent treatment" for a long time, then maybe we will run into each other, see what happens, and let time bring us back together. Evolution is DEFINITELY nonexistent here. That's No Life. 5. We ask someone to bring us together to a dinner table, and try to be in the same room, and maybe that's enough. But kids don't even act like that. 6. Instead of truly forgiving, one side tolerates what happened hoping the other person "grows up" or "change for the better". 7. We buy a gift for the other side, and go visit them, and pretend nothing happened. 8. We just leave or move to another part of the state or country under the pretense of "God led me to go". . . . And a few other misconceptions of what true forgiveness is all about. To the follower of Christ, Jesus said that if we don't truly forgive, our Father in heaven will not forgive us our sins. Besides, He forgives us, and called us to be like Him. There is NOTHING on the human side, and in my condition, that equips me to truly forgive. What now? *(Tuesday, July 15, 2014 at 11:38P.M. CDT)*

The Seven Principles of Forgiveness

From my heart to yours

THERE IS NO TRUE AND FULL EXPERIENCE OF FORGIVENESS UNTIL ONE COME TO THE CROSS OF JESUS CHRIST. There he/she experiences it personally first. No alternative or workaround. 2. FORGIVENESS ALWAYS COSTS. Nothing happens in vacuum. When wrong is done, it cannot be simply dismissed. Someone must pay. 3. THE ONE WHO FORGIVES, PAYS. The sin or error cannot be brushed under the rug and forgotten. Sin always has a price that must be settled. 4. THE ONE WHO FORGIVES IS SET FREE - "From" and "To" - SET FREE FROM fear, attitude driven by pride, distrust (because it's now forgiven and put behind), bitterness (the worst), and other pounding headaches and hounding forces on the heart and soul; and, SET FREE TO worship God and genuinely love and serve others. Absence of forgiveness makes worship NOT in Spirit and truth, meaning, the Spirit of Christ found a way to forgive, and did it, and can teach us to do likewise. 5. THE ONE WHO FORGIVES WILL BE FORGIVEN BY GOD when he/she confesses his sins. It's a promise. Jesus said, "If you forgive peoples their sins, your Heavenly Father will forgive you, and if you don't, He won't." 6. LET THE CIRCLE OF FORGIVENESS BE THE SAME SIZE AS THE CIRCLE OF SIN. If the sin committed is between me and God alone (not against someone else), then true confession is sufficient only to God, and He promised that He will forgive for the sake and on account of Christ's work on the cross. 7. MAKING SACRIFICES AND OFFERING GIFTS TO GOD

DONT REPLACE FORGIVENESS. The wrong must be settled. Jesus teaches me that even if I'm in the innocent party, I should take the first step and go and settle the matter. Didn't Christ do that? So ought we to do likewise, if indeed we are His followers. *(Wednesday, July 16, 2014 at 4:18A.M. CDT)*

JESUS DOWN TO EARTH
From my heart to yours

To be clear, this is not talking about the incarnation (God becoming man), but about the majesty of His Presence with people on earth that made ALL the difference in this world for them. What is amazing about Him alone is that, although he never lectured about doctrines to people (a specialty of the Pharisees of His day), His practical communication always accomplished its objective. Here's why: 1. His conversation revolved around the Gospel and the Kingdom 2. It brought people around to come face to face with Him, many times to make a decision (even No-Decision is a decision, such as the rich young ruler) 3. His conversation always attracted people, not to doctrinal accuracy, but to HIM. 4. He was more intent on the "will of the Father in heaven" than on the emotions of the people on earth. 5. He was always filled with, and dominated by, the Holy Spirit whom He also promised to His followers. Jesus never led people to grasping doctrinal accuracy, but always led people to Him. For He is the embodiment of all doctrine and life. (Col 1:19; 2:3,9; and 2 Peter 1:3). So, it is natural to ask: "So, where is the doctrine if it's so important?" Answer: "All doctrines are wrapped up in Him". 1. Understanding the doctrines never led someone to salvation because it still takes the direct intervention of the Holy Spirit to move someone from death to life in Christ. 2. A true sign of being in Christ, as believer and follower, IS "Abiding in Him, and in His Word". In Him, doctrines come to life, and then they start to make sense. But, without question, life IS in Him. 3. Jesus was the only person who succeeded to merge two critical and generically broad concepts. They are: "Theory" and "Practice". For example, doctrines are and will remain in the category of "Theory" until one truly puts his trust in Christ. Then, once alive, the Holy Spirit begins to give understanding and proper application; and, hence, "Practice". 4. Now He calls us to LIVE HIM on earth, not talk about Him. Meaning, the world is tired of just TALK. Not just that, but the world is TIRED of FAKE FOLLOWERS who are No followers, but Pretenders. So now there is a new generation of God-haters, Church-haters, Religion-haters, Christian-haters. I know there has always been "worldly, sinful, depraved, etc." people who always live in the world. But, what is different with this generation is that they are ANGRY and they HATE anything that has to do with God, and are vocal about it. The reason they give is this: "we hear you and we know how you live. And the two are worlds apart." So, Come on, man!!!!! My friend, Which are you, FOLLOWER or PRETENDER ? *(Thursday, July 17, 2014 at 10:43P.M. CDT)*

SAYING AND SEEING
From my heart to yours

To "speak about Jesus", anyone can do that. It does not define (1) Who I am at all, or (2) whether I have any relationship with Him.

However, to "Speak Jesus", it takes being in UNION and in COMMUNION; *Union with Him and Communion with His Spirit*. And if one thinks that's impossible, he is CORRECT. But when I come to the cross, I come to my end, and begin a new life in Him. Then, as I "abide in Him", He begins to flow out from within me in truth and love. Yes, it's about HIM. *(Thursday, July 17, 2014 at 11:04P.M. CDT)*

FALLING IS BETTER
From my heart to yours

Q: What is the difference between Simon the Pharisee and the fallen woman who broke the alabaster box on Jesus' feet ? (Matt 26 and Lk 7)

A: One word: Glory. Simon self-righteous created his man-made glory and lost, but she placed her glory, her hair, at Jesus feet after she broke the last valuable thing to her in the world. Result: (1) Jesus reached out and saved her. (2) Jesus put her name in "Who's Who list of the Redeemed" because she found herself unworthy in His presence and He made her worthy. (3) She loved much because she was forgiven much. (4) She carried His fragrance with her everywhere after she wiped His feet with her hair . Not bad for a "fallen woman". Those who are a "Nobody", Jesus makes them a "Somebody"! The difference? Jesus! I found myself humming a song I learned many years ago, and it says: - "Turn your eyes upon Jesus, - Look full in His wonderful face; - And the things of earth will grow strangely dim, - In the light of His glory and grace." Give Him glory; He gives grace to the humble. Keep your glory, and you find no grace in time of need. Why? Because God has no place for the proud in His presence! *(Friday, July 18, 2014 at 3:31A.M. CDT)*

MYOB
From my heart to yours

About the fallen woman, Jesus said to the guests in the house, "Leave her alone!" About John the beloved, Jesus said to Peter, "What's that to you? Follow me!" Following Jesus cannot be done right without minding our own business. *(Friday, July 18, 2014 at 4:20A.M. CDT)*

PERFORMANCE SNAPSHOT
From my heart to yours

Church is not a Performance. It is a "Transformance". So, the question is not: What are they doing, but, Is the Holy Spirit changing me? If he's not changing me, then I'm part of the performance. *(Friday, July 18, 2014 at 7:16P.M. CDT)*

ATTRACTION SNAPSHOT
From my heart to yours

We are always drawn toward the object of our affection. Usually, the object of our affection is a secret of the heart. The rest is details. That's why we will always get to the destination we determine in our hearts. "Where your treasure is, there will your heart be also". *(Saturday, July 19, 2014 at 5:05A.M. CDT)*

Always Busy
From my heart to yours

Our conversation day and night is always consumed by the details of our life. We don't give the Holy Spirit a chance to say anything. And there are some who really believe they are in charge. "All we, like sheep, have gone astray, each of us has turned to our own way ..." There is "a better way". *(Saturday, July 19, 2014 at 5:15A.M. CDT)*

Are you In or Out ?
From my heart to yours

Am I part of the deformation and stagnation OR Am I part of the reformation and transformation of the church? The Holy Spirit is not interested in what I CAN do, but in what HE determined to do with or without me, because His eternal desire and commitment is that the Eternal Son is glorified in the Spirit's full power - in the Church! Am I on the team? To be member of the Team, the application is at the cross - the application of the cleansing blood in the heart. It's all about Him! *(Sunday, July 20, 2014 at 9:50A.M. CDT)*

Prayer and Sin
From my heart to yours

> Pray! Pray one for another that you may be healed. If there is sin, confess it, hate it, stay away from it, give it up, and replace it with pure affection for the One who died and rose again! *(Sunday, July 20, 2014 at 5:55P.M. CDT)*

A Good Friend
From my heart to yours

> A dear friend who turns 94 on July 23, still giving and keeping his mind sharp. Yesterday, he fell because there was a piece of mail in his box that belonged to his neighbor, and he didn't want his neighbor to miss it. So he decided to take it in person. On the way back, he fell and bruised the back of his head. He prayed and the next day he showed up to share his heart. I came to the conclusion that they don't make them like that anymore. I thank God for him, my friend, Dr. Labib. *(Sunday, July 20, 2014 at 6:02P.M. CDT)*

Side Benefit of Prayer
From my heart to yours

> It's amazing what prayer does. Among its benefits is that it brings people of God together because their focus is not on each other anymore, but on Him who hears their prayer! Any alternative is NOT better! *(Sunday, July 20, 2014 at 6:04P.M. CDT)*

THE GOSPEL OF JESUS CHRIST
From my heart to yours

The Gospel of Jesus Christ is the most widespread worldwide human spring revolution for life that is guaranteed to have a 100% success rate. The rest are simply imitation margarine that melts under the heat, while the Gospel spreads more effectively when the heat is on. *(Sunday, July 20, 2014 at 10:11P.M. CDT)*

HIM ALONE
From my heart to yours

The real-ness of Christ is found in the truth that He brought heaven to earth to give life in all its abundance, because true life is in Him - Alone! That's why we say: It's all about Him! *(Sunday, July 20, 2014 at 10:14P.M. CDT)*

CENTER AND CIRCUMFERENCE
From my heart to yours

When the Gospel of Jesus Christ ceases to be the Center and Circumference of the church, the church ceases to be the church. And any other name will do. For the Gospel is not an item to discuss, an evolving human effort, a religious blip of human consciousness, or a sublime attainment that lacks touching the fallen, broken, and shattered humans all over the world. But it's the heart and soul of the true Church. *(Sunday, July 20, 2014 at 10:16P.M. CDT)*

ON KNOWING

From my heart to yours

Knowing the Person of Christ, and not just ABOUT Christ, is where old things stop dragging us down, and the newness of everything begins. Isn't this what the world keeps looking for ? Being set free is what Christ is all about. And the journey begins at the cross, and stays there. Maybe that's why it's all about Him! *(Sunday, July 20, 2014 at 10:39P.M. CDT)*

FAILING TO SEE

From my heart to yours

Nothing amazing about the persistence and determination (a.k.a., stubbornness/rebellion) of the world. Christ's amazing grace consists of His truth, His peace, His joy, His hope, His love, and so much more that is all wrapped in Him. He made union and communion possible in both heaven and earth, and has gone past the Garden of Eden right into heaven itself, establishing an eternal covenant and sealing it with the full consent, power, and Name of the Triune God. ALL for love's sake! Isn't this what the world is looking for, and keeps trying to construct, and persistently fails?! *(Sunday, July 20, 2014 at 10:51P.M. CDT)*

BIRD'S EYE VIEW
From my heart to yours

There is a bit of confusion regarding the true meaning of the Christian life. This confusion arises, I think in part, from a chaos in understanding what's involved. So, this results in erroneous or at least misplaced expectations. I trust that delineating these four stages helps clarify, knowing that a true follower of Christ does not graduate out of one stage into another, but they are a continual understanding of the effective work of Christ on the cross. 1. CHRIST FOR ME - this refers to Jesus Christ who died for me to bring me salvation. The fact that He died brings the reality of salvation front and center to mankind, and divides history into two parts. But it does not mean that it became a reality in my personal life automatically, not just yet. 2. CHRIST WITH ME - this refers to Jesus Christ walking with me by means of "the other comforter" who is the Holy Spirit" who gives me the clear sense of His presence in my life and "takes care of me" teaching me to recognize and be thankful, but also eager to want to learn more. 3. CHRIST IN ME - this refers to Jesus Christ who, through the Holy Spirit, teaches me all things. He is not teaching me to be a warehouse of information", but to be changed by the truth of what He leads me to understand. And He brings about change in my life which will often cause in me to experience "growing pains" because He is changing me constantly. But that's not all ... 4. CHRIST AS ME - refers to the part where I become light and salt to the world so that the world will not only "hear" what Christ "sounds like", but "see" what Christ "looks like". These four (4) points are not stages where one graduates from one into another, but are like concentric circles that constitute the sum total of my life. Or one may choose to think of them as four (4) layers that are intertwined with one another all the days of my life. To be sure, there is a starting point at which I consciously interact with Christ. From my angle, not Christ's, I "sense" His desire to interact with me in my life. That's when I begin to discover Him as Savior, and not just a historical fact. From His angle, He may have been preparing the way without me being aware yet. A modest and imperfect analogy or comparison is where the mother is carrying a baby during pregnancy and can sense every movement and becomes increasingly loving and attached to her baby way before the baby is born. Perhaps that's why the Chinese include the nine months of pregnancy as part of the first year of life, so when the baby at three months is in fact one year old. Incidentally, this is not exactly "Made In China" :). (Monday, July 21, 2014 at 7:04A.M. CDT)

THE CROSS, THE CROSSROADS
From my heart to yours

While "evidence" is used to feed arguments, In the cross of Christ is all the evidence one can ask for because from there, real life happens. When a sinner comes face to face with the full expression of God's love on the cross, his sins are forgiven and his life changes inside out, and he's willing to die for the one who saved him, I don't call that a "reality show"; it's simply "Real". Anyway, if something/someone is not worth dying for, he's not worth living for. That's why people fight in the name of Christianity, but others are willing to lay their life for Christ. This is not "Christianese"; this is simply CHRIST. What blows my mind about Him is that when he died, life began for everyone else in Him. In contrast, when anyone else dies, he's just dead! That's why I said the cross has all the evidence one can ask for; but some people want to reject anything and everything that has to do with Christ; and they start unknowingly at the cross and reject it. The rest is just details. May I recommend: (1) Josh McDowell's "Evidence that Demands a Verdict" and "More Than a Carpenter". Also (2) look up on YouTube anything by Ravi Zacharias. He has some good stuff to think about and disturb the comforted who think that Christ-followers are the "whipping boy" of society. Nothing new! *(Tuesday, July 22, 2014 at 1:15P.M. CDT)*

CHOICES SUM IT UP
From my heart to yours

The reality that the world seems to miss (and maybe intentionally) is that God is not about "Religion". Religion is what man is all about. So when man doesn't reach a sound conclusion, man forms a "religion", determined and modified by culture over time or restricted by language or another variable. To compound the confusion, man uses Jesus as the proverbial "whipping boy" throughout human history. In fact they crucified Him because they just couldn't fit Him anywhere in their formulas. And even Christian versions of religion fight and kill others and one another to defend what they do not own. And they still do that even today. I even read articles titled: "Where is Jesus", as if one crucifixion is not enough. God is not about "Religion"; He is about an "Intimate Relationship". Isn't THAT what the world is looking for - a thriving secure loving relationship that they can consider as the solution? But, Alas! They don't seem to come to an agreement on it, and keep running into each other (aka, human conflict in the name of religion). And to be sure, some evangelicals at least have succeeded in making a "religion" out of their evangelicalism (ouch!). But that's the truth. And, even they, have failed, simply they do not reflect the Spirit and character of Christ. To be sure, God doesn't need evangelicals; Evangelicals need God! That's why, thousands upon thousands around the world, regardless of religion, race, gender, affiliation, language, or even sexual orientation (fancy that), are finding truth in Him who said, "I am the way, the truth, and the life". This is what they are testifying. Reason: they asked, and He answered. He promised, saying, "Ask and you will receive". There is always the option of rejecting His offer. The sad thing is that no one, to-date, has brought a better offer. None! And that's sad. The tragedy of all tragedies is that even those who reject the cross of Christ have to come face to face with it, via one medium or another, in one venue or another, and have to intentionally reject Him in the inner sanctum of their hearts. CHOICES - That's what life is all about. The rest are mere consequences of choices people make. "Let the words of my mouth and the meditations of my heart be acceptable to you, my Rock and my Salvation"! *(Tuesday, July 22, 2014 at 2:36P.M. CDT)*

Two Types of Stripes

From my heart to yours

In 1945, Dietrich Bonhoeffer died (39 years old) as a martyr in World War II. Hitler ordered the annihilation. He said that Christians will be seen as "persons who cause divisions, undermine family life, mislead the nation, and disturb the peace" (Cost of Discipleship, 216). That's almost 70 years ago. In 2012, Abubakar Shekau, leader of Boko Haram in Nigeria, said: "You Christians should know that Jesus... is not the son of God." He went on to say, "I am the Shekau that does not like Christians, and I don't like Muslims that relate with Christians." He publicly announced three choices for Christians in northern Nigeria: become Muslims, leave the area, or die. "The time is coming when anyone who kills you will think they are offering a service to God." (John 16 NIV) A leopard's stripes never change. But the stripes Jesus took on His body were sufficient to save whoever comes to Him. That's where complete healing takes place. Whosoever will, to the Lord may come ! It's all about Him, and will forever be! *(Wednesday, July 23, 2014 at 2:08A.M. CDT)*

Praying In Persecution

From my heart to yours

There are over sixty countries where "Christians face the reality of massacre, rape, torture, mutilation, family division, harassment, imprisonment, slavery, discrimination in education and employment, and even death simply for the sake of what they believe." Intercessory Prayer is appreciated. Q: How do I know

I'm engaged in real intercessory prayer? A: When I'm in the Presence, but words can't come out of my mouth because the burden is too heavy. So I choke and sit still for tears and mumblings make more sense before Him who knows everything. Peter, after being asked 3 times "Do u love me", replied "Lord, you know everything." *(Friday, July 25, 2014 at 3:31A.M. CDT)*

GREAT ERRORS LEAVING THE CHURCH ANEMIC (1 OF 2)
From my heart to yours

Jesus called only His followers to accomplish four tasks: 1. To be salt and light in the world, 2. To love God with all of their being, 3. To love the neighbor as oneself, 4. to love one another from a pure heart. NONE HAS A CONDITION OR LIMITATION. The only way any of the four tasks can happen successfully is by becoming a follower of Jesus Christ. I'm defining "successfully" as simply something that brings God exclusive glory when it intersects with people. The practical expression of these tasks has been summarized in what came to be known as the "Great Commission". However, the church failed in general on all counts. So periodically, God sends revival fires, using unknown individuals who begin with concerted prayer for a season, followed by acts of the Holy Spirit, to stir His church back to its original love, calling, and mission. Although Jesus gave what we describe as the "great commission", somehow the majority have settled to a confused Christian life bordering on rebellion at times by choosing Not To Go, and leaving that to "those who are called", missing the point that all who follow Him ARE called, called to accomplish those four tasks. This is manifested in the 72% of evangelical church adults who have serious questions about their faith, and 76% of the 20-something population in the same churches. Grievous errors have been committed throughout church history that left the church anemic and maintained on life support systems devised by human ingenuity but ineffective when it comes to the original purpose and intent. I mention some of the errors in the second post, if you feel led to read on. Thank you for reading to this point. *(Saturday, July 26, 2014 at 4:52A.M. CDT)*

GREAT ERRORS LEAVING THE CHURCH ANEMIC (PART 2A)
From my heart to yours

The first error committed is: SEPARATION BETWEEN EVANGELISM AND DISCIPLESHIP -- as if they are mutually independent. The tendency to pursue evangelism separate from discipleship has left church leaders in what's been lately labeled as "The Christian South" (i.e., south of the equator, referring to the Far East, Africa, and South America) crying out and stating the there is much growth in numbers, but it's all SHALLOW. Current so-called "discipleship programs" affirm this separation and are left wanting because they miss the emphasis on the critical nature and required cost of true discipleship. It's more than finishing a seminar or workshop. It's usually a course, not that we say we "finished", but in fact it's the sort of course that finishes the selfish me, and leads me on a life path of utter dependence on the Holy Spirit to accomplish His purpose. *(Saturday, July 26, 2014 at 5:50A.M. CDT)*

Great Errors Leaving The Church Anemic (Part 2B)
From my heart to yours

> The second error committed is: Ignoring the PRIESTHOOD OF ALL BELIEVERS -- that if one becomes a follower of Jesus Christ, he/she has a role that is vital to their own survival and the health of the general body of the church. Hence, in most cases, churches have grown anemic while they carry the pudgy stomachs of starvation with budgets, numbers, and properties. *(Saturday, July 26, 2014 at 5:51A.M. CDT)*

Great Errors Leaving The Church Anemic (Part 2C)
From my heart to yours

> The third error committed is: NOT ALL BUT FEW ARE GOING (maybe!) -- The go-to verses are Matthew 28:18-20 labeled as the "Great Commission". Question and Comment: The "Question" is: If the text says "Go, Make disciples, Baptize, and Teach", Where is "Evangelize"? The "Comment" is that the word "Go" in the text is not a verb of command, but a "state of being", as if to say "While you are going...", assuming that all are in fact going. This redefines much of what the church's mission ought to have been all along. *(Saturday, July 26, 2014 at 5:51A.M. CDT)*

GREAT ERRORS LEAVING THE CHURCH ANEMIC (PART 2D)
From my heart to yours

> The fourth error committed is: REVIVALS ARE NOT FOR THE DEAD BUT FOR THE COMATOSE -- Most churches are content without revival as OPTIONAL, and attach it to money to pay someone to come and "do a revival". To be sure, churches "hold" revivals for few days, then seemingly release the speaker to go elsewhere, and acknowledging that "at least they tried". Maybe that IS the problem, that they "hold" revival ... from happening. However, the fact is that the church has a BUILDER who said "I will build my church and the gates of hell will not prevail against it". And like a mother who for love's sake nurses a sick child through his dark sleepless nights, so does the Holy Spirit whom Jesus promised from the Father (John 14-16). He stirs the church out of its stupor, and back to its "sanity" and original purpose. (Saturday, July 26, 2014 at 5:51A.M. CDT)

FIVE GREAT ERRORS LEAVING THE CHURCH ANEMIC (PART 2E)
From my heart to yours

> The fifth error committed is: MARRIAGE BETWEEN THE STATE AND THE CHURCH -- This odd couple has institutionalized the church, legislated morality, and made the church the prostitute of the politics of the day. Curses followed in every generation, and that for one simple reason. The Church is a living organism with a life of its own that is designed to throb with the life of God and grow by the Spirit of God to accomplish

the plan of redemption through the ages, and on the other hand the institution has no life of its own, no single purpose beyond what man can devise, no unifying compass, no ability to span human history except by artificial mutations, and all its resources are controlled by the few, the rich, the famous, and the powerful. *(Saturday, July 26, 2014 at 5:52A.M. CDT)*

GREAT ERRORS LEAVING THE CHURCH ANEMIC (PART 2 - SUMMARY)

From my heart to yours

The incomplete list of errors made by the church: 1. SEPARATION BETWEEN EVANGELISM AND DISCIPLESHIP 2. PRIESTHOOD OF ALL BELIEVERS 3. NOT ALL BUT A FEW ARE GOING (maybe!) 4. REVIVALS ARE NOT FOR THE DEAD BUT FOR THE COMATOSE 5. MARRIAGE BETWEEN THE STATE AND THE CHURCH (If you wish to read brief descriptions of each, please visit other posts.). *(Saturday, July 26, 2014 at 5:59A.M. CDT)*

CAN YOU COUNT ?

From my heart to yours

I was arrested the last few days by this scene: 1-2-3-4-5-6-7-8-9-10-11-12-13-14-15-16-17-18-19-20-21-22-23-24-25-26-27-28-29-30-31-32-33-34-35-36-37-38-39. I dare you to take the time and count each number (no cheating, skipping, or saying 'I know how to count'), as you stand there, right beside the Roman soldiers who flogged Jesus! This post is really not for reading but for counting. Think about His face, His eyes, His body, His skin, His stress, His numbing cry. Think about how the whip plowed on his back making deep furrows as He submitted himself willingly. Think about your sins that He bore and for which He laid there and took the 39 lashes willingly. Now think about His amazing love that He shed upon us as He shed His blood willingly. "For God so loved the world that He gave His only begotten Son that whosoever believes in Him should not perish but have everlasting life." Are you still thinking about sinning? Are you still counting? *(Sunday, July 27, 2014 at 8:06P.M. CDT)*

Prayer Snapshot

From my heart to yours

When you pray for rain, do carry the umbrella with you. Otherwise, that prayer is just words that evaporate when they reach the clouds. *(Monday, July 28, 2014 at 8:23A.M. CDT)*

www.ingramcontent.com/pod-product-compliance
Lightning Source LLC
LaVergne TN
LVHW051037080426
835508LV00019B/1571